Other volumes in preparation
ISSN: 0141-1012

This book is part of a series. The publisher will accept continuation
orders which may be cancelled at any time and which provide for
automatic billing and shipping of each title in the series upon publication.
Please write for details.

© 1985 by Gordon and Breach Science Publishers S.A. All rights reserved.

Gordon and Breach Science Publishers

P.O. Box 786
Cooper Station
New York, New York 10276
United States of America

P.O. Box 197
London WC2E 9PX
England

58, rue Lhomond
75005 Paris
France

P.O. Box 161
1820 Montreux 2
Switzerland

14-9 Okubo 3-chome,
Shinjuku-ku
Tokyo 160
Japan

Library of Congress Cataloguing in Publication Data
Shanklin, Eugenia, 1939–
   Donegal's changing traditions.

   (Library of anthropology, ISSN 0141-1012)
   Includes bibliographical references and index.
1. Donegal (County)—Social life and customs.
2. Ethnology—Ireland—Donegal (County) I. Title.
DA990.D6S53   1984   306'.094169'3   84-8093

Cover photo courtesy of the Irish Tourist Board.

ISBN 2-88124-001-1. ISSN 0141-1012. No part of this book may be
reproduced or utilized in any form or by any means, electronic or mechanical, including photocopying, recording, or by any information storage or
retrieval system, without permission in writing from the publishers.
Printed in the United States of America.

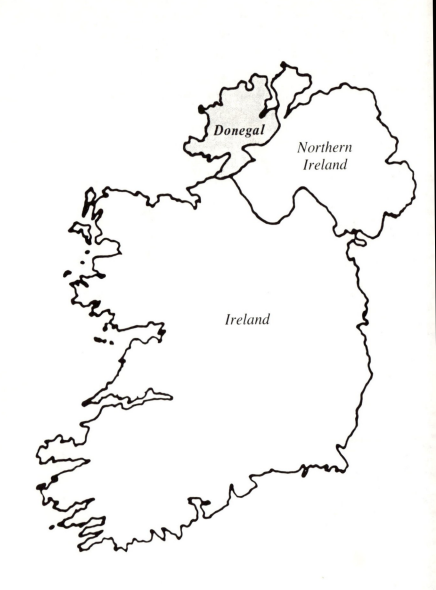

Donegal

Northern
Ireland

Ireland

Though you are in your shining days,
Voices among the crowd
And new friends busy with your praise,
Be not unkind or proud,
But think about old friends the most:
Time's bitter flood will rise,
Your beauty perish and be lost
. . .

W. B. Yeats

Contents

Introduction to the Series

One of the notable objectives of the *Library of Anthropology* is to provide a vehicle for the expression in print of new, controversial, and seemingly "unorthodox" theoretical, methodological, and philosophical approaches to anthropological data. Another objective follows from the multi-dimensional or holistic approach in anthropology which is the discipline's unique contribution toward understanding human behavior. The books in this series will deal with such fields as archaeology, physical anthropology, linguistics, ethnology, and social anthropology. Since no restrictions will be placed on the types of cultures included, a New York or New Delhi setting will be considered as relevant to anthropological theory and methods as the highlands of New Guinea.

The *Library* is designed for a wide audience and, whenever possible, technical terminology will be kept to a minimum. In some instances, however, a book may be unavoidably somewhat esoteric and consequently will appeal only to a small sector of the reading population — advanced undergraduate students in addition to professional social scientists.

My hopes for the readers are twofold: first, that they will enjoy learning about people; second, and perhaps more important, that they will come to experience a feeling of oneness with humankind.

New York, New York   *Anthony L. LaRuffa*

Preface

This is a book about traditions that are changing, not languishing in a moribund state and not dead, as other scholars have suggested, but changing to fit present circumstances. Since many people think of traditions as static or immutable, my assertion that traditions are changing may strike readers as paradoxical, but this book deals with a paradoxical people, the Irish of Southwest Donegal, who simultaneously guard and manipulate their traditions: guarding them against the encroachments of the modern world and manipulating them for their own advantage in that world.

In Yeats's apt phrase, "time's bitter flood" is rising; there are many challenges to traditions, the "old friends" of the people of Southwest Donegal. Changes are coming now, not step by step over a period of years, but daily, leap by leap. Rapid change muffles the voices of the past and lends a desperate note to those of the present. The process of slowly absorbing and recasting innovations as "traditions" is an on-going one, but whether it will be replaced by "modernity," by labelling innovations as good and traditions as bad, is not for me to say; it is a decision that must be, and is being, made by the people themselves.

To only a few of the people of Southwest Donegal does "tradition" seem a static, stultifying notion. For the others, tradition has been a creative force that aided the process of adapting to the changes they and their ancestors have met, sometimes with grace, sometimes with guns. Change may have been inevitable, but the incorporation of a new practice under the rubric of "tradition" made it less disruptive to the people.

Now the flood of innovations swamps and disrupts much that earlier generations held dear. I shall describe some of the traditions I have seen in their death throes and some I have traced to their historical antecedents. To disclose the mechanics of the consensus sometimes called tradition, I will describe both customs that are changing and customs that seem likely to endure.

My description is in the language of anthropology, of ethnographic fieldwork, because the beginning formulations of an explanation for this treatment of tradition took place during the ethnographic fieldwork I began in Southwest Donegal in 1970. After fourteen months of fieldwork, I returned to Columbia University and wrote my dissertation, "Sacred and Profane Livestock in Southwest Donegal" (1973). In 1974, I returned to spend three months in Donegal and since that time have visited the area briefly on other occasions.

Thus, in the ten years that have elapsed between the completion of my doctoral dissertation and the publication of this book, I have had ample opportunity to rethink many of the points I investigated originally, and almost the only issue about which I have not changed my mind is the importance of the study of traditions as they change and are recast.

Throughout any Irish fieldwork, the importance of the past for understanding the present is reiterated over and over. What is difficult is to make sense of the many pasts that are evoked to explain the present, to put these pasts into a perspective that makes their logic apparent to a reader. My focus is thus on "tradition" and not on providing a complete ethnographic account of all aspects of life in Southwest Donegal.

In Section A of the Introduction, Southwest Donegal will be "set" within its wider Irish context in order to illustrate that Donegal traditions are changing, not dying. In Section B this view is set within the context of anthropological views of tradition. Then, in section C, some of the active uses of tradition as practiced in Donegal at the time of my fieldwork, are illustrated.

Also given in section C are four examples of the uses that are made of the word tradition. However, a closer-grained analysis of the interactions of tradition and history requires an understanding of recorded history and the continuities and discontinuities between past and present. This is not an easy matter to present, for there are several levels of understanding involved in labelling a custom as "traditional." It will help if the reader considers that the chapters have a point-counterpoint relationship to each other, within the general time scheme of past, present, and future.

In Chapter 2 the continuities of recorded history in Southwest Donegal are discussed. These include the preoccupation with cattle as prestige products and as recycling agents for scant resources; the use and transmutation of the Celtic calendar as a means of adapting to the environment; the use of landmarks with Celtic and pre-Celtic names enshrined in folklore as a way of delimiting the boundaries of the important townlands, the basic unit of land use; and the development of indigenous hereditary leadership in Southwest Donegal.

The loss of this hereditary leadership and the development of informal mechanisms of leadership in Southwest Donegal are dealt with in Chapter 3, along with the intermediaries that arose out of post-Famine policies in social, ideological, economic, kinship, and political spheres.

In Chapter 4 the results of my own survey of the production decisions made by a sample of 30 farmers in Southwest Donegal are outlined in considerable detail and compared with the findings of the West Donegal Resource Survey report. This entailed a close analysis of the "verifiable" present, and I used the Famine (1845 – 1849) as watershed, distinguishing between pre-Famine and post-Famine customs as these relate to land tenure and livestock production decisions. These in turn were related to the human population numbers and the division of labor within farm families. I hope by this means to indicate some of the complexities of the system.

In Chapter 5, to further illustrate those complexities and to allow the reader to hear the voices of the real people who are making the decisions, 5 farmers from my sample of 30 are allowed to speak for themselves. Each speaker represents a different approach to questions of traditional and modern practices, and I hope that the reader will come away impressed, as I was, with the diversity of views available on this difficult topic.

The farmers' decisions, and particularly their discussions of experiences with both traditional and modern production methods, are far more illuminating, I believe, than any statistical summation could be. Both the farmers and the local historians, whose opinions and renderings of the "traditional" past are given in Chapter 5, illustrate my (counter) point about the way in which traditions are changing.

In the conclusions (Chapter 6) I return to the question of reformulating and recasting traditions, this time in terms of the implications the process has for future studies.

Princeton, New Jersey   *Eugenia Shanklin*

Acknowledgments

This book is based on fieldwork carried out in Southwest Donegal in 1970–1971, work funded by a joint training grant in ecological anthropology from the National Institute of General Medical Sciences and Columbia University, No. 5-TO1-GM-01797. The dissertation that came out of the fieldwork (Shanklin 1973) was gently and carefully supervised by Alexander Alland, Jr. and Conrad M. Arensberg, whose encouragement in the writing of this book I gratefully acknowledge.

The agricultural agencies of the Irish government (*An Foras Taluntais* or the Agricultural Institute, and the Department of Agriculture) cooperated fully in helping me gather whatever information I needed; their employees could not have been more pleasant or understanding. I am also indebted to the Agricultural Institute for permission to include in Chapter 4 data drawn from the West Donegal Resource Survey, Volumes 1–4, as part of my analysis.

My thanks must also be extended to the publishers who have allowed the use of materials published earlier: to the *Anthropological Quarterly* for permission to include in Chapter 3 material from "The Irish Go-Between," which appeared in Volume 53(3):162–172, July, 1980; to the newsjournal *Group* for permission to include in Appendix A material that originally appeared in my article, "Where There Are No Innocent Bystanders," which appeared in July, 1974; to the *Journal of Anthropological Research* for permission to include in Section B of Chapter 1 material from "Two Meanings and Uses of Tradition," which appeared in Volume 37(1):71–89, Spring, 1981; and to *Natural History Magazine* for permission to include in Section A of Chapter 1 material from "Donegal's Lowly Sheep and Exalted Cows," which appeared in Volume 85(3):26–33, March, 1976.

I am also indebted to Ruth Bogia, Yehudi A. Cohen, Cheryl R. Cramer, Sidney W. Mintz, and Alvin H. Schulman for their helpful comments on the numerous early drafts of this book, and to Renate

Fernandez for her help with Chapter 3. Susan Schiffer and Geraldine DiCicco helped with the typing and Nita Krevans with the research, vital tasks that too often demanded great patience.

I am indebted beyond measure to my informants in Ireland; I cannot name most of them but I trust they will find in what I have written about them some recompense for their patient attempts to teach me the rudiments of appropriate social conduct in their part of the world, and, a much more exacting task, the fundamental rules of the game in which they extract a livelihood from a merciless environment. To all, I extend my thanks while claiming full responsibility for my errors.

CHAPTER ONE

Introduction

The Irish "peasant" is the child of time. He is its guardian and
its slave. He will preserve for centuries dull and foolish habits
that those who neither love nor fear time or change will quickly
cast aside; but he will also preserve dear, ancient habits that like
wine and ivory grow more beautiful and precious with age, all
jumbled with the useless lumber in that dusty cockloft which is
his ancestral mind.
     Sean O'Faolain, *The Irish* 1972:80-81.

A. THE SETTING

My aim when I went to Ireland was to gather information about
livestock production strategies, data comparable to that available
from other societies dependent on livestock. Southwest Donegal
has been a livestock-producing area for more than two thousand
years. Its people have survived in a difficult and rigorous
environment under tormenting political circumstances.
Throughout this time, raising livestock was the major way of
making a living. The people have thrived in some years, barely
survived in others, and, weathered the political as well as the
climatic storms, by means of their animals.

Because of its rigors, Southwest Donegal was an ideal place to
do ecological research, but because of its recorded history, its
political upheavals, and the emphasis on livestock production,
the area offered many tempting research directions. As an
anthropologist gathering information on livestock production
strategies, I was fascinated by the many similarities between the
people of Southwest Donegal, with their mixed farming and
pastoral economy, and the "pure" pastoralists, those who live
solely by their herds, in other parts of the world. Despite centuries
of potato cultivation and many decades of settled living, there are
striking parallels between the value systems of the Donegal Irish

1

and the nomadic pastoralists of Africa and Asia. Some of those parallels are intelligible within an ecological framework.

Those customs that do not fit easily into an ecological framework are even more intriguing; to explain them, one must put them in historical perspective against a Celtic backdrop. The Celts were aggressive pastoralists. They conquered Ireland well before the birth of Christ, fought among themselves for a while, and eventually sorted out the land into four provinces — Leinster, Munster, Connacht, and Ulster — each with its own "king." Settling into one of those golden eras about which little is known, the kings spent their time raiding each other's herds. That much *is* known about them because reigns were counted glorious or not according to how many cattle raids had been carried out.

One of the oldest epics in Irish literature, the *Tain bo Chulaigne*, is the story of a cattle raid instigated by the Queen of Connacht against the King of Ulster because of her determination to own the finest bull in Ireland. Kinsella, a translator of this epic, remarks that, "It is possible that the kind of culture the *Tain* describes may have lasted in Ireland up to the introduction of Christianity in the fifth century" (1969:ix).

With the introduction of Christianity, many things changed, but cattle remained a focal point of Irish life. Ways of raising livestock involved customs that predated Christianity: some of those customs were rigorously observed in Southwest Donegal up until the beginning of the twentieth century. At the time of my study there were people alive who still remembered the old customs, still observed many of the "old" traditions. This opportunity to study production strategies through time, as they pertain to current social institutions, was irresistible. As a result, I strayed from my original ecological intent and, in exploring traditions, rummaged through such diverse particulars as Celtic fairs and heroic tales.

Thus the aim of my fieldwork — to study livestock production strategies as practiced in 1970–71 — and the aim of this book — to consider through time the development of "traditional"practices in livestock keeping — differ. Fieldwork involved careful scrutiny of livestock keeping, and of both traditional and modern ways of keeping cattle and sheep. The data gathered in that study form only part of the basis for this book, however; I went on to consider the origins of those "traditional" techniques and the processes involved in labelling a custom a "tradition." This necessarily involves other aspects of Donegal life and here I am concerned primarily with illustrating the changes in those traditions that have served the people of Southwest Donegal so well so long.

But first we must explore the position of Donegal within the Irish Republic, as well as some of the political and economic characteristics of the area. To understand the position of Donegal, it is necessary to understand first of all that it is remote — geographically, politically, and economically.

To borrow the geographers' phrase, Ireland can be likened to a saucer, the mountainous rim of which drains into a central basin. As a whole, Donegal is part of the northwest's mountainous rim and it borders mostly on what is now the political entity of Northern Ireland. For a tourist, the coast of southwest Donegal is one of the most beautiful and austere in the world and the interior of the region scarcely less picturesque. The area resembles a high desert — windswept and barren except for an occasional tree bent in the direction of the prevailing winds. As a local priest put it, "When God was creating the earth, He had used up most of the fertile land by the time He got to Donegal and He had to save what He had left for America. So He compensated by giving us all the scenery He had left over; we got cliffs rising out of the sea, high mountains, waterfalls, and white beaches, while the Europeans and the Americans got the rich soil."

Such sentiments are privileges reserved for the tourist or for one who does not make his living from the land. It is difficult to find a Donegal farmer who appreciates either God's afterthoughts or the grandeur of the landscape. Inland the dual impression of beauty and cruelty persists. The deep valleys are dotted with thatched cottages, thatch that is tied down against the gale-force winds, and cottages are set not at the top of hills but just beneath the crest to avoid those persistent winds. In addition, every stone, brae, and valley has a name and a legend, usually commemorating some murderous occasion. A study of the local place-ghosts reveals a long history of conquests and rebellions.

The land has been dominated in turn by chieftains, armies with holy causes, kings, absentee landlords, and today, by government bureaucrats. For two thousand years, the population persisted while the conquerors came and went; some conquerors went quickly, once they realized the cruel beauty of the land, while others lingered and were assimilated. Departure or assimilation were practically the only choices available, for the climate is almost as poor as the soil. Gale-force winds, a growing season bounded more by rainfall than by temperature variations — with the heaviest rains coming during the harvest season — and extreme variation from year to year in both rainfall and duration of the frost-free season make the region a poor one for agricultural purposes.

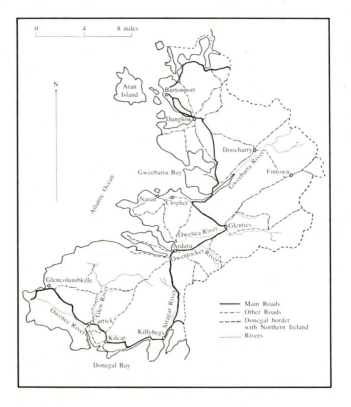

Figure 1.1 Glenties Rural District, geographical location and principal towns and villages.

For centuries Donegal was tied politically and economically to Ulster, the northernmost province of ancient Ireland, by virtue of its rivers and its roads, which fed produce into the interior (see Figure 1.1). Consumer goods came in from other parts of Ulster, and Donegal produce (mainly livestock) was destined for the central basin. In 1922, Donegal was separated from what had been its market and trade region and made part of the Republic of Ireland. The effect of this separation has been to isolate Donegal from its natural trade region, the interior of Ulster, and to force the people of Donegal to rely on the south for most of their manufactured goods, as well as markets for their agricultural produce. This meant that high transport costs had to be paid on anything not locally produced and that markets for such things as agricultural produce could not be established easily since out-of-area transport costs had to be absorbed. For the people of Donegal, one of the effects of the separation has been a reduced standard of living compared to most other parts of Ireland.

In 1971 livestock was still largely sold into Northern Ireland but most manufactured goods had to come from the Irish Republic. Having always been an agricultural area with few resources for the development of manufacturing, the present separation from Ulster further augments the remoteness of Donegal but the economic privations created by Donegal's isolation within the Republic did not eliminate the feeling of cultural identity with Ulster that the people of Donegal manifest. Official Irish government publications include Donegal as part of the West of Ireland, that is the Gaelic-speaking and backward region of Ireland. But Donegal people do not see themselves as such and they speak disdainfully of the people of the West. In their view, they are Northerners and they gleefully describe the differences between themselves and the Westerners: in the North, people are said to be more industrious, more helpful and hospitable, as well as more straightforward and honest. In the West, the people are believed to be unfriendly, dishonest, lazy, and prone to all kinds of superstitions, including beliefs in fairies and leprechauns.

The cultural differences that Donegal people assert between themselves and the people of the West is borne out linguistically — Ulster Gaelic differs from that spoken in the Southern provinces, so much so that the Gaelic programs broadcast on national radio and television are often not understood by many

Gaelic speakers in Donegal. Officially, however, much of Donegal is considered to be part of the Gaeltacht region, of which Freeman says:

> The areas with which the [Gaeltacht] Commission dealt were similar to those studied by the Congested Districts Board some thirty years earlier, and admitted to be the poorest in the land. In 1956 the Gaeltacht was redefined to cover areas in which the vast majority of the population spoke Irish, with a general average of 87%. . . . the population of the new Gaeltacht was 85,700 in 1956 and 78,500 in 1961. In Co. Donegal it included a population of 28,900 in 1956, reduced to 26,400 by 1961, located in the northwest and west (Freeman 1969:166,167,169).

In Banagh, the name I will use for the area in which I worked and part of the former Congested Districts, the proportion of Irish speakers to English speakers is about three out of five in rural areas, less in the villages, but older farmers are more likely to speak Gaelic than their younger counterparts. Most people in the rural areas command both English and Gaelic without difficulty, (this is not so true in the villages) and in my sample of thirty, there was only one household in which spoken English was not understood by a majority of members.

Today Donegal is isolated by its curiously artificial position, sharing only a few miles of its lengthy border with the Irish Republic. Three thousand years ago its remoteness was a natural consequence of its geographical position, the difficulty of its terrain, and the paucity of its resources.

Remoteness has advantages. In the past, remoteness from government control accounted for the region's status as one of the last subdued by the Celts, one of the last to become fully Christian, and one of the last areas of active rebellion, in the name of the Irish chieftains, against the British. Sentimental Irish patriots often see Donegal as a repository of traditional Irish culture, and this culture is one that has come to be regarded as especially virtuous (because Irish and "traditional"), especially by those who live apart from it. This view is based on the retention of the Gaelic language and the system of small farms in the area; but these are also virtues peculiar to a region largely cut off from foreign trade (as well as influence) and one that existed for centuries beyond the effective sphere of active governmental interference and control. Because in Ireland as in most other countries there is a certain sentimental value to the supposed "retention" of native customs, the government has been willing to invest large sums of money in maintaining the integrity of the area as a stronghold of Irish values. Underlying the sentiment, however, may have been the recognition that to undertake redevelopment would require even greater sums of money than are spent on maintenance. Now, as in the past, the area's remoteness is a large factor in governmental premises and policies.

It may be useful to say a few words here about my reasons for choosing Southwest Donegal, as opposed to Northwest Donegal, as the area of my study. I have said that my primary interest in going to Ireland was to study livestock production methods. Wherever I went in Donegal, I was assured that the Northwestern area was the more interesting, for one or more of the following reasons: most of the population was supported by migratory labor and/or overseas contributions; Gaelic was still the spoken language and the area was therefore more important for historical reasons; such things as "tribal" names persisted, along with other archaic customs. My inquiries about livestock holdings in the Northwest revealed a serious drawback, however: there is no longer any need for the average householder in the Northwest to keep animals, by virtue of migratory labor and modern dairy production. The report on livestock holdings in the West Donegal Resource Survey Report indicated this clearly and I chose to work in the Southwest region where livestock were kept as a critical part of the production system.

The study area was one in which, as I have said, domestic animal production has been the focus of economic and prestige activities for more than two thousand years. The region has long been known for its dense population and scant resources, but recent improvements in pasturage techniques may increase the carrying capacity of the area's most extensive resource, bog lands for grazing animals. What is perhaps most intriguing about the system of livestock production is that it is the end product of a long-standing pastoral adaptation but it must be borne in mind that many changes have occurred as a result of economic and political activities that were largely unrelated to the changes in the system of livestock production. Of these, the most significant probably was the isolation of County Donegal from its natural market region — the ancient province of Ulster. Livestock production systems have been seriously affected by these changes, and the question now is whether the long-standing pastoral adaptation is flexible enough to incorporate modern economic conditions. My hunch, based on the careful observation of more than thirty farmers in the region, is that livestock production systems may be transformed but they will not be eradicated or destroyed by "modern" conditions. Further, many of what I now describe as innovative practices will be incorporated into the systems as "traditional" methods. This is neither cynical nor foolhardy behavior on the part of the farmers; it is one of the ways in which a long-standing pastoral adaptation is maintained.

B. TRADITION IN ANTHROPOLOGICAL THEORY

There are numerous explanations in the anthropological literature for the retention of "traditional" customs and ideas, but the issue is by no means resolved. Elsewhere (Shanklin 1981) I have reviewed the meanings and uses of tradition, especially the notion of tradition as a passive immutable force, brought into the social science literature by Durkheim, Weber, Marx and Tönnies. I will reiterate a few points from that survey here with particular emphasis on one: I believe the most exciting work on the study of traditions is being done right now, work that assumes that traditions are active agents in the process of modernization and I believe that Ireland is one of the most exciting places in the world in which to study these active, on-going revisions of tradition.

Early ethnographers recorded traditions with an eye to discovering or demonstrating their own (the ethnographers') origins or origin myths, whether Egyptian, Babylonian, Hebrew, or just plain primeval horde. Tylor, who systematized a good deal of anthropological thinking, referred to those customs that seemed out of place, that persisted through time despite new religions and new governments, as "survivals." Survivals were atavisms, time-honored beliefs that withstood the ravages of time, but Tylor's interest was not in explaining them; rather, he hoped to use them to retrace the steps by which cultures had evolved and he noted that proof of the development of civilization could be traced through history and through survivals (1960:11 *et seq.* [1881]). By combining the study of history and survivals, it was possible to trace back to their origins many customs or whole bodies of knowledge.

The premise that earlier stages had to be (or even could be) reconstructed caused Tylor's notions to be disregarded, once the premise had been taken to its most extreme conclusion by those who traced all "survivals" to Egyptian origins and found traces of Egyptiana in every custom.

At the same time it became unfashionable to discuss origins, Tylor's theories about survivals were also discredited by a new generation of anthropologists who called themselves functionalists and liked to insist that everything had a purpose, usually an ecological or structural purpose. Under this reasoning, no culture trait was carried over generations without having some purpose in the survival mechanisms of the culture. Those trained in the functionalist school of Malinowski and Radcliffe-Brown denounced the idea of survivals because every cultural item — no matter how trivial or unlikely — had some relation to the system in which it was found. Its significance was most probably to be found in the relationship between resources and human exploitation or between political institutions and ambition.

Malinowski, who liked to refer to himself as the "arch-functionalist," suggested that traditions or legends among the Trobriand Islanders were recited to satisfy social ambition:

> Moreover, since they record singularly great achievements ... they redound to the credit of some individual and his descendants or of a whole community; and hence they are kept alive by the ambition of those whose ancestry they glorify (Malinowski 1948:106).

This is one functionalist view of what tradition does; others have noted that traditions may "function" as part of a society's environmental adaptation, retaining or incorporating customs that are useful within a particular ecosystem. Of course there is no reason that traditions cannot do both, and more. I believe that the greatest problem with functional anthropological definitions of tradition is not with their teleology but with their assertion of unicausal explanations. As we will see, it is possible for traditions to function in order to retain or incorporate useful customs, to serve social ambitions, or to preserve the internal solidarity of a group. At the height of the popularity of the functionalist paradigm, in the 1930's, Irish studies had their brilliant beginnings in the hands of Conrad Arensberg and Solon Kimball. Arensberg and Kimball were committed to a formal functionalist viewpoint and their emphasis was on the workings of the system, the connections between the important institutions in rural Irish life — farming, family, communities and relationships in the towns or villages. They acknowledged (1968:xxix) their debt to the formulations from preliterate societies of Malinowski and Radcliffe-Brown and at the time (1932) they were carrying out ethnological fieldwork in County Clare, they were among the first anthropologists to bring their insights to the study of "modern civilized communities" (*ibid.*:xxx). Subsequently other modern communities were studied but Ireland was not much "revisited" by anthropologists until the sixties, when Fox (1962; 1963; 1968), Kane (1968), and Messenger (1962; 1968; 1969) began work in different communities in the West.

In the sixties, anthropologists began to discard the functionalist paradigm in favor of a processual emphasis in social studies generally. But before the paradigm was discarded, the living cell that was the basis of the functionalist metaphor was carried to its logical conclusion in Irish studies, i.e., the cell/community that earlier had functioned to meet the needs of its constituent parts/members now met its death. Arensberg and Kimball had studied an ongoing community in Clare; those who came after them found matters greatly altered by the incursion of modernity and the breakdown of the "traditional" ways of doing things. They believed it was their duty to proclaim the "death" of Ireland and along with it went the equally premature proclamation of the death of Irish traditions. Thus Messenger wrote of the anomic Irish countryman, whose way of life was disappearing because of emigration, and Nancy Scheper-Hughes announced, "I bear the sad tidings that on a certain grey, windy day in March in the year of Our Lord 1975, Ireland passed away," and "I share with other recent ethnographers, among them Hugh Brody (1973) and Robert Cresswell (1969), the belief that rural Ireland is dying and its people are consequently infused with a spirit of anomie and despair" (1982:xv, 4).

Aalen and Brody (1969) described "The Life and Last Days of an Island Community" in their book, *Gola*, but it was Brody alone in his (1974) book, *Inishkillane*, who first drove home the idea of the death of a rural Western community and thereby gained the attention of the anthropological community.

The seventies witnessed the arrival of several would-be pallbearers to the West of Ireland, but there were others who came to look with a more measured gaze. Among them was Philip Snyder, who worked in Connemara and recorded the following impression of community members:

> Although they are quick to point out the drawbacks of their existence in this remote and often harsh landscape, in general they seem to derive considerable satisfaction from their life-work. Rooted in a familiar world and an all-encompassing Faith, the people I came to know have a strong sense of who they are and what life is about. There is an indefinable certainty to their actions, and they possess a great capacity for taking each day and moment as it comes, pausing from their work to enjoy a brief interval of sunshine, and accepting the inevitable return of the rain (1975:21).

Another was Mart Bax, who did a masterful study of politics in rural Ireland (the precise location is disguised), and concluded that:

> Thus, the general pattern, . . . seems a spiral: a rise and fall of rural-based machine politics. Where the political culture is a carrier of machine political patterns of behavior — and this will be so in Ireland for as long as the electoral system is maintained — the disintegration of rural based machine politics does not mark the end of the generic pattern. Indeed, urban based machine politics may proliferate. They will be more subtle and disguised, but they will function in basically the same way (1973:256).

Snyder's and Bax's studies are at odds with the pronouncements of the death of Irish rural life and traditions. But they are, like my own, in keeping with the observations of the folklorists, among them Henry Glassie's (1982 a and b) recent studies in Ulster; and with the findings of the historians who have looked closely at the mechanics of changing traditions in the British Isles, e.g., Trevor-Roper's analysis of invented Scottish Highland traditions or Cannadine's study of the British monarchy (in Hobsbawm and Ranger 1983).

In other words, not all assessments of changing traditions in general or of Ireland in particular are so dismal. If Ireland died in 1975, what were Bax, Snyder, and other scholars witnessing? It seems that Irish studies have taken a wrong turn and have embraced the idea of the death of a culture without bothering to check on what the "corpse" was up to. This is one reason for disagreeing with the presentiments of death that are offered as fact in Irish studies; another is that such presentiments are at odds with my own findings and, for better or worse, anthropologists are socialized by their informants. My Donegal informants do not believe that their traditions are dead or dying. Nonetheless the depressing views of Ireland that are currently broadcast by anthropologists and others reflect very closely preoccupations some Irish people have. Whether such pessimistic views are accurate for other parts of Ireland in this century, I do not know but I do know that one reads over and over in Irish literature that Irish traditions are dead — whether the century is the14th, 15th, 16th, 17th, 18th, or 19th. The 20th century preoccupation with the death of Irish tradition therefore seems to me a better subject for investigation than for proclamation and unquestioning acceptance.

I agree with Maybury-Lewis's (1970:134) rumination on Lévi-Strauss that "The job of the social anthropologist was . . . to find out what a society was trying, either consciously or unconsciously, to 'say,'" and I think that anthropologists who looked critically at what was being said and at the style of the performance might find that they were witnessing, not a funeral, but the performance of an Irish custom, that of announcing the death of Irish traditions. Anthropologists might be better advised to emulate a different Irish custom, that of borrowing/parodying English phrases, and to say "Irish tradition is dead; long live Irish tradition."

I have said that my aim in this book is to show how some of Donegal's traditions are changing, especially the ways in which "traditional" methods of livestock keeping are being transmuted to suit modern circumstances. To understand these changes, it is necessary to take into account the active uses of tradition that have been pointed out in other parts of the world as well as some other theoretical conceptions and definitions of tradition. Many authors have made suggestions about the dynamics of the process wherein modernity supplants or supersedes "tradition," but there are three I find especially illuminating, Cohn's (1961), Lévi-Strauss's (1966;1976) and Hobsbawm and Ranger's (1983).

Cohn (1961:242) has suggested that rather than seeking to determine "the" past, researchers must look for two types of past: "a traditional past, which grows out of the mythology and sacred traditions . . ., and a historic past, which is a set of ideas about the remembered experiences of a group of people in a local region." He speculates that, "a society is modern when it does have a past, when this past is shared by the vast majority of the society, and when it can be used on a national basis to determine and validate behavior" (1961:249).

This is one of several possibilities for dealing with "tradition." Traditions become part of a national ideology; the Irish "centuries of British oppression" explanation tends in this direction, and binds the people of Southwest Donegal to the Irish Republic.

Another hypothesis about the relation between traditions and modernity or between tradition and history has been put forth by Lévi-Strauss. Traditions, Lévi-Strauss says, closely approximate myths, in being timeless explanations of present, past, and future while history is sequential. He uses the French Revolution to illustrate this point, noting that the French Revolution is both a sequence and a timeless pattern to a French politician, a pattern that "can be detected in the contemporary French social structure and which provides a clue for its interpretation, a lead from which to infer future developments" (1966:250).

According to this view, anthropologists should expect to find that traditions are an active, creative force in societies. In "How Myths Die," Lévi-Strauss notes that the transformations a myth undergoes will eventually exhaust it but the myth will not disappear. Rather, it will be fictionally elaborated or reactivated "with a view to legitimizing history. This history, in its turn, may be of two types: retrospective, to found a traditional order on a distant past; or prospective, to make this past the beginning of a future which is starting to take shape" (1976:268).

In Lévi-Strauss's conception, then, traditions are not faulty understandings of history: they are instead history in the making. Lévi-Strauss's interpretation of traditions as history in the making accords closely with my own observations of the Irish uses of their traditions, as will be seen. Cohn and Lévi-Strauss hinted at the ways in which myth or tradition was transformed to become history but it has since been historians, not anthropologists, who have begun to systematize thinking about those transformations,

especially with respect to "invented traditions." In 1983, Eric
Hobsbawm discussed the issues lucidly and suggested that
invented traditions should be studied by historians because they
are symptoms or indicators of problems not otherwise recognized.
They are evidence, he says, and because they "use history as a
legitimator of action and cement of group cohesion" (1983:12),
they are clues to the understanding of the human relation to the
past. Further, the study is an interdisciplinary one, demanding
collaboration between historians, social anthropologists and others
in the human or social sciences (*ibid.*).

By and large, anthropologists working in Ireland have not yet
begun to collaborate in the study of invented traditions. It is my
hope that future anthropological fieldworkers will find this a
productive enterprise in Ireland, for it has certainly yielded many
insights into change in other parts of the world. Before going on
to explicate the many-faceted uses of tradition in Ireland, it is
useful to review some of the ways in which traditions have been
used to sanction modern ideas.

Current ethnographic definitions of tradition generally follow
one of the two directions — active and passive — that may be
culled from Williams's discussion:

> Tradition in its most general modern sense is a particularly
> difficult word. . . . It is sometimes observed, by those who have
> looked into particular traditions, that it only takes two
> generations to make anything traditional: naturally enough, since
> that is the sense of tradition as active process. But the word
> moves again and again towards age-old and towards ceremony,
> duty and respect. Considering only how much has been handed
> down to us, and how various it actually is, this, in its own way,
> is both a betrayal and a surrender (Williams 1976:268-269).

The emphasis in anthropological writing and ethnographic
reporting, however, has shifted only recently away from the passive
aspects of tradition. With a few brilliant exceptions, the active
uses were generally ignored. This neglect may be due to
anthropological training and theory, i.e., to the bias in favor of
preliterate societies in which oral traditions are viewed as sketchy
and unreliable, or to a persistent functionalist bias in which history
is regarded as unimportant to what is going on at the moment.
Whatever the reason, these biases will probably diminish and

disappear as anthropologists come to grips with history in complex societies.

Traditional beliefs may sometimes serve as a basis or focal point for conservatism or innovation; religious beliefs, particularly, are susceptible to numerous interpretations. Leach (1972) and Tambiah (1972) point to the ambiguities of the Buddhist tradition in Burma, Ceylon, and Thailand. Leach illustrates with several examples the ambiguity "present in all 'nationalistic' symbolism" (1972:42), an ambiguity that provides a context in which Buddhism can flourish.

Tambiah also illustrates the paradoxes of nationalist sentiments in his references to the "consciousness of historical continuity" shared by all three countries, a consciousness that is based on "an understanding of history that conceived each country's national destiny to be the protection and guardianship of the religion" (1972:56).

In general, British or British-trained anthropologists have approached tradition less reverently and more analytically than Americans, while political scientists have viewed tradition as a form of "political religion" and treated the dynamics of developing nations, with their selective reliance on tradition, accordingly. In anthropology, concentration on the active meanings and uses of tradition was begun by J. A. Barnes, who studied the Ngoni and found that they were making numerous uses of their traditions. Barnes examined Ngoni history and oral traditions, and found some curious distortions between the two (Barnes 1951:295-303). According to their legend, the Ngoni defeated all other groups until the British came in 1898. Historical accounts indicate that the Ngoni were by no means undefeated before this time, but, says Barnes, "the distortion introduced is not only the elimination of defeat . . . the Ngoni conquerors of yesterday are made to look like the European conquerors of today . . ." (1951:296-297). The legends have been modified to conform to modern values; Barnes's informants even assured him that the old Ngoni language was closer to English than to Nyanja (1951:296-297).

The Ngoni also use tradition to evaluate their present circumstances: their defeat by the British explains present failures and expresses tribal identity. When Barnes asked about Ngoni marriage payments and confronted informants with the reality that such payments were often not made, even before the British conquest of 1898, "Ngoni do not deny these facts but they do deny their relevance. To them, the distinctively Ngoni way of marrying is with these two payments . . . . They regret that people no longer marry in this way and blame the Europeans for it, but it remains part of the distinctive cultural heritage of the tribe" (1951:298-299). Tribal identity is emphasized by having — but not necessarily by following — such distinctive customs.

Another use of tradition is made in the law courts, where Ngoni appeal to traditional practice in a different way: judges may maintain that a decision is in keeping with tribal custom without quoting specific precedents and, "in this undocumented environment new decisions, if they are not soon challenged, become part of what has always been the custom since time immemorial" (1951:300).

Barnes's findings are borne out by many other ethnographers, among them Stevens (1975), who has documented the spread of what he calls the "Kisra tradition" in Africa, a legend that finds favor in societies under threat from outside; Fernandez (1972:3-8), who has shown that a traditional migration legend is used among the Fang "to foster a sense of community and political unity," and Orans (1965:35), who shows that the Santal distort their traditions in order to establish a basis of solidarity, from which they may counter threats of assimilation.

Traditions serve both evaluative and sanctifying functions in these instances and, while the authors begin from different points of view, they end by describing similar phenomena. Stevens is interested in history; Orans and Fernandez in political processes. A different perspective is offered by Collier, in his ecological analysis of the Tzotzil. Collier extends the ecological concept of environment to include the larger system in which the Tzotzil of Mexico occupy a peripheral position and notes that "ethnic tradition is an adaptive response by which exploited groups establish and defend a protective niche . . . . (1975:212). Collier believes that "peripheral ethnicity" has emerged in situations in which colonialism brought "dominated peripheral groups" into larger systems and that these groups adapted by becoming ethnic groups and clinging firmly to their traditions. Schwartz (1977) also emphasizes ecological factors in his description of changing conceptualizations of the past in Guatemala, and notes that the changes may have been triggered by rapid changes "in the demographic, economic, and political environment" (1977:339).

Insights such as these, insights into the intricate balance between tradition and modernity, must be sought in Irish studies, as must a careful delineation of the principles that govern current Irish views of these subjects. To illustrate the complexity, let us begin with a consideration of the many meanings of tradition in Southwest Donegal.

C. TRADITION IN SOUTHWEST DONEGAL

In Donegal, the meanings of tradition are numerous, as are its uses. Ask anyone why something is done in a particular way and your informant, who may never have thought about it, will probably reply that it's a tradition and add as an afterthought that it undoubtedly has something to do with centuries of British oppression. So it may, but long before the English (who were then the Anglo-Normans) ever set foot on Irish soil, there were Irish (then Celtic) customs and I have no doubt that a revenant would report that there were people who answered questions with the "We've always done it that way" explanation. The current variant that the people of Donegal use, "We've done it that way ever since the British came," does not explain either the endless revisions of custom that can be documented in the historical record or the curious lapses in informant memories of the past.

I mentioned above Williams's definition of tradition as having two senses, an active and a passive sense, but I should point out that while the English language may have only two meanings of the word, the Irish use tradition to mean far more than two things.

I believe these uses can be broken down into four (non-exclusive) categories: first, tradition can be used as a sanction for innovation or new customs, as we will see is the case with the "traditional" fair of Magheramore. Second, tradition may be used as a storage device for preserving important components of the behavioral or ecological system; here my example will be a story I think of as Pat's story (actually a myth) of The Warrior and The Pig. Third, tradition may be used as a way of identifying the people who share a common heritage, as a means of establishing

ethnic identity. To illuminate this use, I will discuss the standard
Donegal explanation for traditional practices, the "centuries of
British oppression" explanation. The fourth use is allied to the
third, the use of tradition as a way of comparing the "glorious
past" with the realities of the present, and I will use as example
the writings of one of the local historians of Southwest Donegal,
Patrick McGill, as he ruminates about the effects of the Famine
in the area.

The Fair of Magheramore originated in the Celtic era as a ritual
assembly, celebrating the beginning of the Celtic year. In Donegal,
this festival lasted for three days, beginning on November 1st.
The customs associated with the fair of Magheramore were
changed radically in the nineteenth century, but the name has
persisted. The assembly site was moved from Magheramore to
Ardara; the date was changed from the first of November to the
first of October; the cattle that were displayed on the old festival
date were replaced by sheep sales.

The "traditional" fair of Magheramore, in other words, was
changed beyond recognition. Nevertheless, the people of Donegal
still speak of the fair of Magheramore as a traditional one, and
they assert that sheep were always sold on the first of October in
the village of Ardara. This belief persists in spite of published
evidence to the contrary. During my stay, a local historian wrote
a column about this fair for a newspaper and many people pointed
it out to me as an impressive piece of scholarship. It did not
disturb their assessment of the October 1st sheep fair as a
traditional one, though the historian traced the provenance of the
fair as a cattle fair, held on the Celtic holiday of November 1.

Most people saw the article as "proving" that the fair had its
origins in tradition (in the passive sense Williams gives the term),
a time-honored, respected set of beliefs. The changes had not
occurred during the lifetimes of my informants, and to them,
prior to the publication of the article, the October first sheep fair
was the tradition and the name Magheramore a curious
attachment. Their grandfathers and fathers had done it that way
and they were pleased to know that they, too, were following the
"traditional" custom. That there had been an active
transformation of this fair during the 19th century was
unimportant.

It might be argued that since these changes had taken place before my informants were born, their labelling of the event as traditional was reasonably accurate; here I must point out that other changes, changes that had occurred within my informants' lifetimes, were also labelled by them as traditions and were considered to be in accord with age-old practice. For example, a few people remembered the changes in livestock breeds that had come about during their own lifetimes. Those who did remember were exceptional but accurate; those who did not remember were in the majority, however, and their assumption that what they were doing was the "traditional" thing might, in the absence of written records, be taken as definitive. My point here is that whether the changes have occurred within "living memory," or not, what matters is the consensus that something is traditional, and not whether it can in fact be shown to be a time-honored custom.

The use I have talked about involves the "internal" approval of a custom by labeling it as a tradition, but there is another external sanction to this labeling. Elizabeth Colson (1974) has pointed out that in those areas of the world colonized by the British, the people who were colonized quickly learned that their new rulers had great respect for tradition. When the "natives" wished to innovate, they told the adminstrators that they had always done it that way, that it was a tradition, and the administrators, not being authorities on local "traditions," accepted this explanation more readily than they might have accepted the explanation that the locals wished to try something new. "It's traditional" became a convenient rubric for dealing with foreign administrators, and once again, tradition served as a sanction for innovation. This first use of tradition, then, as a sanction for "new" customs or to sanction old customs revised almost beyond recognition, has served the Irish very well for centuries.

The second use of tradition is as a storage device for certain components of the behavioral or ecological system. To illustrate this use, I will tell Pat's story about the Warrior and the Pig.

One day I was driving along a remote mountain road on my way to a sheep dipping near Finntown. Pat, the dipping inspector, was my companion and we had been quiet for a while, as I concentrated on dodging the sheep that wandered onto the road.

Pat was a taciturn man and he and I often drove for miles in friendly silence; occasionally he would point out an interesting feature of the landscape or tell me a story about someone whose house we were passing.

We had passed no houses for some time when Pat mentioned that we would soon pass the grave of a man who had been killed by a pig. Preoccupied with dodging sheep, I answered in monosyllables and Pat went on talking about how the man had chased the pig up and down the valley, how the man's dogs had been killed in the chase and precisely where they had fallen, and how, eventually. both pig and man died of their terrible wounds. I listened absent-mindedly and interrupted occasionally to ask where the man's neighbors were when all this was happening (Pat was not sure but he thought they were all away), and who kept pigs in the area (no one had tried, after that man's awful death). or why the man hadn't fetched a gun to shoot the pig (he hadn't had a gun, only the dogs and a stick). The details of the story were clear; the first dog had died near a large rock, the second had died near the valley floor, and the man himself several miles further on, near the top of the cliffs overlooking Lake Finn.

Pat finished the story and lapsed back into silence, while I dodged sheep and puzzled over this extraordinary sequence of events. Then one anomaly struck me forcibly and I said, "Pat, there's no church in this valley [hence no consecrated ground for burial]. Who was this man?" Pat didn't answer immediately; he thought for a while and said that he hadn't known the man personally. In fact, it had all happened before his time but there might be others who would know more of the details. The story was told as if it had happened in the last few weeks and Pat related it with all the assurance of an eye-witness. There was no clue that it was a myth, except a negative one: when stories are told about real people, the story-teller often adds that the person has been dead "these hundred years" or so. Pat had added no such marker; he was relating a myth.

The myth is part of the Finn Cycle, the stories that are told about Finn McCool and his warrior band, the Fianna. Finn and the Fianna are celebrated in legend as the defenders of Ireland against the Viking invasions that began at the end of the eighth century A.D. The Finn cycle is said to date from the third century but most of the stories about Finn are recorded in 12th century manuscripts (Cross and Slover 1969:355).

The warrior and the pig story has two parts: first, the fight with the "pig," and second, the death of the warrior and his sister. One version begins with Finn McCool hunting a wild boar; Finn locates the fierce boar in one valley and chases it through the pass between the mountains into another, losing his dogs in the struggle. Finally, exhausted, Finn and the boar battle to the death at the other end of the valley. Another version of the first part recounts the story of Fergoman, one of the Fianna, who had thougthlessly killed a litter of "pigs" and was then attacked by the wild sow. Fergoman and his dogs battled the sow through one valley and into another, the dogs being killed along the way. Finally Fergoman and the sow confronted each other near the cliff top and both were fatally wounded (Swan 1965:160).

In the second part of the story, Fergoman, mortally wounded, raises a cry for help and the cry is heard by his sister, Finna, who is on the shores of a lake below the cliff. The cry she hears, however, is an echo and, believing her brother to be on the opposite side of the lake, she swims across only to hear him calling from the opposite side. Confused and exhausted, she swam the lake several times before sinking and drowning. In her honor, the lake is called Lake Finn.

I later checked Pat's story with people who lived nearby; almost everyone knew the story. for it had been printed in an elementary school textbook after it was collected in the area. The recitations of it, however. were different: either the hero was Finn or Fergoman; the hero died or didn't: the pig died or got away. People who lived in the first valley knew the first part of the story and some had heard the second; those who lived near Finntown knew the second part of the story and were unfamiliar with the first part. In the first valley, only one feature of the story was invariant: the place names were always invoked in the right order. The place names corresponded to the townland boundaries or boundary markers, and although the details of the story might vary widely, the boundary markers never did. In each story, the dogs were killed near the large rock and on the valley floor.

There is another interesting feature of this story, the grave site that is located where Pat said it was. The *Shell Guide to Ireland* identifies this grave site as "Crocam Giants Grave, a ruined prehistoric chamber tomb" (1967:297). The grave was built during the Bronze Age, somewhere between 2500 B.C. and 500 A.D., and it is located between Lake Finn and Lake Muck (*muc* is the Gaelic word for pig). One informant suggested that he and I should go and dig up the grave site, a suggestion I declined, but others had undoubtedly been there long before to engage in amateur excavations. These Bronze Age graves often contained remains of the native Irish boar, a species that died out in the 12th century (Orme 1970:57).

The "events" and the participants in this myth are confused as are the times — a third century hero, famed for fighting eighth century Vikings, is said to be buried in a prehistoric, pre-Celtic tomb. But the Celtic place names are not confused, nor is their sequence ever skewed in the recounting.

Myths serve several purposes, among them entertainment and education of the young: this particular myth teaches the boundaries of the townlands and does so in such a vivid way that even though the details of the story may be forgotten or misremembered, the boundary markers are recalled in correct sequence in every retelling. Time has been collapsed or ignored as an unimportant detail, but the boundary markers, the important features of the story, are clearly delineated.

One point often made in the literature on Ireland is that the Irish do not bother to distinguish between time periods when telling stories, that myths and rumors are told in precisely the same way. Morton observes that in the West of Ireland, "If you miss the beginning of a story you never know whether a countryman is talking about a man in the next village or a saint in the next world" (1931:228). The point is well taken but in my example, the mnemonic function of myth or of "traditional" stories is also clear. I said earlier that every landmark in Donegal, every stone, brae, and valley has its own name and legend; in these names and legends, which are easily remembered, one can see how traditions are preserved or stored. The traditional story identifies the boundary markers, names them in specific order, and "explains" the origin of the place names. Further, children enjoy learning the story: it is a pleasant educational package.

Before I leave this second use, I will add one more point about the storage function of tradition, with respect to the ecological system. There is sound ecological reasoning behind some traditions, such as the "tradition" of bringing the sheep down from the hill on St. Patrick's Day. Until the beginning of the twentieth century, the custom was to bring the cattle up to the hill on St. Patrick's Day, March 17th. The custom was then inverted or reversed (as was the case with the Fair of Magheramore); sheep were brought down instead of cattle being brought up. The new tradition has two good outcomes: it gets good grass to the ewes before lambing (a practice called "flushing") and it removes the sheep from the higher lands at a time when the grass there is at its least nutritious. Grass comes in earlier in the valleys than on the hilltops, and this "extra bite," as the Irish call it, probably reduces the mortality rates for sheep considerably.

Bringing the sheep down on a "traditional" day is a very effective storage device and many other traditional practices can be viewed in this way; the care given to cattle has the effect of recycling resources. Keeping the cattle inside at night yields manure, which is used to fertilize the fields on which the cattle graze. But cattle are kept in at night, if one asks a farmer, because it's a tradition and "we've always done it that way."

There is another way in which tradition is a storage device that works to the farmers' advantage: if there were no tradition of bringing the sheep down on a particular day, then each individual farmer would have to decide when to bring his sheep down. Some farmers might bring them down too early, in which case the sheep would damage the early grass; some might bring them down too late, in which case many more sheep would die of starvation. St. Patrick's Day is an effective solution; in most years the early grass is well established in the valleys by this time and the mistakes that could be made by bringing them down too early or too late are minimized. Tradition protects farmers against themselves, in effect, given their difficult, unpredictable environment.

Where traditions of this kind do not operate, farmers run the risk of great losses. In "saving the hay," or harvesting the hay crop, the owners of the farms in each townland decide among themselves when to begin the cutting of the hay. Making the decision jointly is the tradition; there is no traditional day on which saving the hay is begun. The effect of this practice is that the farmers all work together but the problem with it is that they may make the wrong decision. Not all traditions work to the advantage of the community all of the time, especially in an uncertain environment, but it is likely that the customs that are considered to be "traditions" are often those that worked, and that they are retained for that reason, not for sentimental reasons.

By serving a storage function — or as a mnemonic or decision-making device — and by being sanctioned by the community as a whole, traditions are also effective regulators of community action and behavior. The emphasis in the statement, "We've always done it that way," might profitably be placed by analysts on the "we" rather than on the "always." By aligning their customs and traditions with those of the ancestors, the farmers are identifying themselves as a group. This is the third function or use of tradition and there are two ways of stating it, either as "our grandfathers did it that way" or as "we've done it that way ever since the British came." Both the "grandfather" response, as Alland (1972) calls it, and the "centuries of British oppression" (COBO) response, as I recorded it in my notes, have tradition as their referent but they were used to explain different phenomena.

The grandfather response was used to explain customs that informants liked or approved; the COBO response was used to explain all the rest, i.e., any custom that was disliked, disapproved of, or not completely understood. Southwest Donegal is largely treeless, for example, and the deforestation process began in the first millenium A.D., as a result of the cultivation techniques in common use then and the moist climatic phase.

The people of Donegal now attribute the lack of trees in the landscape to "centuries of British oppression," and some even go so far as to maintain that the English cut down all the trees and sent them to England. However, the deforestation of the area is attributable to the agricultural practices of the Irish "grandfathers," and to the third-century introduction of the iron plow. Regeneration of the forest was afterwards prevented by grazing livestock, and there is no sense in which the British (who assumed control of Donegal in the 17th century) can be held responsible for the lack of trees in the landscape. Nevertheless, because the lack of trees is something that people deplore, the British are thought to be responsible.

The COBO explanation appeared frequently in my notes, as did the grandfather explanation. Neither of these explanations is necessarily accurate. As I shall elaborate further on, most Irish farmers are not acquainted with their grandfathers (for reasons to do with land tenure and inheritance) and it is likely that many customs that Donegal farmers now claim as part of their ancestral heritage would bewilder an Irish grandfather. Before I return to the question of the reasons underlying the grandfather/COBO responses, I want to discuss the reaction people had to specific disconfirmations of these responses.

Often, after having gone through their own elaborate explanation of a "traditional" custom, informants would turn to me and ask why I thought they had begun doing it that way. The "traditional fair of Magheramore," which informants insisted on explaining as belonging to the traditions of the grandfathers, was among these and, just as insistently, informants would ask what I knew about the tradition and especially about the designation, "Magheramore." They knew that the fair was a "traditional" one and they knew its name, but they knew very little in fact about what its referents were and they hoped that my research would turn up something to shed light on the matter.

When I told people about the fair of Magheramore having been a Celtic fair that took place on the plain at Magheramore, they were interested — but disbelieving. I also pointed out that the "tradition" of selling sheep on the first of October in Ardara had displaced the Celtic practice of showing cattle on the first of November in Magheramore. I doubt that anyone remembered my "explanation," and I am sure that few believed I knew what I was talking about. An outsider cannot be expected to have a feeling for the traditional ways.

Another of my discoveries about these traditional ways came about because I have a poor sense of direction. When attending fairs in the villages in the area, I had to find the place where the cattle were sold. At first I asked directions to the cattle fair in each village but I soon discovered that I didn't have to bother: I simply made my way to the highest hill in the town and there were the cattle. In this way I noticed a regularity that people were surprised to hear pointed out: cattle were always sold on the highest hill in the village, and part of the hill was set aside for this purpose. [The only exception to the rule of the "cattle hill" was one village in which the Protestant Church had been built on the highest spot in town; cattle were sold, like sheep, in the streets below.]

Why were cattle sold on a hill, and why was the hill set aside for this purpose? When I inquired, most people said they had never noticed it. It was a custom that sounded Celtic, because the Celtic penchant for heights was well illustrated by the *raths*. But the Celts did not sell cattle, they traded or raided for them. Further, the Plain of Magheramore, where the Celtic cattle would have been paraded for show, was a plain and not a hill. The chief advantage of Magheramore was that it was flat and therefore afforded a large, level area for games, tents and such.

Though informants were surprised, they quickly rallied and came up with an explanation for the "cattle hill." Some suggested it was for ecological reasons (drainage was better on the hills and cattle would not stir up so much mud); others believed it might have something to do with the town councils, which set aside places for cattle sales — but why would nearly every town council in the area set aside the highest spot for selling cattle? Was there a precedent for it in earlier times? As usual, when questioning and cross-questioning people, I was treated to the full range of Irish volubility and imagination but, having dismissed the explanations one by one, I persisted and we arrived eventually at "tradition" as the full and final explanation. This custom, not having been noticed before by the people, could not be blamed easily on the British and, anyway, there was no particular harm in it. One informant made a weak attempt at the COBO explanation, noting that the English always insisted on removing matters Irish to the least accessible part of the town, but even he admitted that this was illogical for, he said, the British dearly loved to watch over the Irish carefully, especially when they were gathered for some event. It is still the case that the *Garda* post (police station) is situated on a hill, and often next to the "cattle hill," as it is called in every village. This did not explain the custom of leaving a choice plot of land free all year round, except for twelve days of the year, and I began searching the literature for a more likely origin for this custom.

It did not take long to find it, but had I not become attuned to the levels of explanations and to the many purposes that "tradition" could be made to serve, it would have been difficult to recognize the origin of the "cattle hill."

The fair sites, such as the fair of Magheramore, were assembly sites for conducting a great deal of business, with the chief passing judgment on transgressors and marriages being performed. According to Evans the logical place for transacting business would have been these hilltop sites; but Magheramore is not a hilltop and every other fair site in Donegal villages (save the one with the Protestant Church on it) is on a hilltop. There had to be another explanation; I found it in P.W. Joyce's account of ancient Irish customs (1913). In each village a small hill was set aside for business purposes; councils of representatives held their debates on local matters there (Joyce 1913:449), a custom that was continued to the end of the sixteenth century. These "meeting hills" were governed by special regulations and a fine was levied against any individual who permitted his cows to graze there. Joyce notes that Ferflatha O'Gnive, the *ollav* poet (court poet) of the O'Neills of Clannaboy in the time of Elizabeth I, "lamenting the decay of the old Gaelic customs, says that now, alas, the sacred meeting hills are no longer frequented: they are tilled and cropped and used as common market-places" (1913:450).

The cattle hill, then, was part of the tradition of the area but its present uses and its original purposes were quite disparate. Cattle hills were places apart, specially regulated, but for Donegal at least, O'Gnive was partially wrong: the "decay of the old Gaelic customs" led to the creation of a set of new traditions.

I have said that the difference between these two rationales, the grandfather response and the COBO response, has to do with whether the custom or feature under discussion is liked or not by informants. Alland suggests that the grandfather response is made in situations in which traits have no particular basis in the theories of the informants, and while I think he is right, I believe there is a further implication to be drawn here, an implication that has to do with ethnic identity. It is all well and good to align oneself with the grandfathers but to evoke the Centuries of British Oppression explanation is to identify oneself and one's activities as the direct result of COBO is to formulate the predicates of ethnic identity. Throughout this book, I will have much to say about this process and the often curious forms that it takes but the reader should note at this juncture that the separation of Donegal from its natural market region in Ulster was probably the precipitating event that made many of these revisions necessary. So long as they are economically dependent on livestock, which are marketed in Northern Ireland, and politically dependent on the Republic to the south, the people of Donegal will have a "mixed" ethnic identity, will continue to see themselves both as "men of Ulster," as they like to say, and as patriots of the Republic, sufferers of many Centuries of British Oppression.

The fourth use of tradition has to do with the discrepancies between "living memory" and the written record. Lévi-Strauss has said of myth that it is a way of reconciling unwelcome contradictions and I think tradition does the same for the people of Southwest Donegal. It is a way of reconciling past and present, ideal and real behavior. Anthropologists are much given to discussing the differences between ideal and real behavior as if they (the anthropologists) were the only ones who perceived these differences. I think, on the contrary, that "tradition" is often used as a way of reconciling these disparities, and that, while it is very useful as a mnemonic device, a storage device, and a sanctioning device, tradition as a "final" explanation for the way things are now is most important in its use as a means of reconciling differences between past and present, between ideal and reality and, equally important, as a way of making claims on a better future.

By claiming that a new custom is a tradition, continuity between past and present is established, that is, "We" are doing things the way they have always been done. By claiming that tradition accounts for a great deal of present behavior and that traditional behavior is good, many innovations and practices that the Irish do not like (and that cannot be attributed to Centuries of British Oppression) or that have not been firmly established because of the high risk involved, can be denounced. "Ideal" behavior is traditional behavior; "real" behavior is nontraditional and introduced from outside.

This is a view that incorporates into "tradition" a way of reconciling ideal/real disparities, because everything that is not good, that is disturbing about the present, is due to interference with the "traditional" ways. It is, in some ways, an irrefutable argument, especially if one is able to disregard the written records that disprove it.

It is customary in Southwest Donegal to regard the "old days" as the good times, the present as the bad times. A common belief is that everyone was happier in the past than today, and less isolated.

That there is more isolation is undoubtedly true, but the isolation results from heavy outmigration rates among young people, and outmigration, in turn, has been caused by changing standards of living and expectations. These are external factors that have changed the pattern of social relations in Donegal and they are the realities. Tradition has nothing to do with the matter, but tradition is used as the referent for the "good old days" of the past and modernity for the "bad new days" of the present. The "good old days" included gombeenmen, debt slavery, high infant mortality rates and dirt floors, as well as few men "who ever got their fill of bacon." They also included Cromwell's War, as it is called in Ireland; the rebellion that culminated in the Flight of the Earls; the Land Wars; the "Trouble Times" and the Civil War of the 1920s (to name only a few conflicts)' and the Great Potato Famine of 1845-1849. But all these have become part of the honored traditions of the good old days.

Even the Great Famine — which probably accounted for a population loss of 2,500,000 due to starvation or outmigration (Woodham-Smith 1962:409) — can be used to illustrate the good old days and the ingenious hardy ways of the ancestors. After recounting the centuries of British oppression that led up to the Great Famine, Patrick McGill writes:

> Despite the evidence of famine and distress in the parish [of Ardara] in those tragic years, the writer is of opinion that conditions were not quite so severe as in many similar areas, and that fewer people died. Almost every townland had famine survivors down to 1914 and later, yet their most harrowing accounts seldom had a local provenance, and were mainly based on the tales of "travelling men" (McGill n.d.:98).

It may be true that the people of Southwest Donegal were not so hard hit by the Great Famine as were people in other parts of Ireland, but the historical account that McGill himself gives indicates the contrary. Seven soup kitchens were operated in the parish of Ardara and, according to an eyewitness report to the Relief Commissioners, "of the entire population seven-eighths of the householders are small farmers and occupiers whose existence at all times depended upon (the potato) . . ." (McGill n.d.:96).

Why does McGill see the Famine as less severe in Southwest Donegal? Presumably because its survivors were his ancestors and the ancestors, by definition, were the source of all good things, while the British were the source of all bad things. With these premises, written history can be denied easily.

Estyn Evans gives a delightful example of the tendency to "purify" the past, in his discussion of plowing by the tail, a practice apparently common in Ireland during the 17th century. It is no mean feat to attach a plow to a horse's tail but, assuming that the ancestors did it, later generations proved even more ingenious in their denials that the ancestors did it.

Evidence for the practice of plowing by the tail is adduced from Parliamentary Acts banning it and by artistic representations of ploughmen walking backwards in front of their draft animals (1976:34). Acting out of what Evans calls a need to "purify the past," several Irish authors have denied that the custom ever existed; their denials take most fanciful forms:

> It is argued that since ploughing by the tail was impossible, and if possible then extremely cruel, it could not have been practised by the Irish, and that the various Acts of Parliament passed against it from 1635 onwards were instigated not by any pretended concern for the horses but by hostility to the Irish people and the wish to demonstrate how degraded they were (Evans 1976:34).

Although ploughing by the tail seems to have disappeared by the 19th century, Evans believes that a number of associated customs persisted, including the custom of walking backward in front of the plough horses. He notes that one author, writing in 1858, explained the custom of walking backwards by referring to the opinion of a County Galway ploughman that "it was necessary for the horses to speak to the leader" (Evans 1976:35).

This kind of reasoning is the quintessence of Irish thinking about tradition; the past may be purified, as Evans terms it, or it may be disregarded or the practices may be inverted. Whatever happens, "tradition" is the winner.

I have traced here four uses of tradition: first, as a sanction for new customs or for old customs newly revised or inverted; second, as a storage device for preserving important components of the behavioral or ecological system; third, as a way of identifying the people who share a common heritage; and fourth, as a way of comparing the "glorious past" with the realities of the present. From what has been said it should be apparent that tradition can be and is both an active and a passive force in the lives of the people of Southwest Donegal, that tradition as a general category can be creative, in the sense that new and useful customs can be incorporated into the category of tradition, and thereby preserved.

The rubric "tradition" helps, rather than hinders, the creation of new modes of adapting, either to the political or the physical environment.

What I have not said, and would not say, is that tradition is dead or that it is a stultifying force that prevents innovation and causes irrational rejection of new adaptive modes. Over and over again, the people of Southwest Donegal have coped with crises and I agree with Rose when he says that "crises of authority are nothing new to the Irish. They could almost claim to have discovered them" (1971:17). But I would add that crises of most types are not new to the Irish and that includes crises over new customs. If the real history of the area serves as a guide to its future, the likelihood is that the people of Donegal will also cope with modernity. They will undoubtedly cope in their own way and on their own terms; they may translate new practices into "traditions" or they may alter their vision of the past. Whatever else, it seems likely that they will continue to cope with the present and add to past glories. Some modern practices may be environmentally unsound and lead to environmental degradation — a bitter accompaniment of modernity elsewhere. Some new ideas may facilitate already heavy outmigration, the true peril to the region's social and economic integrity. Though it is fashionable to decry the passing of the "traditional" system, I have some faith in the ability of the people of Southwest Donegal to make wise choices, to resynthesize old and new and to recast modernity in their own "traditional" terms.

CHAPTER TWO

The Distant Past:

Continuities in Recorded History

" . . . and yet I often think it odd that [history] should be so dull,
for a great deal of it must be invention."
Jane Austen, *Northanger Abbey*

Along with the South Sea Islanders and the Arabs, the Celts
are among literature's most over-romanticized peoples. Though
it is not my task to add to the glorification of the Erin-that-was,
it is important to establish that pastoralism or livestock keeping,
the basic adaptive mode of the Celts, had and continues to have
an enormous influence in Irish lives and landscapes, particularly
in Southwest Donegal. In addition to Donegal's remoteness and
its pastoral base, there are other continuities between past and
present. Two such are the calendrical system and land tenure
practices. A major discontinuity is the post-1600 loss of local
secular leadership. All have an impact on present practices and
perceptions.

It is usual in recounting Irish history, to begin with an early
conquest — say the Norse invasion of 800 A.D., or the Norman
Conquest that began in 1170 A.D. — and then to elaborate on
the changes brought by the conquerors. However, in Southwest
Donegal, the most important conquest was that made by the Celts
in the third century before Christ and the implications of some
of the changes they brought continue into the present. I will deviate
slightly from the practice of beginning with a conquest and outline
what I see as the continuities of history in the region before and
after the appearance of the Celts and recorded government. Such
a deviation is made easier by the facts: the Norse never invaded
Donegal and the impact of the Norman invasion was not felt in
the area for almost 400 years. Remoteness, then, was a factor long
before the arrival of the Celts and their livestock. Southwest
Donegal has always been removed from the centers of political
activity and has seldom been of interest to conquerors bent on
plunder and exploitation.

PreCeltic Times

Prior to the Celtic invasion of the third century B.C., successive human occupations of Ireland brought about an environment in which the Celts could flourish. The prehistoric, preCeltic background of livestock production is most graphically described by pollen analysis, the best indicator of land-use patterns.

The earliest inhabitants of Ireland's dense mixed woodlands were Mesolithic hunters and gatherers. As in most of Western Europe, the hazel, elm, oak, and pine forests provided cover for game, as well as abundant forage.

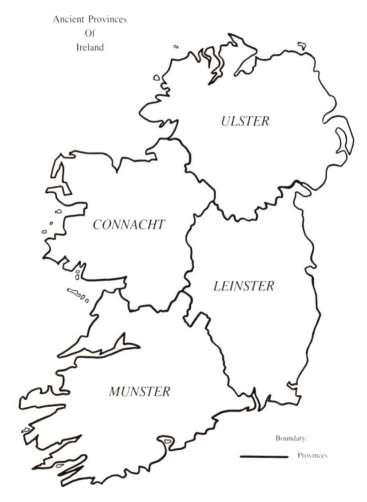

Ancient Provinces
Of
Ireland

ULSTER

CONNACHT

LEINSTER

MUNSTER

Boundary:

—————— Provinces

About 3500 B.C. Neolithic invaders arrived. As they began to clear the woodlands, the Mesolithic people were driven deep into the forests or reduced to year-round dependence on fish (Mitchell 1971:282). The Neolithic farmers chose the lightly forested uplands as cultivation sites, and accompanying the decline of elm pollen was an increase in open pasture species such as ribwort and bracken. "The evidence points to small co-operating communities of farmers, presumably kin groups occupying clusters of from 10 to 20 houses, who cleared successive patches of forest over a fairly extensive area and sent out daughter colonies to repeat the process" (Evans 1957:225).

The Neolithic peoples were exploiting a new niche and, like most animal populations in similar circumstances, their population expanded rapidly. The effect of this expansion on the environment was not irremediable. Slash-and-burn agriculture did not prohibit forest regeneration; elm, which occupied the sites most easily utilized by the colonists, once more reasserted itself and the landscape was little changed. "Gradually the landscape became a mosaic of virgin forest, tillage patches, rough pastures and secondary woodlands in various stages of regeneration until elm, oak, and alder once again predominated" (Orme 1970:79).

Domesticated animals were introduced during the Neolithic. Archaeological remains indicate that these animals were smaller than, but otherwise similar to, those of the present (Orme 1970:58). Sheep resembled the present mountain breeds and cattle remains show similarities to the modern Kerry breed, small animals noted for their hardiness.

The Bronze Age people who began to arrive about 1800 B.C. were, with their metal tools, able to clear the forests more easily and effectively than had their predecessors. The pollen record shows a great increase in those species common to over-grazed plots, for example, bracken, gorse, nettles, and ribwort. Elm pollen declines drastically at this stage, along with other, hardier species that had not been disrupted previously.

All this took place in a climatic phase well suited for agriculture, the warm, dry sub-Boreal. In parts of Donegal, crops were grown that have not been successful there since. After 500 B.C. the climate deteriorated and the sub-Atlantic phase, a cooler, moister period, began. This brought the conditions the Celts found almost ideal for their pastoral economy, but even before the Celtic conquests, the indigenous economy shows a greater emphasis on livestock than on agricultural produce, an undoubted consequence of the climatic shift.

The moist climate accelerated the formation of peat bogs and, as virgin forests were further assaulted, regeneration of trees slowed up considerably. Under the new climatic conditions, the upland areas, which had been cleared for cultivation, were unsuited to forests and to agriculture; but some authorities believe that human interference alone would have disrupted regeneration. Whatever the cause, the effect was leaching of the soil, rapid runoff of surface water, and poor drainage.

To summarize the pre-Celtic period, then, the Celts who came to Donegal in the third century B.C. found small communities — probably kin groups — in nucleated settlements or clusters of houses surrounded by land of varying types and uses. Because of the climatic shift toward moister conditions, livestock were already more important in the economy than agriculture; bog formation, a consequence of high rainfall, may have been accelerated by clearing of land for pastures. Evidence of the settlements in which these pre-Celtic peoples lived survives today mainly in the pre-Celtic townland and place names still in use.

The Celts

The sub-Atlantic climatic phase, which extends through the present, is sometimes divided into two zones, one of general deforestation from 300 to 1700 A.D. and a second of afforestation, from 1700 onwards. This last is accompanied by the introduction of alien species. From 250 B.C. the Celts transformed the landscape to suit their own purposes, a process that was aided by a millennium of relatively undisturbed rule. Orme observes that, "as Celtic settlement and land-use practices spread through the country, man's impact on the landscape became more uniform" (1970:85). Forest decline continued but was accelerated after the introduction of the heavy iron plow in 300 A.D., a date that coincides with the zone of deforestation.

During the Celtic invasions, fortified settlements had appeared for the first time. These were stone or earthen ringforts (*raths*) built on heights; although their builders are unknown, it is certain that these structures later served as the base from which the local overlords ruled. Because the *raths* lack permanent water supplies, it is unlikely that they were intended for more than temporary defensive purposes. There are 28,000 raths in Ireland (Evans 1942:32) and twenty-four in one of the parishes of Southwest Donegal. The town of Ardara takes its name from the fort prominently located there; *Ard an Ratha* means "hill of the fort" and the earthen fort commands a spectacular view of West Donegal, a view now enjoyed largely by the cows grazing on the slopes of the inner wall (20' high) of the enclosure.

The largest of the forts in the parish is about 80 yards in diameter. There are many smaller ones which also must have served, 2,000 years ago as now, as sheep pens. The usual pattern seems to have been to locate one or more houses at one end of the enclosure and leave the rest of the space for animals. Although the *raths* may have been inconvenient dwellings or hopeless ones in the event of a long siege, they are ideally suited for protection against cattle raids.

The Celtic aristocracy, which occupied the *raths* or forts, was in the minority, and a chief held his power by alliances. A system of cattle lending not unlike that of the Southern Bantu (Schapera 1937) seems to have been in operation. Little is known about the surviving pre-Celtic peoples, but it is thought that they continued to live in kin group settlements (*clachans*[1]) on their open fields, cultivating grain crops and caring for a number of the chief's cattle in exchange for the animals' produce. The peasant's wattle and daub houses do not survive in the archaeological records; townlands and place names are the remnants of these settlements. *Raths* are found only on the best lands. Loughros Point, one of the most fertile areas in Southwest Donegal, has seven forts, including the traditional "castle" of the O'Boyles.

Orme suggests that there were two "pivotal" institutions in Celtic society, the *fine* or joint family (a landholding unit) and the *tuath*, sometimes translated as a petty kingdom but more closely resembling a chiefdom. The Celts were strongly patrilineal and the joint family included all relations in the male line for five generations. Land was divided equally among brothers and an individual had legal rights only as a member of the joint family. This may have been the origin of the naming system that persists today; the Celts called people by their given names and by their fathers' names, so Conal McGlynn was Conal, son of Glynn. The prefix O' is attached to a clan name, and surnames, which were often clan names, came much later in Irish history. The landholding units and the chiefdoms were probably the major sources of individual identity in Celtic times, and loyalties may have been much the same: first to the family or landholding unit, then to the *tuath* or chiefdom of the area. The *tuatha* proliferated and factionalism was rife.

Rank in Celtic society was dependent on birth, wealth, or learning. Judges, poets, druids and later, Christian clergy, were equal in rank to the petty kings or chiefs (Orme 1970:88-92). The wealth of a landowner was measured in *sets*, a unit equivalent to a young heifer. After the Celtic hold on the country was secured:

> Ireland became a land of cattle. Wealth was counted in heads of cattle, not in land. Lacking currency, the cow was a basic unit of value and exchange. It was also the main source of meat, dairy produce — the principal summer food — leather and hides. The rath (ringfort) was a ranch in which a mainly pastoral economy that was not nomadic but which involved short-range transhumance, or booleying, designed to use summer hill pastures for the cattle.... Most cattle were killed and salted in the autumn for winter food, because of the scarcity of winter animal fodder.... Inevitably, cattle-rustling became a popular and violent blood-sport, a test of manhood and noble status (Orme 1970:95).

Recorded government first appeared in the middle of the fifth century when three sons of Niall of the Nine Hostages, High King of Ireland, began the conquest of Donegal. Eoin, Conall Gulban, and Eanna divided the area among themselves. The southern and western parts were given to Conall, from whom the area takes its name — Tir Chonaill, or the land of Conall. Having claimed the land, Conall's descendants had then to spend a century subduing it. Conall's second son, Eanna Boghaine, established for himself a sizable portion of Tir Chonaill, known as the Barony of Banagh. Later the Barony of Banagh was split in two; the modern southwestern portion of Donegal (the area I studied) was called the Barony of Boylagh after another of Conall Gulban's descendants, Baoighill, a chief of the thirteenth generation after Conall. (Boylagh was reduced considerably by the Scottish MacSweeneys in the 13th century, and again in the 14th century by a southern branch of these same MacSweeneys.)

The incursion of the sons of the Celtic High King into the farthest northwestern corner of Ireland did not change the land's

allegiance to its natural geographical center, the province of Ulster.
The chieftains allied themselves, as had their predecessors, with
other Ulster chiefs. Another continuity of the area's history, one
of equal importance, is religion: the sons of Niall of the Nine
Hostages brought with them Christianity. Conal Caol (590-627
A.D.), the grandson of Eanna Boghaine, established an island
monastery and began the missionary work that took another
hundred years to complete. Almost from the beginning, then,
religious and political control were consolidated, and continued
to be so until the end of secular rule by the O'Boyles and the
O'Donnells. The last O'Boyle chieftain to be inaugurated, Tadg
Og O'Boyle, died in 1607. A few years later the remains of Niall
O'Boyle, Bishop of Raphoe from 1591 until 1611, were interred
along with the O'Boyle chieftains, a fact that suggests that Bishop
O'Boyle may have been of noble ancestry (McGill n.d.: 40).

The Celts were colorful people, happily given to boasting about
their exploits. Heroism was judged by daring cattle raids and the
Annals of Ulster record 274 cattle raids between the ninth and
fifteenth centuries (probably only a portion of those carried out),
recorded to enhance the prestige of chiefs. Over time the numbers
given by the annalists increase: in 1044 one chief took 1,200 cows,
and another is recorded as having taken 6,000. In 1593 the Earl
of Tyrone offered 20,000 cows in payment for a fine, and 10,000
were reported stolen in a raid.

Religious literature also indicates the importance of livestock.
St. Naile is supposed to have demanded "a full-grown beef of
every lasting capture in the raids of your neighbours," from all
who paid tribute to him, and a cow from every raid seems to have
been a standard tithe (Lucas 1957:75-87).

In the 12th century the Celtic landscape is described as
containing innumerable *raths*, forts in which pastoralism was
practiced, several thousand farm clusters in their open fields, and
about 200 self-sufficient monastic settlements. The forests had
diminished considerably and most lowland agricultural areas were
surrounded by rough grazings. There was no central government,
nothing resembling a town or city, and few trade or communication
networks.

The *rath* of the nobility and the *clachan* of the peasant were
economically self-sufficient units, with the *raths* maintaining
something of a monopoly on luxury goods. The Anglo-Norman
invaders who arrived in Ireland in 1169 displaced the Celtic

nobility (although not in Donegal until 1600) in most of Ireland but encouraged the common farmers to remain on their lands.

The Celts shared most of the beliefs and practices with regard to their animals that anthropologists are accustomed to finding among African pastoralists today. The use of blood for food, the belief that a cow would not give milk unless her calf was near, the custom of blowing in a cow's vagina to make her let down her milk — all these were known to the Irish. Most disappeared with the advent of English rule. The last mention of bloodletting is during Famine times when travelers regarded it with horror.

Although many Celtic customs relating to livestock may have been lost owing to English abhorrence (or perhaps to a newfound Irish delicacy), the Celtic calendar was deeply imbedded in the ritual cycle of the Catholic Church and this calendrical system survives even to the present. The Celtic year began with All Hallows Day, November 1. This was the day when the family was reunited after some of its members returned from the hills where they had cared for the cattle over the summer. Cattle were given free run of the land after November 1, new fires were lit, and rituals included a great fair, the predecessor of the modern fair day:

> From very early times the major ritual assemblies of the year provided opportunity for exchange of goods, of livestock and of news, and for the maintenance of folk tradition and bardic skill. In ancient Ireland it is recorded that there were two kinds of assemblies, the "*aonach*" for pleasure and the "*aireacht*" for business, but it seems probable that, like the great fairs of recent times, they served both purposes. It is suggestive of the ritual and religious elements in the old assemblies that they generally met upon hill-tops — often the site of prehistoric burials — and that they took place at the fixed times marking the beginning of the Celtic seasons (Evans 1942:157).

The November first fairs, which lasted for three days, were held throughout Ireland and the ancient roads led to these assembly sites. Feasting, fighting, and athletic contests usually took place on a plain large enough to accommodate thousands of visitors. In Southwest Donegal the assembly site was Magheramore, which means large plain. When new roads were constructed in 1750 the old fair sites were bypassed and although the fair of Magheramore continued for several decades it did not survive the Famine intact. As mentioned earlier, the date was changed from November 1 to

October 1 and the fair was moved to Ardara where the October 1 fair is still referred to as the traditional fair of Magheramore.

The next major holiday in the Celtic calendar was February 1, St. Brigid's Day. On the eve of this day rushes were pulled and woven into crosses which were hung up in houses and byres to bring luck (Figure 2.2). "Some of them are very elaborate, but the oldest style, to judge from its Celtic form, is the three-legged cross which is specially associated with cattle and is not, like the other shapes, taken to church to be blessed . . ." (Evans 1942:154). These crosses are still woven and hung in Donegal as, for that matter, they are in parts of Belfast. The ritual significance of St. Brigid's Day, however, is overshadowed by its agricultural significance, for it is the first day of spring and therefore the day when preparation of the land is supposed to begin. St. Brigid's Day is also the time from which most of my informants reckoned the beginning of the year.

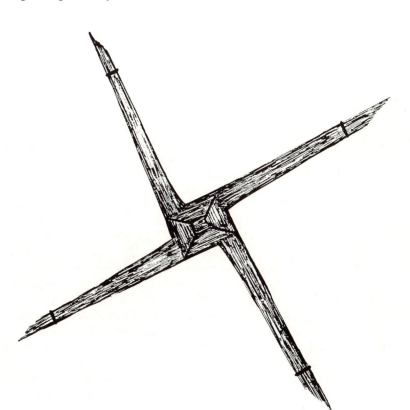

Figure 2.2. St. Brigid's Cross

According to the historians, Brigid was a native Irish goddess and patroness of poets before she became a Christian cowherd and saint (Dillon and Chadwick 1973:184). Chadwick specifies that the Celts adopted earlier practices, such as those to do with Brigid, for their own purposes:

> The persistent recurrence in the literature of certain days in the year on which particularly important events took place makes it possible to identify the four major peaks of the Celtic ritual calendar. This is reinforced by later folk tradition, particularly that concerning *Lugnasadh*, and Christian attempts to efface pagan practice by adopting and adapting to Christian usage well-established cult-practices, as in the case of *Imbolc*. Samhain (1 November) was the beginning of the Celtic year, at which time any barriers between man and the supernatural were lowered. *Imbolc* followed on 1 February. This appears to have been involved primarily with fertility ritual, traditionally associated with the lactation of ewes. Christianity, in an attempt to reconcile the strong attraction of this feast with its own teaching and ritual, made it the feast of St. Bridgid, who in the Irish Christian tradition was made the midwife of the Virgin Mary. St. Bridgid herself, if she ever existed, appears to have taken over the functions of a Celtic goddess of the same name and comparable attributes (Chadwick 1970:180-181).

The first of February no longer has the importance in the pastoral year that it once held, though February 1 is still the day when preparation of the land is supposed to be begun. St. Brigid's crosses commemorate this day and, in the making of the crosses, their fashioning from left to right, i.e., with the sun, commemorates the probable origins of the practice. The crosses themselves serve no useful purpose beyond an aesthetic one, and the practices with which they are associated are no longer useful; in this sense, the crosses can be seen as a survival. Until recently, perhaps, the Celtic calendrical system had some efficacy in the adaptation of the population to its environment and therefore there is some functional value that could be assigned to the commemoration of the first of February. The crosses symbolize a past activity, or set of activities, and they are part of a set of time-honored beliefs that withstood the ravages of time because of their utility to the believers. Both Tylor and Malinowski would have liked St. Brigid's crosses, no doubt, for they "prove" both their theories.

St. Patrick's Day, March 17, is the day on which sowing is begun. In the Celtic year this was the time cattle and sheep were removed to rough grazing lands in the hills; the practice is reversed today in Donegal and sheep are brought from their winter grazings.

Both May 1 and June 23 were associated with fire and with the blessing of the cattle; St. John's Eve (June 23) had a special significance: ceremonies performed kept the sun on its course. August 1, along with November 1, February 1 and May 1 were the beginnings of new seasons and were celebrated with feasting and with a fair.

Many assumptions about Celtic husbandry are probably based on later custom. For example, it is assumed that the Celts were transhumant pastoralists when they arrived in Ireland and that they spread this custom. "In all the Celtic lands the life of the aristocracy centered largely on hunting and all that goes with it: that of the lower classes in waiting on them, and in carrying on such agriculture as prevailed" (Chadwick 1970:122). Transhumance survived the Celts and it may have preceded them; too little is known about the life of the pre-Celtic peasants to make a definite statement on the subject.

Another custom attributed to the Celts is that of keeping cattle in the home. "This custom of keeping cows in the dwelling house in winter is so widely attested in the country from the 16th to the 19th century that it must be an ancient usage although there do not appear to be many explicit early references to it" (Lucas 1957:80). The author goes on to say that cattle "were sometimes shut up at night in an enclosure called a *tuar*. In some parts of the country this word is a common component of place names, . . . Not much appears to be discoverable about the *tuar* but in recent times at all events, it seems to have been chiefly used as a means of collecting supplies of manure" (Lucas 1957:80).

Cattle were subject to many dangers — from wolves, raiding parties, and the like — and were probably kept under close surveillance at all times, but the reasons for keeping them penned up both at night and over the winter may have been closer to modern ones, that is, manure would have become more valuable with an increase in population and the introduction of the potato. Wolves were eradicated by the 18th century and raiding parties a century before that, yet the custom of keeping cattle in at night and during the winter remains to the present day. Under the rundale system the supply of manure accruing to each household would have insured its livelihood; prior to the introduction of dispersed housing the best way of safeguarding this would have been to keep the cows in the house, in the case of a peasant or, in the case of an aristocrat, within the ring fort.

That the Celts put great emphasis on their cattle is well documented; the lives of the early saints are filled with miraculous episodes that illustrate their power over cattle. The commonplaces of animal husbandry are not so well known but in this discussion of the Celts I have tried to outline some of the features of Celtic society that survived its leaders: the primary dependence on cattle and cattle products, the peasant *clachan* with its mixed agricultural-pastoral base, the calendrical system of holidays that still demarcates the seasonal activities associated with livestock, the rituals from which the livestock fairs took their time and place. Though I would not disagree with the authors who claim that the Celtic legacy persists, I would suggest that it is the pastoral elements of this legacy that persist. The Celtic social and legal systems have disappeared; what remain are certain features of the Celtic economy.

Perhaps the most curious aspect of this legacy is the bias in favor of cattle. Though sheep and other domestic animals were kept before and during the period of Celtic domination, wealth is always recorded in kine (cows), and other domestic animals are translated into livestock equivalents (5 sheep = 1 cow). Although this bias is common to Indo-European peoples, it seems to have reached its logical conclusion among the Celts, for whom cattle were the measure of all things.

There remains to be discussed one discontinuity since 1600, the loss of local secular leadership. There is no better comment on the role of the chiefs at the end of Celtic rule than a eulogy written for one of them, one of the "earls," Red Hugh O'Donnell who died in 1505:

> This O'Donnell was the full moon of the hospitality and nobility of the north, the most jovial and valiant, the most prudent in war and peace, and of the best jurisdiction, law and rule of all the Gaels of Ireland. There was no defence made in Tyrconnell during his time except to close the door against the wind only; the best protector of the church and the learned; a man who had given great alms in honour of the Lord of the Elements; a man by whom a castle was first raised and erected at Donegal that it might serve as a sustaining bulwark for his descendents; and a monastery of Friars de Observantia in Tyrconnell, namely the Monastery of Donegal; a man who had made many predatory

excursions around through Ireland, and a man who may be justly styled the Augustus of the north-west of Europe (from *The Annals of the Four Masters*, quoted in O'Faolain 1942:1).

Emphasis is placed here on Red Hugh's virtues as ruler, his protection of his people, his services to the church. The O'Donnells were the ruling clan of Donegal, the O'Boyles lesser chieftains and rulers of the Barony of Boylagh. All exacted tribute from their subjects and were in turn expected to provide protection. This, along with intricate networks of kinship and fealty, was the basis for their secular power. As there is no description on record of Red Hugh's functioning in this capacity we can borrow such a description from a biography of a kinsman and neighboring chief, the Earl of Tyrone:

> But it is not merely of buildings that he would think as he set out on some long ride through his demesnes but of his *urraghs*, or lieges, bound to him by bonds of service and fealty, or by those links of fosterage and gossipred which form a stronger alliance than blood ... the inextricable network of Gaelic society from which every captain like himself gets his lawful dues of oats and oatmeal, butter, and hogs, and mutton, and rents. He would see every one of these at least twice a year, at May and Hallowtide, when he weaves his way with his retinue of swordsmen and horsemen, lawyers, chroniclers, and poets around the spring-to-autumn woodland camps. At these camps O'Neill would dismount. The food would be laid out on great stone slabs or on the beaten fern.... After the meal O'Neill would settle down to business, to the discussion of crops, and cattle, and rents, and raids, for the whole source of his power was his capacity to protect his liegemen against other men, and that nexus bound them to him, and him to them in a bond of mutual advantage (O'Faolain 1942:19).

This was the nature of the secular rule and of the society of the Celts. The leadership that persisted for more than 12 centuries (from the fifth to the seventeenth century) was always fragile and subject to infighting over inheritance of the title of chieftain. Closely bound to the rulers and dependent on them for protection were the monastic establishments of this era. It has been emphasized that, although there was a Gaelic society, there was no Gaelic nation, hence no state organization to undertake the defense of the region (O'Faolain 1942:11). When the British attack came in earnest the O'Boyles joined the O'Donnells (or rather that branch of the O'Donnells to which they owed allegiance) and the O'Donnells allied themselves with the O'Neills; all were defeated at the Battle of Kinsale in 1601.

Bishop Niall O'Boyle was imprisoned for intriguing with the Spanish king to overthrow the English government, a charge that may have had its foundation in fact. In 1607 came the "Flight of the Earls" from Ulster and the native rulers left Ireland forever.

Both secular and religious leadership had been firmly under the control of the indigenous establishment. In the absence of its rulers the church probably drew what power remained into its own hands. This proposition helps to explain why the church continued in power for so many years and it may partially explain why even now people look to the church for leadership in secular matters such as economic development and material improvement in life-styles. Once the earls, the local political leaders, had gone, no secular leaders arose.

Plantation

After Kinsale, the British were determined that no such uprising would occur again. Three hundred years of governing the Irish had taught the British "that it was not enough to defeat the Irish in time of war; their influence seeped back again in time of peace" (Inglis 1956:52). The earls who had fled forfeited their lands to the Crown, so that almost all Ulster was open to plantation (colonization) by the English.

In 1610 the lists of the divisions available for planting were made public. Land was issued to "Undertakers," each of whom undertook to plant English or Scottish tenants on his lands within two years. A detailed study of Southwest Donegal in the seventeenth century sets out in full the conditions of plantation grants:

> It was a condition of the plantation grants that an undertaker of a small proportion of 1,000 acres should build a stone or brick house or castle with a strongbawn on a demesne within his lands, should plant at least 10 British families including 24 able, adult men, and should establish 2 fee-farmers and 3 lease-holders for three lives on farms of 50 or 60 acres, together with other husbandmen or cottagers to live in villages (Graham 1970:143).

The "mere Irish[2]" were ordered to disperse and to vacate the lands they had formerly held. The scattered relatives of Tadg Og

O'Boyle, the last chieftain, were removed from the area and resettled on barren lands in the north. The Irish population was to be placed in small communities under the supervision of Servitors and was to occupy the very poorest lands.

In Donegal the plantation system was difficult to put into practice, for the region had few inducements and fertile land was not one of them; elsewhere in Ulster the system took hold because the available land was better. Many English and Scottish tenants who came to the Barony of Banagh (called by the English the Proportion of Monargan) were dismayed by what they found, and left almost as rapidly as they had come.

There was almost as much difficulty in keeping landlords as there was in keeping tenants, and the land patent changed hands a number of times because of neglect in fulfilling the patent conditions. In 1618-19, a survey revealed that "few British tenants, but a great many Irish dwelt upon the lands" (McGill n.d.:46). The whole of Southern Donegal was divided into three proportions, each of which contained 1,000 acres of arable land (the whole area containing 330,000 acres). On only one of these had the requisite "bawne" (a fortified enclosure) been built. One proportion had only one British family, and the other had been sold three times with little evidence of any but native occupation (McGill n.d.:46).

In Graham's study of 17th century Donegal, an important conclusion is that the large land units of the area with their summer grazing lands had an economic validity that was undisturbed even by the political upheaval of plantation. She offers considerable evidence to support her belief that, although the system of tenure was changed by the influx of landlords and agents, the agricultural system did not undergo significant changes. The "planted population" had little effect:

> The actual influx of persons of British origin was small, and of these the majority were connected with the town of Killybegs. Farming in this poor environment was unattractive and, with tenure insecure, very few British farmers must have wished to compete with the Irish whose long established agricultural system represented a suitable adjustment to the local environment. Since farming practices were in no way affected by the change in tenure of the Irish farmers, and since there was no great influx of land-seeking foreigners, they were continued as before (Graham 1970:151).

What changed, then, was the political system; ownership of land was forbidden to Catholics and the "mere Irish" had to pay fixed rentals on the land they had formerly occupied by customary right and for which they had paid tribute to their chief. Money replaced payments in kind. Under the chief a man had paid his debts either with produce or by keeping a number of the chief's cattle.

The religious system changed, too, at least outwardly. Catholicism was outlawed, so masses were said in the open air; priests were hunted and killed; the population remained avowedly Catholic. A point made before bears repetition because it relates to the continuity of religion in the area. Once the native secular leaders were removed, the church remained the only source of native leadership. Recruitment policies for the priesthood bear this out; only the wealthiest families could afford to educate a man to become a priest. Hence the church assumed many of the functions normally relegated to government, and its members in Donegal continue to do so to the present day. The greatest churchman the area has produced was Cardinal-Archbishop O'Donnell, a lineal descendant of Red Hugh O'Donnell, mentioned above, the chieftain who built Donegal Castle.

The O'Boyles and their strongest rivals, the O'Gallaghers, produced the largest number of priests in the area. The O'Boyles seem to have had a near monopoly on the profession, and historians note that for two centuries, the parish priest of Ardara was an O'Boyle (McGill n.d.:113). In an account of the 50 priests and bishops of the area, nine bear the surname Gallagher and six the name of Boyle. No other surname appears more than twice.

Plantation had little success in the area, as noted. In 1641 Southwest Donegal joined the rest of Ulster in the rebellion known as Cromwell's War. Because the remaining leaders had been removed to the north, the rebels defended their western sector only briefly. The O'Boyles were prominent in this uprising but organization was poor and Cromwell's forces swept through the countryside. Massacre sites are still pointed out in many townlands and, in Southwest Donegal, the most famous of these, a cave in Maghera, is said to be the scene of the slaughter of 500 people.

After this war the value of rents from land declined drastically (Graham 1970:150), perhaps due to depopulation and a decline in agriculture or perhaps due to a natural reluctance on the part of the landlords to enter the area to collect rents. The rent received on one tract of land in Glencolumbkille in 1640 was £96 sterling; in 1655 it dropped to £25 because, it was said, some of the land was no longer inhabited or had gone to waste.

After the Pynnar Survey of 1618-19 revealed the situation of the Baronies of Banagh and Boylagh, the proportions were declared forfeit to the Crown and reassigned to a Scotsman who promptly leased the lands to a "papist", causing it to be forfeit once more. The grant terms were for 10,000 arable acres and a new arrangement, whereby one-quarter of the land would be allotted to the native Irish, was made. This too failed to take effect. In 1665 there was only one Planter family in the area and historians believe that the Protestant population of the district left during the rebellion in order to insure their own safety and to join forces with Protestants to the north in putting down the rebels.

A descendant of the Scotsman who lost and then recovered his land claimed it and then sold half of the two baronies to a cousin, Sir Albert Conyngham, who began the Cunningham estate which lasted well into the 19th century. The origins of this estate are hinted at in a letter written by Sir Albert to King William's Secretary of War:

> If I had my dragoons all together I would be able to scour the mountains of this cuntry which I heare are possessed by some Ulster rapparies with their cattle, most of them of the County of Donegall where I live. I chased them out of that cuntry and would out of this if I had men fit to scoure the mountains [quoted in McGill n.d.:50].

Sir Albert's methods probably caused some of the depopulation and his means of rewarding his dragoons may have been to settle them on the lands that had been vacated. This would account for the sudden swelling of the Protestant population. From the one family of Planters in 1665 the population rose until in 1715, it was noted in the Protestant Church records that 90 children with Planter surnames had been confirmed in the parish. Many of the cattle farmers of Boylagh were said to have gone "on creaght," to have become migrant cattle breeders, wandering through the mountains in search of temporary pasture.

From this time on, the history of Donegal is much the same as that of the rest of Ireland. The potato was introduced early in the seventeenth century and, by the end of Cromwell's War, was being cultivated throughout the country. This phenomenon has been fully documented elsewhere and need not be dwelt upon here; the changes it induced in the agricultural system included the fragmentation of landholdings, the year-round occupation of land previously used for summer grazing, and the growth of population — all well-known and well-documented processes.

The political, religious, and economic history of the region illuminates the continuities in its history. There was little change in the years between 1665 and 1891. In 1890 land tenure was as insecure as it was in 1665. The authority of the native leaders continued to be vested in the priesthood, as it was after 1665, and secular power was in the hands of the landlords and their officers. Even at present the "government" is often regarded in this light as a body of indifferent officials whose effects on local affairs are both minimal and repressive — minimal because the distance involved created difficulties in enforcing legislation, and repressive in intent if not in effect.

One other continuity should be mentioned: the Irish feeling for the continuities between their own lives and those of their ancestors. This sentiment can be and often has been mistaken for patriotism, a label that seems to me at best doubtful. The people of Southwest Donegal do not lack patriotism; it is expressed in ways other than those discussed in this chapter. Their feeling for the land is more a sense of the history attaching to it than a sense of devotion to a nationalistic ideal. O'Faolain, writing about the sixteenth-century Irish, remarks:

> Anybody who knows the life of the Gaelic-speaking parts of Ireland in our own day will guess how centred they were in their own rural world and the slight extent of their interest in the distant towns. And that would be more true of Ulster than of any other part of Ireland: because it was more remote it was more archaic (1942:20).

Along with the recently (1641) acquired massacre sites, each townland has a long history. Mountains, rivers, lakes, bogs, and even stones are more than natural phenomena — they are sites of events that are described as if they occurred only last month. The day before I left Donegal I was paid a visit by a descendant of the O'Gallaghers, the O'Boyles' rivals for leadership in the Barony of Boylagh. In the course of conversation he remarked that he had been at school in the north where, being "Boylagh," he had had to fight for the honor of his area against the northerners, who were "Banagh." I had thought of this distinction as one

remembered only in the historians' notebooks, for it has not
appeared on an official document in more than three centuries.
Its retention in the oral literature of children and its continued
use as an indicator of identity, a demarcation according to place
of origin, demonstrates that the Irish feeling for the continuities
of their own history must never be disregarded in a study of their
present circumstances.

NOTES

1   Whether the term *clachan* is Gaelic or not is a matter of dispute among
    scholars. I use the term here as my informants in Southwest Donegal use it,
    to mean a group of kinspeople settled on their agricultural land and, as Fox
    (1978) uses it, to indicate a rundale system of land use.
2   Scholars point out that the historical meaning of "mere" in the phrase,
    "mere Irish", meant pure or unmixed race or language, and that the phrase
    did not have its present, pejorative meaning.

CHAPTER THREE

The Recent Past:

Discontinuities in Recorded History

> Crises of authority are nothing new to the Irish. They could almost claim to have discovered them.
> Richard Rose 1971:17.

Having indicated some of the continuities between social life in the distant past and in the present, I will now turn to a consideration of political and economic discontinuities, changes that have affected Donegal social life profoundly. The discontinuities to be discussed in this chapter came after the loss of indigenous hereditary leadership; there followed a rise of intermediaries as a ubiquitous part of the social landscape. Here I will look at the development of the role of intermediaries and their use in economic, political, social and ideological matters. This development may have been the florescence of what was a common practice in the 18th century or it may have been a genuinely new way of doing things. Whichever it was, its effects were profound.

Once power and authority were vested in the colonizers, usually the landlords, one of the conditions of owning land was that the owner be Protestant. The Catholic population on the land was disenfranchised. Its leadership, once hereditary, became ephemeral, for the "mere Irish," as the English called them, had no means of gaining power and keeping it. This is one of the areas of Irish life in which the "centuries of British oppression" explanation works very well; the response to the crisis of authority was the use of intermediaries in most areas of social life, especially where there was potential for conflict.

The role of the intermediary has probably changed considerably in the last century and at least some of those changes can be documented.

I will consider the intermediary's role in numerous contexts: in the social context (matchmaking and fighting), in the ideological context (worshipping and spying), in the political context (party secretaries and bureaucrats), and in the economic context (cattle-sale intermediaries and "gombeenmen"). "Gombeen" is the Gaelic word for interest on a loan. (It should be noted that I use the word "gombeeman" in the generic sense; there were gombeenwomen as well.) The gombeenman was primarily a usurer who extended credit to poor people, then charged high rates of interest that made repayment impossible for most. Those so indebted were obliged to work for the gombeenman for whatever "wages" he offered; the system amounted to debt slavery. Particular attention is paid to the provenance, career, and virtual demise of the gombeenman in the west of Ireland; changes in the role of economic intermediary over the last century exemplify the changes that have come about as a result of increasingly centralized government and economic development.

SOCIAL AND IDEOLOGICAL INTERMEDIARIES

An anthropologist studying Ireland a century ago would have found several types of intermediary. The Irish intermediary was generally as ephemeral as he was ubiquitous and, in social relations, only the role of matchmaker was fully developed.

Arensberg and Kimball (1968) provided classic descriptions of an intermediary's function in arranging marriages. In the words of one of their informants:

> If I wanted to give my farm over to my son and I would be worth, say, two hundred pounds, I would know a fellow up the hill, for instance, that would be worth three hundred pounds. I would send up a neighbor fellow to him and ask him if he would like to join my family in marriage (1968:105).

In matchmaking the intermediary was a neighbor, not a relative. Arensberg and Kimball go on to point out that the role of matchmaker became a specialty: "Certain individuals become well known locally as successful negotiators. In former days there was once a fully developed 'matchmaker' or marriage broker. . . . Quite often a well-known shopkeeper or local politician comes to play the role" (1968:107). Bargaining over the amount of the dowry was in the hands of the matchmaker; the task of "dividing the difference" between the amount asked and that offered was lengthy and involved, and from this occasion came the matchmaker's only reward. Financial arrangements were discussed over a series of drinks and "the speaker [intermediary] gets plenty and has a good day" (1968:108).

In the field of social relations a similar event was the apprenticing of a youth from the country by a village shopkeeper:

> First there is a period of negotiation and investigation by both the youth's father and his prospective master. If both parties are satisfied with their findings they sign a contract which indentures the youth and in which the mutual obligations of each party are stipulated. . . .
>
> Many of the preliminaries remind one of matchmaking, where every precaution is taken to reduce the possibilities of failure or dispute (1968:348-351).

In apprenticing as in matchmaking the intermediary was a neighbor, not a relative. With an apprenticeship, the shopkeeper himself served as intermediary between the town and the countryside, indoctrinating a rural boy into the village and teaching him a useful trade. In Southwest Donegal the formal role of matchmaker — never very well developed — has disappeared, in part because of high outmigration rates and in part because of automobile transportation that enables young people to attend dances in villages up to fifty miles away.

When shops were small, as in Southwest Donegal, an apprenticeship was unheard of but an alternative was practiced in Donegal, as well as in Clare. Arensberg and Kimball (1968:366) mention that the small shopkeeper hopes to marry a woman from the surrounding countryside, preferably a woman with a large family and one who will bring him her kinsmen's trade. In the village where I lived, the shopkeepers were almost all married to country women and the one exception to whom I spoke believed that marrying a country woman was a sensible thing for a man to do, for kinship relations still determine a large proportion of the shopkeeper's business.

In drawing up a contract the aim is to reduce the possibilities of conflict and the task of "dividing the difference" is undertaken by a neighbor, not a relative. Where conflict has already erupted its resolution must be undertaken by a relative, not a neighbor. This is the other social arena in Donegal in which the role of intermediary figures heavily.

At a dance on Tory Island (Robin Fox, personal communication) a fight begins between Wee Johnny and Old Paddy. After shouting threats at each other the two drift back into the dance hall. One of them sits on the side muttering, then rushes out again to verbally assault his opponent. He is restrained, but

the two stand, held by their supporters, and shout insults at once
another.

> [Then] the priest came out and told everyone to go home. No
> one was listening and soon, still protesting, he was brushed
> aside . . . [After some scuffles and shouts of "Hold me back or
> I'll kill him."] There was a last flurry, again the principals were
> pulled back, and now someone was bringing Wee Johnny's
> mother forward weeping; the crowd parted for the old lady. With
> prayers and admonitions she pleaded with Wee Johnny to come
> home and not disgrace her like this in front of her friends and
> neighbors. Saints were liberally invoked and the blessed Virgin
> implored often. People hung their heads. Johnny, looking dazed,
> told her to quiet herself — she didn't — and hurled at Paddy
> and his group, "I'd have had yer blood if me mother hadn't
> come. Ye can thank her that you're not in pieces on the road,
> ye scum . . ."

After the fight had been resolved by the intervention of Johnny's
mother the priest again attempted to intervene. He announced
that he would ban dances if such a fight happened again, "but he
was told that the hall was built by Tory men and that they would
settle their affairs in their own way, according to 'the custom of
the island'". The appropriate intermediary in a fight between local
men is a relative (a "friend" in Donegal usage); on Tory Island
this intermediary may be the mother of one of the parties but,
says Fox, in most cases the mother is drawn in only at the last
moment as a sort of symbol of family unity, while it is the members
of the kin group who attempt mediation or, as a last resort, hold
back the protagonists.

The epilogue to Fox's story is that Fox, on a walk, found himself
between Johnny and Paddy who were approaching from opposite
directions. While Fox pondered what he should do, the two passed
each other, one looking out to sea and the other toward the hills.
Fox was not an appropriate intermediary, nor was there the
requisite crowd to hold them back.

I witnessed several fights of the sort Fox describes and was told
about many more; the "hold me back or I'll kill him" syndrome
was always in full operation, and there was always someone to
hold back the antagonists. The only fight I heard about in which
damage was actually inflicted was between a group of local men
and a group of tourists from Northern Ireland. This fight took
place in a pub and damage was restricted to the pub owner's

glassware and furnishings. I did not see the fight but it was under discussion for the better part of a week. Those who commented on it agreed on only one detail, that the village policeman should have intervened to stop the fight.

The local policeman was called when the fight began but he refused to come, claiming that he was sick in bed; finally, the police from a neighboring town had to be called. They broke up the fight and took away the one person who was injured, a man from Northern Ireland who suffered a bloody nose after being hit by a piece of flying crockery. In the village everyone believed that the local policeman should have come and they deplored his conduct, even though the damage was mostly to the pub owner's property. Most seemed apprehensive, not about what *had* happened but about what *might* have happened.

Nor was the policeman's conduct in fact deplorable; it was the norm he applied to all local fights. When local men fought between themselves, as they often did, these same people would have been outraged if the police had intervened. Those I questioned said it would not be right to call the police when local men fought, for the policeman was a "stranger" and it was no affair of his. When local people fight among themselves, the policeman is supposed to turn away and he regularly does so; he remarked to me that the people of the North (he is himself from the South of Ireland) have an odd way of fighting, that the fights are mostly between families and thus no affair of his.

In Southwest Donegal the appropriate intermediary is always a kinsman when locals fight; this man will break up the fight on the grounds mentioned above — injury to the family name, the humiliation of it all, and so on. In my example, the appropriate intermediary in a situation involving local men and outsiders was the policeman — else he would not have been called. His refusal to become involved was censured by the villagers but, on his part, it was probably an erroneous extension of the general principle that policemen should not be involved in local fighting.

It is apparent from Fox's example that the priest was not considered an appropriate intermediary: he was quickly told that the matter had to be settled "according to the 'custom of the island" (1975:149-153). The same people who quaff their Guinness on the sly because the priest would not approve have no qualms about telling the priest that his intervention is inappropriate when quarrels between families are at issue.

The intervention of a protagonist's mother as a symbolic gesture and the invocation of the blessed Virgin bring up another point about the use of the intermediary. The intermediary in a cattle sale (as will be seen) freely invokes the name of Mother Ireland, and both the protagonist's mother and the cattle-sale intermediary are making use of symbolic forms well understood by their audiences. It is not surprising to find the pattern of the intermediary reiterated in the Catholic Church's doctrine of "holy intercession." The Virgin and the patron saints (especially the Irish ones) can intercede with God on behalf of a petitioner. Messenger observes that "there is a marked tendency toward polytheism in the manner in which they [Irish islanders] relate to the Blessed Virgin and certain Irish saints . . ." (1969:88). He also notes that "the islanders know little of church dogma and the purport of rituals and feast days" (1969:89). I suspect that the doctrine of holy intercession is very well understood by parishioners in Southwest Donegal, and that the devotion to Irish patron saints is a cultural representation of the intermediary pattern.

Some mention must be made of the darker side of the intermediary pattern, the dread of an intermediary whose loyalties are suspect. Initially unaware of the aversion to the public role of "informant," I was puzzled when strong men became faint at the sight of my pencil and notebook. I was sternly reprimanded and advised that if I wanted information I would have to abandon all thought of writing down anything in the presence of an informant. I took this seriously, and later, when my memory had improved considerably and my position as harmless crank was firmly established, I discovered that it only applied in public. Privately, I was often admonished to write things down so that I would get them straight. Never after the initial attempts did I write anything down publicly; to do so is not merely a serious breach of etiquette, it could threaten the informant's social position for life.

The negative aspects of the intermediary pattern are brought into play and fears are exacerbated by the prospect of being seen "giving evidence" to an outsider. Only a people sensitized to the potential damage to be done by an informer would be so sensitive in the matter of public recording.

Another instance of the dread of an intermediary with questionable loyalties concerns the belief in the evil eye, a belief formerly prevalent in the area. The evil eye affected livestock, causing cattle to behave strangely or some accident to befall them. (The priest was called in to mediate between the forces of evil and the aggrieved owner.) Although the belief is no longer prevalent and most people will swear (quite convincingly) that they never heard of it, one man was quietly accused by his neighbors of possessing the evil eye. This trait is inherited through the mother, and seems to work in the same manner as the X and Y chromosomes, that is, the mother is a carrier only and does not necessarily possess the trait herself. While the so-called possessor of the evil eye was described to me as "always looking," there was nothing obviously strange or especially alert about this man. He seemed no more and no less interested in livestock than anyone else. He was a farmer and the only unusual thing about him was that he was frequently employed as a guide to tourists interested in fishing. Many men did this casually; he did it regularly. Apart from matters relating to livestock, the only anecdotes I was told about him concerned his wide range of acquaintances in Northern Ireland.

It would be overstating my case to say that the evil eye accusation was leveled against him because he was in regular contact with outsiders, but if it is a coincidence, it is an interesting one. This man was not actively disliked by his neighbors, and had none of the attributes that might have caused him to be disliked. He was never excluded from any social group he wished to join, though many people deliberately misidentified their own cattle in response to his inquiries. He was not a particularly successful farmer; he was not especially articulate; he had no outstanding qualities of leadership. While this is not the usual anthropological explanation,the evil eye accusation may have been an acknowledgment of his numerous connections in Northern Ireland (cf. Maloney 1976).

The darker side of the intermediary role illustrates an important point about the social and ideological functions of intermediaries. When the issue is one of "dividing the difference," that is, a money or property transaction, the appropriate intermediary is a neighbor, not a relative of the parties. The loyalties of this individual must not lie with either group. In family matters the appropriate intermediary is a relative, whose loyalties are assumed to lie with one of the protagonists. Intermediaries must not only be loyal, they must be "seen to be" loyal, in the English phrase. Those who regularly violate the social conventions by associating with "strangers" or non-kin are suspected of questionable loyalties.

This discussion of intermediaries in social and ideological realms bears directly on recent analyses of intermediaries generally and of patron-client relationships in particular (Gilmore 1977; Galt 1974). The debate centers around whether intermediaries reduce or exacerbate conflict within a society and, when considered within only the political or economic spheres, the question appears to have some validity. However, when the use of intermediaries in many contexts is considered, it appears that while intermediaries can easily exacerbate conflicts, their primary function is to reduce the potentially disruptive consequences of conflict. A dual potential — either for conflict exacerbation or conflict avoidance — is apparent in the specificity of the recruitment rules for intermediaries in social and ideological realms; it becomes even more apparent in the role of the party secretary.

POLITICAL INTERMEDIARIES

In the foregoing section I have used the term "intermediary" in the way Silverman (1965:173) uses it; intermediaries are persons who provide contact between two systems but who have no critical interests or exclusivity of position to defend. In Donegal, people use the terms intermediary or go-between (Shanklin 1980). Mediators in Silverman's usage (1965:173) do have critical interests to defend and must guard their exclusive positions; in considering more ephemeral positions of authority — such as matchmaker or fight intermediary — the term intermediary is appropriate, but in considering the roles of party secretary and bureaucrat, the distinction between patron and broker is useful. Paine (1971:21) defines a patron as an individual who chooses the values or prestations to be put into circulation and brokers as those who have some purposive function in processing information.

The Irish party secretary is a patron, in these terms, for he chooses the favors he will confer; the Irish bureaucrat is a broker, serving as information conduit for the national government. The political realm within which these individuals operate usually involves government subsidies and the "dole" (unemployment compensation). Both patron (party secretary) and broker (bureaucrat) attempt to serve local interests in their dealings with the national government.

The position of party secretary is an elective one and each party has its secretary in every voting district. In villages there are no elective offices; the party secretary represents the district, not the village alone. Status in Irish communities is determined by wealth and education. Priest and schoolmaster always enjoy high prestige; after them, wealthy cattle farmers and merchants occupy high status positions, and it is from this high status group that party secretaries are most often chosen. Schoolmasters often become party secretaries (priests do not); the village in which I lived had three schoolmasters, all of whom had been or were secretaries to their parties.

During the period of my fieldwork in Southwest Donegal the party secretary of the dominant party was both a wealthy cattle farmer and a merchant; the position had been occupied in the recent past by a man of similar attainments. The chief duty of the secretary is to secure for each applicant what he desires from the government. This may involve petitioning the county representative in the government for restoration of a man's dole, or asking the representative to intercede with the appropriate agency to secure an old-age pension. Any activity in which an individual petitioner has a case to bring before an agency of the county or national government is a legitimate sphere of operation for the party secretary; local matters and agricultural development are not part of this sphere of operation, and the secretary's role is to act as liaison between the local people and the party officials. If the secretary does express an opinion on local matters or on agricultural development, he does so on his own, not in the name of the party he serves.

It is the secretary's responsibility to keep his constituents happy, and that is how he perceives his role; the party expects in return that votes will be the results of his actions. Not only his own party members apply to him for aid, however; members of other parties may come to him for favors, but they ordinarily do so only after their own party secretary's efforts have proved ineffectual.

Western Ireland has a high literacy rate and in theory any individual could petition the government for any compensation to which he thought he was entitled. No one does so, however, and no one expects that it would be efficacious to do so. I first became aware of this when the local party secretary (of the dominant party) offered to obtain the children's allowance for my dependent child. Even as I declined the offer[1], it was made clear that the appropriate procedure was for *him* to make the request, even for local residents who were entitled to benefits under the law.

Members of minority parties often believe that the patronage system extends further than it does; they do not apply for agricultural subsidies, for example, which are offered on a non-partisan basis. They perceive the role of the agricultural agent as a partisan one and will not call upon their agent for badly needed information, assuming (erroneously) that the agent would have no interest in their problems because they vote the "wrong" way. Because the party secretaries are perceived as patrons, that is, those who can dispense favors in return for votes, employees of government agencies are often perceived as patrons, too, whereas in fact they are brokers and have a purposive function in processing information but do not expect a local compensation for their efforts.

Local bureaucrats, especially employees of the agricultural services, are civil servants, not political appointees; their duties include the impartial administration of government loans and grants for farm improvements. They transmit information between local and national agencies but their primary function is to provide information about such grants and loans at the local level, to help the local farmers in making application. Grants are awarded on the basis of eligibility, not party affiliation. Accustomed to the system of patronage embodied in the party secretary, many farmers believe that their agricultural agent is just one more official whose function it is to see to it that the party faithful get the rewards. This misapprehension can be corrected by the diligent work of the agent himself. In one district the agricultural agent had been at pains to contact everyone he believed to be eligible for a particular program and, despite initial resistance and mistrust, he successfully put together a development program that was widely admired. In the adjoining district a less energetic agricultural agent accomplished almost nothing, for he believed it was the farmers' responsibility to contact him. Those who voted with the dominant party did contact him; those who did not belong to the dominant party had seldom heard his name. In his district, two brothers who were members of a minority party had applied for and received farm improvement grants; they were exceptionally well informed about the granting agencies, information they garnered from wide reading and not from their agricultural agent.

Bureaucratic rewards come from the national agencies in the form of promotions, pay increases, and the like. The party secretary's rewards may involve import-export privileges, business loans, or simply a large network of useful acquaintances in government. The party secretary is a local man and his loyalties are supposed to be with his locality, though grudging recognition is given to his "higher" party affiliations. Those who have served as secretary to the dominant party are careful to tell any inquirer about the "favors" they have done for minority party secretaries and members, a form of boasting that simultaneously underlines their superior position and their local, not party, ties.

The national government has taken steps to insure that bureaucrats do not act as patrons. One of these steps is the civil service examination; another is the policy, similar to that of the *Gardai* (police), of assigning to each locality individuals who have no local "connections," or relatives. These disconnected people, it is thought, are less apt to become involved in local politics and feuding, for outsiders are believed to be excluded automatically from the indigenous authority structures, hence they can act impartially. In the case of the agricultural agents, the policy is beginning to work, and ultimately, the very fact of the agricultural agent's "outsider" status may cause the perception of his role to change. In Ireland, there is great interest in an individual's place of birth and his family; most of my informants had considerable knowledge of the connections of all the people within their social networks, and often this knowledge extended far beyond their own region to include the family and social origins of well-known politicians, or television stars.

When a sufficient number of agricultural agents have passed through the western regions and all of them have "been seen" to be from far-off counties, the perception of the agents as party representatives will also change. The national government will have successfully broken down at least one aspect of the patronage role played by the party secretaries and supported by the parties themselves. The misperception of bureaucrats as patrons has undoubtedly hampered government efforts at economic development.

ECONOMIC INTERMEDIARIES

In economic transactions, too, there existed an intermediary or go-between, who served only as a contact between two sides, and a patron, who specified the goods and services to be put into circulation and who guarded his critical functions and exclusivity. Once again the intermediary, this time in a cattle sale, was called upon to "divide the difference."

My interest in this role was first stimulated by a young informant who, after denouncing what he considered to be old-fashioned and obsolete in the system of livestock marketing, declared that one "couldn't sell an animal without a go-between." Livestock are sold in Southwest Donegal in three ways, in fact: privately, on the farm; and publicly, either at a livestock fair or at an auction mart. Farmers who regularly sell animals on the farm do so without benefit of an intermediary and must "divide the difference" themselves. Publicly, at a cattle fair, this would be regarded as a serious breach of etiquette.

At the time of my fieldwork most cattle raised in Donegal were sold into Northern Ireland. Cattle fairs were held in towns once a month and buyers from Northern Ireland attended these fairs. The buyer is usually accompanied by an assistant who blends more easily into the human landscape than does the buyer — buyers wear hats instead of caps and are much given to Irish tweeds, which the people of Donegal make but do not wear. The assistant attempts to join the conversation(s) of the assembled sellers. After a conference with his assistant — at which the probable going price for cattle is discussed — the buyer approaches the owner of the cattle he is interested in. A discussion of the weather follows, and the would-be buyer then makes some flattering remarks about the seller's cattle and asks him his price. The seller looks discomfited and astonished at the suggestion, managing to give the impression that the thought of parting with his cattle had not occurred to him. He reluctantly agrees to give the matter some thought and, after more impersonal conversation, he names a price well above what he has already decided upon. The buyer counters with an offer well below what he is willing to pay. The seller appears to be greatly offended by such a low estimation of his animals' worth and to the onlooker it seems that the transaction will break down at this point. But an intermediary now materializes out of the group that has formed around buyer and seller.

The intermediary's first task is to persuade the seller that no offense was intended by the buyer's initial bid; his second is to convince the seller that the initial asking price was perhaps a bit unreasonable (in view of current prices, world conditions, or whatever). He persuades the seller to suggest another price and the buyer to make another offer. Successful conclusion of the transaction often depends on the intermediary's abilities as a speaker; his performance is a brilliant verbal display of relevant and irrelevant adjectives and analogies. He points out the virtues of the cattle, their approximate weights, their fine coats, their breeding superiority. He stresses the seller's talents at cattle raising, the importance of maintaining amicable relations between the region and the buyer's home province, the virtues of both men's parents (whether he knows them or not), and so on. Throughout, the buyer maintains an air of indifference and the seller one of sulky disappointment.

A practiced go-between delivers a rapid-fire monologue, interspersed with irrelevant comments and jokes. One go-between asked me the precise meaning of the Mary Poppins word "supercalifragilisticexpialidosius," and when I told him that it had no precise meaning, he decided that he would work it into his next monologue. He did so, to the great amusement of his audience. Because note-taking in public was forbidden, I was unable to record these monologues as they occurred, and those intermediaries I asked to repeat their statements for me privately were greatly embarrassed by the request. Their attempts were wooden, and they maintained that it was impossible to reproduce all the exaggerations without the stimulus of an audience.

I offer here a reconstruction of the comments that experienced go-betweens believe to be indispensable. I will confine myself to a rendering of the substance of the remarks, as directed to the participants: first, to the buyer, then to the seller, whom I shall call Sean, and finally, to the audience.

To the buyer:

> Now here we have as fine an animal as we've seen at this fair in many a day, as fine an animal as ever I've seen here, and that's not surprising since Sean here has a reputation for being an outstanding man with the cattle, a man like his father before him who is known for being a wonderful man for the cattle. A man known to his friends [relatives] and to his neighbors as a man with the right touch with animals. This cow, I can safely say, was raised by Sean's own hand and treated almost like a member of his family.

To the seller:

This gentleman [the buyer] has come a long way in search of the right animals and we'd not want to disappoint him in the quality of animals he'll find here, nor in the price we're asking for them. He is known by reputation from his home county [if known, it will be mentioned] throughout the length and breadth of County Donegal, and if we disappoint him, we will also be known far and wide but we'll not be happy with the word that goes out on us and our prices at the fair.

To the audience:

Now. gentlemen, you know the importance of having both parties to a sale happy about that sale. And you also know the value of the good relations between Donegal and the North [Northern Ireland]. And, sure, we're all Ulstermen here. We've two men before us this day whose parents would be proud to see two men of Ulster resolving their differences in this peaceable way. And their own mothers would weep for joy to see it; Sean's mother was a very devout woman, may she rest in peace, and blessed in the memory of all who knew her. She'd be proud to see her son, Sean, taking the part of a man and helping to uphold the fine reputation of this fair and this village. And you can see from the very look of him what a fine woman this man's [the buyer's] mother was. what a fine son she brought into the world and reared with her own hand. Indeed we know that Mother Ireland herself will be watching what goes on here and hoping these two gentlemen will make the right decision.

The generalities gone through and all the blessings of Mother Ireland called down upon the participants *if* they make the right decision, the intermediary hands out cigarettes to all the onlookers and there is a pause while everyone smokes. During this interlude the group breaks up into smaller conversational units; neighbors and relatives of the seller may take him aside to offer advice, and the buyer confers earnestly with his assistant. The intermediary speaks privately to each man, then again draws the crowd together by announcing that a higher offer has been made and the seller has indicated that he is at least willing to discuss the matter.

The difference between the two prices is now the focus of the intermediary's efforts; he must arrange for the difference to be divided. Toward this end he pleads and cajoles until, sensing agreement, he grasps the right hand of each of the parties and tries to force them into final agreement on a price. A each new bid he brings their hands together and when the bargain is struck he brings the hands together with a fierce blow.

Several hours elapse between agreement and payment and, for cattle, payment takes place in a pub. This rule is not inviolable but it is customary, and a man who prefers to be paid in the street will be denounced by the villagers as a scoundrel. In the pub the buyer hands over the money and buys a few rounds of drinks for the seller and the onlookers; the seller must reciprocate. After the buyer leaves the intermediary often presides, attempting to get other men to join in the rounds of drink-buying. The first rule for an intermediary, informants say, is that he must be a good talker; the second seems to be that he must be fond of liquor. No one had ever heard of an intermediary who was a teetotaler.

While anyone can serve as an intermediary in a cattle sale, some men do so regularly and are recognized for their talents. They are not wealthy, nor are they influential in any special way. But the rules specify that they cannot be relatives of the seller; a recognized intermediary who is related to a seller will not intervene in a sale on his kinsman's behalf. To do so, it is thought, might cause the sale to be nullified, for the buyer would be incensed to learn that an intermediary was a relative of the seller. In fact, it is the local rules that specify that intermediaries and sallers must not be related. Buyers have little interest in the intricacies of local genealogies and would not be the least concerned about this information. Most cattle fairs are attended by at least two "regular" intermediaries and, as occasionally happened, if both men were related to the seller, another person had to be pressed into service. The seller himself usually solicited this service and, after displaying his reluctance and timidity about the prospective sale, proceeded to tell the intermediary what to say.

A sale is a dramatic event and it is good theatre, containing elements of tragedy (the seller's loss of his cattle), comedy (the intermediary's running commentary on everything), and high tension (Will they agree? Who will come closer to his announced price?). As an event, the sale is highly satisfactory and engrossing; a successful outcome insures the redistributive ceremony that guarantees a happy afternoon to all.

The entire ceremony, however, has considerable symbolic significance, and the intermediary's role is crucial in making the symbolism explicit. The status of an intermediary in a cattle sale is as ephemeral as his brief service; his reward is an afternoon of drinking in the pub. He may be,and often is, a person with considerable talent for overstatement but his exaggerations in this context are regarded with amusement, not with disapprobation. His overt gestures of friendliness to the buyer from Northern Ireland are regarded as matters of politeness, not as genuine attempts at cultivating the buyer's acquaintance. Nor is the friendliness displayed genuine; in every other respect the buyers are treated cooly and as non-persons who do not even register in the locals' field of vision. For example, when the buyer comes to collect the animals he has bought, the people standing around disperse; no one offers to help the buyer load his animals onto the truck. This is one of the reasons the buyer comes with an assistant, but it is the assistant at whom most disapproval is directed.

The assistants are younger men who normally have relatives in the area; they are employed by the cattle buyer only during his brief stay in the area and may attend several fairs with him. The assistant may also be a neighbor of some of the cattle sellers, and his loyalties are suspect because he is in the pay of the cattle buyer from Northern Ireland.

The cattle sale intermediary operates with local loyalties uppermost, but outside his own kin obligations. The potential oppositions are thus apparent. The intermediary at a cattle sale may not intervene on behalf of a kinsman, and can offer his services only to neighbors and acquaintances. Kinsmen fight together, and relatives must defend each other in the event of an offense. Neighbors can act to soothe feelings on both sides of a cattle sale, but a kinsman would be obliged to fight on the side of the seller, should offense occur.[2] A neighbor can pretend to be on the side of the buyer for the duration of the bargaining but, should things go wrong and the seller really become angry, only a neighbor could intervene between buyer and seller — a kinsman would have to take the seller's side in the event of conflict.

In contrast to the cattle-sale intermediary, a true intermediary whose role as contact between two individuals or groups lasts a day, the gombeenman's role as a mediator involved serving his own critical interests and protecting his exclusivity (Silverman 1965). The gombeenman was a usurer, whose role, in Paine's (1971) terms, shifted from that of broker to patron and back to broker. The gombeenman who reigned supreme in the Irish countryside during the late 19th century has all but disappeared from the 20th-century landscape, and these shifts between brokerage and patronage, between political power and economic node, demand further attention.

Intermediaries — whether patrons, mediators, or brokers — are often described as if they were timeless but necessary links in the social structure. Silverman, however, predicts the conditions of their decline:

> ... the mediator represents a general form of community-nation relationship characteristic of an early phase of development of nation-states, a form which regularly gives way as the process of integration of the total society advances (1965:188).

An investigation of the provenance, florescence, and virtual demise of the gombeenman illustrates the point that mediating relationships give way as community-nation integration advances, but it is posited here that the origins of the gombeenman's power lie in the colonial government's attempts to help the small farmer of Ireland.

To trace the provenance of the gombeenman it is necessary to consider Irish history from the time of the Great Famine. There were gombeenmen before the Great Famine but they do not seem to have exercised control beyond moneylending. When the Famine (1845–49) began, Irish land was controlled by (mostly absentee) landlords and administered by landlords' agents. Even as late as 1870 "one-fifth of Ireland's 19,000 proprietors still owned 80 per cent of the cultivated area" (Orme 1970:155).

Landlords, not gombeenmen, held sway. According to MacManus (1969:625-626), "The Landlord was 'the master.' ... the landlord owned his tenant, and his tenant's land, and his tenant's vote, and, as he thought, sometimes even his tenant's women-folk." The first Land Act, passed in 1870, was intended to return ownership of the land to the farmers but it accomplished little. In 1880 another Land Act was passed but this too was ineffective. Freeman notes that "the failure of the Acts was due to the lack of capital among the farmers, who had to find one-third (1870) or one-quarter (1881) of the purchase price: only 1,600 holdings were transferred ..." (1969:1-7).

The Land Acts gave power to the landlords' agents:

> There were five classes of tenants under the landlords — leaseholders, middlemen, annual tenants, cottiers and labourers. The leaseholders, in all numbering 135,000, held the land in perpetuity, ... the descendants of these leaseholders survive as farmers of substantial holdings. The middlemen were the agents of the landlords and let off land to the remaining three classes (Freeman 1969:177).

In the West, the Land Acts did little to alleviate the misery of the farmers and in 1879-82, violence erupted. It is noteworthy that most of the casualties of these "land wars" were landlords' agents. During this time the process now known as boycotting was developed and Captain Boycott, a landlord's agent in County Mayo, was its first sufferer (MacManus 1969:637).

The Acts of 1885 and 1891 made loans available for the entire purchase price and were more successful; still, purchases under these Acts seem to have been restricted largely to the more prosperous regions of Ireland and were not common in the poorer western areas. In 1890 the Congested Districts Act was passed, setting up a Board to devise and implement plans to help the poor farmers of the West in buying their land and improving their standard of living. The major hindrance to the efforts of the Congested Districts Board (hereafter the C.D.B.) was the prevalence of gombeenmen, who readily adopted any profit-making scheme for their own purposes.

The evidence of the Acts and of the C.D.B.'s difficulties with well-established gombeenmen prompts the speculation that the government's actions, however well intentioned, may have contributed to the florescence of the gombeenmen. If landlords were the patrons of the 19th century and agents served as their brokers, it seems reasonable to infer that as the government moved to reduce the power of the landlords, it delivered, albeit inadvertently, that power into the hands of the agents. With political power and experience the agents may have become gombeenmen. Agents were paid in money, a rare commodity in 19th century Donegal, and thus would have had the two things necessary to allow them to quickly convert their brokerage role into one of patronage: they were in possession of capital from their wages and whatever abuses absenteeism had allowed them, and they had control of the land, guaranteed by the various Land Acts.

Some authors would take issue with my suggestion that the colonial government "created" the gombeenman with the Land Acts and that the C.D.B. greatly enhanced his profits. Bax (1970) believes that landlords were the principal patrons and brokers until 1922, after which they were displaced by professional politicians. Gibbon and Higgins (1974) believe that the landlords' power was diminished, but that shopkeepers became gombeenmen after the Famine. Sacks endorses the view that landlords were patrons, but cites different evidence and draws what I believe to be an unjustified conclusion: "In most of Ireland, relations between landlord and tenant involved a transaction between a Protestant and a Catholic. No socially unifying 'patron-client relationship' grew up that provided the political and economic security that traditional society was decreasingly able to offer . . ." (1976:24).

The evidence of the Land Acts and the conscious attempts to diminish the landlords' power is sufficient to contradict Bax's position that landlords remained patrons until the politicians took over. Gibbon and Higgins may be right in suggesting that shopkeepers became gombeenmen, but I believe it to be more likely that agents became shopkeepers and then gombeenmen. In 19th century Donegal shopkeepers were often paid in kind, not in money; they would not have accumulated considerable capital. Nor had they any political expertise; the agents who had previously controlled votes for the landlord's benefit were, after 1870, in a position to do so for their own benefit. I take issue with Sacks' statement that there were no patron-client ties because of a religious difference. Landlords certainly appear to have acted as patrons and agents as brokers; the landlords were mostly Protestant and their agents mostly Catholic.

Whatever the provenance of the gombeenman, his patronage role was well established by 1910. With the aid of the priests, gombeenmen exercised considerable political influence. Gibbon and Higgins quote O'Donnell (1910), whom they describe as the "first serious historian" of the Irish parliamentary party, as saying that party conventions were composed of "half gombeenmen and half political priests" (Gibbon and Higgins 1974:33n).

Gibbon and Higgins also provide a description of the economic activities of the gombeenman between 1870 and 1930:

> The gombeenman of the period 1870-1930 typically exercised economic patronage through credit retailing in combination with moneylending. In order to secure a dependent clientele he made cash loans and credit freely available to small farmers, ostensibly without reference to security. In return, he charged both interest and insisted that his debtors bought goods only from his store. Having established dependence, he would then charge inflated retail prices to his customer in order both to secure as much profit as possible and to keep the customer falling further into debt. This secured tied clientele for both purchasing and retailing.

It enabled the gombeenman to attain a monopoly in marketing the produce of clients, and further enabled him not only to pay for them below market price but to make a second profit by insisting that the produce be bartered for shop-goods. The gombeenman was also enabled to create a bonded labour-market, the most famed example of which was that for the knitting industry in west Donegal (Gibbon and Higgins 1974:32).

The gombeenman was the bane of the C.D.B.'s existence.[3] No sooner did the C.D.B. devise a scheme by which a tenant farmer's wife might earn money than the gombeenman devised a scheme by which he turned a profit several ways on the innovation. The well-known "Aran" sweaters knitted in Donegal were developed by the C.D.B. as a cottage industry but their manufacture came rapidly under the supervision of the gombeenman, who imported the wool, supplied it to farmers' wives for knitting and, in return for their labor, paid in shop goods. "MacGill ... estimated that a woman working sixteen hours would earn about 1 1/4 d. worth of shopgoods after the gombeenman had made his four separate profits from the transaction" (Gibbon and Higgins 1974:32).

The gombeenman did not restrict his activities to local trade, however. Using his political power he converted the crafts industry into a national, later international, business. Irish tweeds, woven in the west, also came under the gombeenman's purview. Gombeenmen reigned supreme for several decades; seasonal overseas labor was practically the only other form of income for many tenant farmers. Permanent outmigration — but with remittances sent home regularly — and the dole eventually put an end to the debt-bondage system through which the gombeenman had wielded so much power.

Gibbon and Higgins also claim that gombeenmen "are still disproportionately prominent in local and national government," and cite Chubb's analysis as evidence (1974:35). Chubb shows that "publicans, small shopkeepers and small businessmen, who make up to 3.2 per cent of the employed adult population, represented 31 per cent of county councillors, 34 per cent of parliamentary deputies and 20 per cent of ministers in the last (Fianna Fail) government" (Chubb's figures, cited in Gibbon and Higgins 1974:35). I believe this to be a misapplication of the term "gombeenman," for while all gombeenmen may have been shopkeepers, it is most emphatically not the case in Donegal that all shopkeepers are gombeenmen.

To rely once more on the ethnographic evidence: the word gombeenman is more often whispered in Southwest Donegal than spoken aloud. When it is spoken aloud, it is used only in relation to the dead. It may be said of a certain shopkeeper that "he's a bit of a gombeenman," but this means that his credit terms are harsh, and does not imply the political patronage role of past decades. Only one individual in all of Southwest Donegal was regularly identified as a gombeenman; he was a merchant, a buyer of wool, and his political "connections" were hinted at but not otherwise manifested in voting or in favors granted to him by the national government. Another individual was sometimes spoken of as a gombeenman; he was a small shopkeeper and sometimes worked for the government as a road foreman; this last may have caused him to be identified as a gombeenman but after his death there was no agreement as to whether he *had* been a gombeenman. This lack of unanimity probably means that his credit terms were harsh, that he dispensed road repair jobs in a way thought to be unfair, and that he was generally disliked — but he was not harsh enough, unfair enough, or disliked enough to be termed a gombeenman. The hesitation in using the term or in speaking it aloud suggest the seriousness of the label; the consensus in applying it to only one man in a wide area indicates the scarcity of gombeenmen in southwest Donegal today.[4]

The power of the gombeenman was based on economic and political privilege. With support from his dependent electorate, he could obtain favors from the party and the state; with economic resources (donations to the church, etc.), he could obtain the support of the local notables (Gibbon and Higgins 1974:33). The political privileges accorded him were taken over by party secretaries and Home Assistance Officers (those who supervised the granting of the dole when a "means" test was the standard). Other political concessions came under the control of bureaucrats from different agencies of the national government, and although it is still possible for someone to become a gombeenman in the West of Ireland, it is far more difficult than in the 19th century when sources of capital were few for the local farmers.

If agents became gombeenmen, then the role of the gombeenman may have shifted again from broker in economic and political spheres to patron in economic and political spheres and then back again to broker, but only in economic spheres, as in the case of the current gombeenman who trades in wool. Along with other intermediaries whose powers are reduced, the gombeenman fell victim to increasing centralization of government and the growth of federally regulated bureaucracies.

Shifts in the intermediary's role have been considered in many contexts in the west of Ireland and they are important for understanding the permutations of traditional ways of doing things. In social and economic contexts, the specialized matchmaker and the cattle-sale intermediary have almost disappeared but the fight intermediary is very much a part of the current social scene. Ideologically, the intermediary role — whether as patron saint or spy — still commands respect. Politically, the party secretary and the bureaucrats share power between them, with a shift in the direction of bureaucratic control. The specificity of recruitment rules and the fear of intermediaries with ambiguous loyalties suggests that the position of intermediary is an important one in those areas of life on which government does not impinge.

Much remains to be done on the subject of Irish social relations. On the basis of his work in Northern Ireland, Leyton points to "a dualistic organisation of society, whose structure is based on both integrative and oppositional social forms" (1977:8). Leyton's suggestive comments have as their primary referents the Protestant-Catholic dichotomy, about which I have said little, but I join Leyton in wondering — perversely and paradoxically — by what means the Irish have maintained amicable social relations between opposing groups for so many centuries. My discussion of intermediaries is a preliminary formulation of one possible solution to the problem of keeping the peace. A study of godparent choices in rural and urban Ireland would add considerably to our knowledge of the underpinnings of Irish social life. And, as Leyton points out (1977:8), not much is known about the shopkeepers of rural Ireland. The impact of bureaucrats at the local level is another area for fruitful study; recognition of bureaucrats as impartial mediators will bring about profound changes in patterns of social relations in Ireland.

It is clear from the foregoing that economic and political modes of integration have changed drastically since the Great Famine, and that other changes are in the offing. New traditions or revised "old" traditions have served as a means of internal integration among the people of Southwest Donegal for centuries; whether this can continue depends on how fast the changes take place.

Slow changes can be incorporated under the rubric of "tradition" without difficulty; rapid changes may have to be incorporated under a different set of premises, in which "Progress!" is the watchword, and modernity the goal.

NOTES

1   I declined on the ground that, since I was not an Irish citizen, it would be illegal for me to collect the allowance; this was regarded as a quibble.

2   Leyton (1977) records the graphic expression of this phenomenon as, "If you kick one of them, the rest of them limp." On this point, too, I take issue with Nancy Scheper-Hughes who says, "Silence and avoidance are, in any case, the 'typical' way of handling conflict in Irish villages" (1982b:13).

3   Kennedy (1977:217) from a confidential set of reports compiled by the C.D.B. in 1898: "This consists of 84 local surveys conducted in the West of Ireland. Most of the surveys were completed in the early 1890s. From evidence assembled on interest charged on credit transactions it is clear that fairly extensive areas of high interest rates were to be found in such counties as Galway, Mayo and Donegal.... One may take two of the previously mentioned counties, Donegal and Galway, to illustrate the contention of a wide dispersion of interest rates. Thus in the districts of 'The Rosses' and Glenties (Donegal) and the Aran Islands and Clifden (Galway) charges of 20 per cent or more per annum are reported." See also Micks 1925.

4   Kennedy (1977:217) refutes suggestions made by Brody and Messenger (and restated by Gibbon and Higgins) to the effect that the gombeenman is still a powerful figure in Ireland. Kennedy cites Gilmore's 1959 study of agricultural credit in Ireland, and his finding that "the ratio of total debts to total assets in Irish farming in that year was only 8.5 per cent.... Nor were trader interest rates particularly high, being reported as averaging about 10 per cent per annum" (Kennedy 1977:214).

CHAPTER FOUR

The Verifiable Present:

Sample Findings

> In fact, the trouble with Ireland is that a tradition, once established, never stops.
> Frank O'Connor, 1959: ix.

Having looked at continuities and discontinuities between past and present in Southwest Donegal, we can now turn to a close consideration of the "verifiable" present, those present customs that yield to statistical analysis. My primary source for this analysis is my own sample of thirty households. After discussing the methods I used to select my sample and the characteristics of the sample members, I will contrast my findings with those of the West Donegal Resource Survey reports. The data include settlement patterns as well as land tenure and inheritance systems, and practices to do with livestock production. Here I find it useful to distinguish between pre-Famine customs, those established before the Great Potato Famine (1845-1849) and post-Famine customs. This distinction fits the facts that I will be concerned with and facilitates discussion of the genesis of traditions. Rather than never stopping, as O'Connor would have it, traditions in Ireland are transmuted to become part of the adaptive system.

SAMPLE SELECTION AND CHARACTERISTICS

Shortly before I began fieldwork in 1970, the West Donegal Resource Survey was published; it proved an exhaustive and excellent source of recent information on the region. This West Donegal region is one of the problem areas in Ireland and at the time of my fieldwork, it was one of the few that had been thoroughly surveyed by a team of government experts. My final selection of a field site followed an evaluation of the reliability and completeness of resource estimates, of census data related to agricultural production and resource allocation, and of marketing allocation. These evaluations left me with a choice of two possible sites near the center of the Southwest Donegal area, and the choice between the two was made on a whim, as indicated in Appendix A.

Within a fifteen-mile radius of the village in which I lived, in the area I am calling Banagh, farmers could be found whose holding size and livestock provided material for testing hypotheses. Also within this radius was a range of farms on which innovations had been tried and met with varying degrees of success.

Guided by these considerations, I made a preliminary regional survey and located farmers willing to participate. Initially this was done through inquiries made of the local agricultural agent and, after a time, through the people of the community (whose assessments tended to be more accurate). It was necessary to begin by interviewing the "model" farmers of the area and to contact all the officials to whom either my project or my presence might have been of any conceivable interest. After having established my intent, I was able to ask about people whose farms were not model properties and whose efforts were not outstanding.

Ideally, a community small enough (not more than sixty to seventy-five households) for anthropological study would have been chosen but no such "community" existed within this very diverse region. The community had to contain at least thirty farms with varied landholding sizes and domesticated animals. The initial survey revealed that no such community existed, that the smallest units were townlands of perhaps five to ten households, and that these townlands tended to have similar household composition and livestock holdings. Since there were no ready-made communities for study, the region as a whole had to be taken as the sampling unit and farmers were selected in order to test hypotheses.

I believed at first that this would complicate the study greatly, since it would be more traditional in the anthropological sense and much simpler in terms of participant-observation to live in a community where all sample members might engage in face-to-face interaction daily. I later discovered that it made little difference since most of the interactions I was concerned with were common knowledge throughout the region. Participant-observation was of course severely restricted and I could not keep a daily record of activities, nor could I keep abreast of all the events in the lives of the people I was studying.

But this seeming drawback also had its advantages. Despite my initial resistance, I was quickly drawn into the gossip circuits and

I discovered that one of my primary functions — from my informants' viewpoint — was that of newsbearer. It was not a responsibility I could evade and after some preliminary fumbling efforts on my part and careful tutoring on my informants' part, I managed to learn what were considered the important details of any story. Eventually I put this knowledge to use in tracing patterns of influence. The study of these informal communication networks provided valuable insights exclusive of the more usual participant observation methods and would doubtless provide material for several doctoral dissertations.

My sample differs markedly from the random one drawn by the West Donegal Resource Survey workers, but before I elaborate on these statistical differences, I must add a caveat in the form of an Irish story that aptly illustrates the limitations of all statistical methods in Ireland.

A delegation from a western district came before a public works commissioner to ask for necessary funds to build a factory in their area. They presented the commissioner with a carefully documented report on the amount of manpower available in the district, the promising nature of the available resources, and their assurances that the area awaited only the commission's subsidy before springing into full participation in the modern economy.

The commissioner, being of a logical turn of mind, produced another equally well-documented report given him a year earlier. This report showed that, far from being on the verge of becoming another Manchester or Birmingham, the district in question was in such dire straits that the government's choice was between providing welfare or coffins, there being not an able-bodied man in the area capable of tilling the fields for the many widows and orphans residing there. The commissioner demanded an explanation for the discrepancy between the two reports and the head of the delegation replied sanguinely, "Those statistics were gathered for a different purpose altogether" (Birmingham n.d.).

The story illustrates a point that must be considered in any discussion of data gathering in West Donegal. The West Donegal Resource Survey report was based on a sample of 249 farmers, a sample drawn from the records of the Land Commission. The Agricultural Institute's workers then proceeded to summarize the major aspects of agricultural production in the area, after extensive interviews and questionnaires. The statistics gathered were intended to provide a composite picture after an exhaustive survey of physical resources had been made and a similar survey of demographic, economic, and sociological features of the area had been conducted. The "problem orientation" of the survey was the description of the modal characteristics of production — as things then stood and as they might be developed in the future.

My statistics were gathered for a different but related purpose. A non-random but representative sample of thirty farmers was chosen in order to contrast agricultural production methods within the population. My problem orientation was to describe the characteristics of a sample of people who, faced with a difficult environment, respond and have responded over a long period of time with different production strategies. I concentrated on comparisons of production strategies. In further contrast to the W.D.R.S., I attempted to produce a dynamic picture of production methods; thus the response to changing conditions in production, labor, and marketing was an important dimension in my sample.

My sample can be immediately broken down into three groups based on landholding size. The first group is made up of "small" farmers who own thirty acres of land or less, the second consists of farmers with holdings between thirty and seventy-five acres, and the third includes farmers with more than seventy-five acres.

Division according to landholding size is standard procedure in Irish studies (see Table 4.1) and I hoped to produce data that were comparable with those of other studies made in the country. Such a division is nevertheless somewhat arbitrary because the quality of the land varies widely. Following an ancient Irish practice, it is easier to discuss holdings in terms of carrying capacity. The Irish used to say that a farm had "the grass of so many cows;" ecologists now say that a given plot of land can carry so many livestock units: one livestock unit = one cow.

On the basis of livestock units and carrying capacities, actual and potential, the distinction between the three groups of farmers is somewhat blurred. This will be taken up further in the section relating to specific dimensions of animal production and resources.

Having established the size of the sample and some initial parameters, fieldwork proceeded by gathering three types of data — documentary, interview and questionnaire data — and by participant observation. Quantification of variables directly or indirectly related to the production of domestic animal biomass was done by delineating the decision points in production strategies pertaining to domestic animals. Directed interviews

(Appendix B) on these decision points were used in combination with observation and analysis.

Originally a census of human and livestock populations was planned as the first step; this proved not only a difficult thing to accomplish but a foolhardy first step due to the sensitivity of the people of the area to a stranger's inquiries. I therefore abandoned this idea and sought the requisite data from other sources. The Irish government conducts its human census by questionnaire and there is little reason to believe that census results are inaccurate. The livestock census is carried out by the *Gardai* (police), who approach one person in each townland and inquire about the holdings of every household in that townland. By this method, it is likely that only one man's holdings (the informant's) will be falsified and the results are probably close to accurate.

Historical data on livestock was gathered in this way and I will make use of that data here but I chose a different method for contemporary purposes, the records kept by the Department of Agriculture for its various subsidy schemes. Because animals must be accounted for in order that the owner will be eligible for subsidies, these records are about as accurate as one could hope in Ireland.

Data-collection also consisted of estimation of productivity of different types of soils and differential utilization of these, as well as estimation of the productivity of biomass in different seasons, of delineation of male-female and familial divisions of labor, and membership in cooperative labor groups. Data relating to marketing practices was collected by recording of transactions related to livestock, especially at livestock fairs and auctions.

To summarize then, the sample of thirty farmers was chosen initially through the recommendation of agricultural agents (who suggested model farmers) and eventually through the suggestions of local people who were familiar with all types of farms and farmers. The primary criteria were landholding size and the types of domestic animals kept, and, beyond this, when given a choice, I sought to vary the household composition in order to learn more about production units with similar resources and varying labor inputs.

There will be more to add to a discussion of working methods as the problems with each kind of data come up. Here I shall only note that I often envied colleagues who study naive, pre-literate peoples, to whom the idea of a written language is amusing or

TABLE 4.1 Number of Agricultural Holdings
Classified According to Size

Number of Acres

Year	No more than 1	1+ to 5	5+ to 10	10+ to 15	15+ to 30	30+ to 50	50+ to 100	100+ to 200	200+	Total	200+ to 300	300+
1939	1917	3109	4360	3178	5912	3579	2608	1010	380	26,053		
1944	2016	3163	4298	3098	5835	3518	2643	1042	388	26,001		
1949	1975	3138	4173	2977	5594	3433	2717	1098	386	25,491		
1952	2009	3302	4048	2818	5421	3392	2715	1119	393	25,217		
1953	1993	3297	4044	2841	5403	3384	2734	1126	388	25,210		
1954	2008	3267	3944	2845	5431	3420	2741	1148	379	25,183		
1960	2485	2817	3242	2343	4714	3179	2768	1181		23,168	219	220
1965			8270		1565	3027	2715	1677		20,254		

County

	Year	No more than 1	1+ to 5	5+ to 10	10+ to 15	15+ to 30	30+ to 50	50+ to 100	100+ to 200	200+	Total
Glenties Rural District	1960			2380		817	543	441	317		4,498
	1965			2414		801	483	412	346		4,456

Sources: C.S.O. 1934–1956; C.S.O. 1960; W.D.R.S. Vol. III, p.4 (1965).

intriguing. The Irish find it terrifying, and not without reason. A stranger requesting information, particularly about livestock, has in the past been either a tax collector, a landlord's agent, or a means inspector. More recently, information given has been used to "demonstrate" the people's backwardness or to ridicule them. What is remarkable is not their paranoia about the dangers of the role of informant; it is that they make such excellent informants.

SETTLEMENT PATTERNS AND LAND TENURE

In looking at settlement patterns and land tenure and inheritance systems, it must be borne in mind that in Southwest Donegal, the old system of *clachans* or the rundale system, and land tenure have changed drastically since 1850, but they did not assume their present form until the early years of the 20th century. Modes of political and economic integration also changed, and although there were political upheavals after 1850 — the Land Wars; the Uprising; the Civil War; the establishment of the Irish Republic and Northern Ireland — these upheavals had less effect on Southwest Donegal settlement patterns than the post-Famine policies to do with land tenure. I will deal here with two of these post-Famine innovations: 1) the dispersed housing now common in Donegal, as opposed to the *clachans* or nucleated settlements of the pre-Famine years; and 2) the system of impartible inheritance and late marriages that has replaced the earlier system of subdivision of landholdings (partible inheritance) and early marriage.

In Southwest Donegal, townlands are the basis of local ties: houses are dispersed or located at some distance from one another and they are set in locations convenient to the agricultural land that surrounds them. The townland boundaries predate the Celtic invasion but the settlement configuration is more recent. The dispersed housing now common in most of Donegal is one of the many aftereffects of the Famine, and though the townlands may be part of an ancient "tradition" of settlement, the present configuration of settlements bears little relation to the "traditional" or pre-Famine ways. The dispersed housing, the isolated farms, are little more than a century old. Evans describes the development of the current situation:

The truth is that, taking the country as a whole, most of the farms are too small to be truly independent of their neighbours. Bitter experience and the traditional land-hunger of a community where the land has been almost the sole available resource go far to explain the jealousy with which established rights are maintained, but there are deeper needs and bonds in the rural community . . . for jobs requiring traction-implements or expensive tools the help of neighbours is necessary . . . there is a good deal of co-operation, perforce, among neighbours in tilling the ground, in harvest work and other operations. Both seedtime and harvest are, in the Irish climate, seasons of heavy pressure, when the work must be got through speedily, and nothing is so conducive to speed as a 'gathering' of neighbours among whom a spirit of rivalry acts as a spur . . .

In this and other ways the isolated houses are bound by ties of neighbourhood and friendship so that one may think of them as forming close-knit communities lacking only the physical nucleation of former times (Evans 1957: 21-23).

Under the pre-Famine *clachan* system, the nucleated or close-built houses were tenanted by families who regularly drew lots for the right to use the land; with dispersed housing, fences came to be an important part of the landscape and individuals were responsible for their own land. The pre-Famine system survives only in the system of cooperation that is still practiced; the "modern" aspects of the system include fences, isolated farms, and the right to autonomy, a right that was probably not so common in the *clachan*.

In the current system, an individual, preferably a son, inherits land from his father. Before the Famine, plots of land could be subdivided amongst all of a man's heirs, a system of partible inheritance. This subdivision of land was thought to be one of the causes of the Famine, when too many people owned small plots of land on which they could grow only potatoes; their dependence on the potato crop made them particularly vulnerable to its failure. Early marriage, and many children, along with the system of tiny plots resulting from endless divisions, had contributed to Famine conditions. After the Famine, legislation was enacted to prevent subdivision of plots, legislation that demanded that a single heir be selected by the parents. Most of the land in Ireland was owned by landlords and the legislation had little immediate effect, except to increase outmigration. But it had curious social effects over the century: from a system of early marriage, there emerged a system of late marriage, and a concomitant belief system. If only one child could inherit, then the rest of the children had to find livelihoods elsewhere; this increased the outmigration rates that even before the Famine had been high. Further, the one son who stayed at home had to remain celibate until he inherited the land, partly in order to care for his parents, and partly because of the belief that "two women cannot share the same kitchen." No son could marry while his mother was still alive, therefore, and the number of unmarried people in rural Ireland went from 10 percent among men, 12 percent among women in pre-Famine (1841 census) times (Freeman 1957: 16), to its current high percentages of more than 30 percent unmarried men, and more than 32 percent unmarried women.

In Donegal, the celibacy rate was higher. A survey taken from the 1966 census showed that while the national percentages were 27.6 percent never-married males and 24.3 percent never-married females, the West Donegal rates were 38.4 percent for males and 29.5 percent for females (W.D.R.S. 1969 Pt. 3:38). Most of my informants believed that the system of late marriages was "traditional" and, in their reasoning, because they lived in the more "traditional" area of Ireland, the custom of late marriage was practiced more intensively there. Late age at marriage, however, is not a traditional practice but a post-Famine one. Most people marry between the ages of thirty and forty-four, as opposed to the pre-Famine norm in which two-thirds of the population were married in the 26-35 age group (Freeman 1957: 16; W.D.R.S. 1969 Pt. 3: 38).

Late marriage, then, is an innovation brought about by the changes in tenure laws from partible to impartible inheritance. It is also an adaptive response to the problem of too many children; a woman's reproductive years span 33 years, on average; if she is celibate through the first half of that time, her fertility rate (otherwise unchecked, according to Catholic doctrine) is reduced by half, in theory at least. Lifelong celibacy and late age at marriage support the current, single-heir system; low celibacy rates and early age at marriage supported the pre-Famine multiple-heir system.

Many of my informants believed that late marriage was "traditional;" knowing something of Irish history, I was suspicious of this idea. Connell's data (1950) show clearly that in pre-Famine Ireland late marriages were uncommon, and that most women were married before they reached age 26 (1950: 40). I was suspicious, too, of the idea that certain things were being done because that was the way they were always done. I recognized the "grandfather response" in many of my informants' replies, but the land tenure system currently practiced in Donegal was one that discouraged — almost forbade — knowledge of one's (paternal) grandparents. My informants' knowledge of the traditional customs was severely limited by their system of late marriage and impartible inheritance.

A simple example will indicate why this is so. If a man marries at age 32, produces ten children, and dies at age 70, one of his sons inherits the land, according to his deathbed wish. His wife, presumably a bit younger than he, stands a good chance of living to be 75 years old, so it is likely that there are seven years beyond inheritance in which the heir could not marry. Only when both parents are dead can the son propose marriage to his sweetheart. According to the formal system, then, the son's children would never know their paternal grandparents.

There are two rules that govern inheritance: the first is that only one heir will inherit, and the second is that the name must be kept on the land, i.e., a son or a nephew (who bears the same name) should inherit. Informants are careful to specify that the heir need not be the youngest son (ultimogeniture) or the eldest son (primogeniture); all sons are eligible. The consequences of these rules are of interest and, to follow the example just given, if the eldest son should inherit the land, he would be 45 years old when his mother died (assuming that he was born within two years of his parents' marriage, and that all other children were born after similar intervals). His bride-to-be, two years his junior, would be 43, nearly past childbearing years. If, however, the heir were the youngest son, he would be 22 years old when he inherited the land and 29 when his mother died. The rule of ultimogeniture would work best, but informants, especially those with several sons, vehemently deny that there is any such rule.

Not having such a rule is useful in keeping the sons hard at work on the farm, in the hope that they may inherit, but there is a tendency to favor the youngest son. The formal system of impartible inheritance is observed in Donegal with many informal variations, however, and to understand how these work, one need only think of the possibilities for variation in the family I have described above. There is the possibility that only one son (or no sons) will be born; there is the possibility that the mother will live long beyond 75; and there is the possibility that the son, after his mother's death, will discover that bachelor living suits him better than marriage might.

In my sample of thirty farmers, many informants were younger sons whose elder siblings had left Ireland before the informants had come of age. The breakdown within the sample was as follows:

Bought land	6
Eldest son	3
Eldest with younger son	5
Younger son	11
Only child	3
Relative (nephews)	2
	30

To test further the "pattern" that exists in actual land transfers, I chose two townlands, one in a very remote part of Southwest Donegal, and the other in an English-speaking area near a good-sized town (Table 4.2). In the former, the outmigration rate has exceeded forty-five percent over the last two decades, while in the latter, the rate for the same time period has been slightly over sixteen percent. These two townlands were selected because my informants in each were knowledgeable older people with good memories and an interest in the question of land inheritance. In the English-speaking area, there were twelve landholders (tenants) as of 1857; according to my informant, there were twelve inhabited houses in his youth some thirty years ago. The Griffith Valuation lists the total acreage of the townland as slightly more than 247; my informant estimated that each of the twelve farms had twenty acres. Of the twelve families he knew in his youth, five "died off," and the population dropped from fifty to thirteen over three decades. In addition to the fifty regular inhabitants, there were seasonal laborers (elder sons) who returned home for the winter. Now, he says, "they all marry across the water and raise their families there," returning only for holidays. Of the five abandoned farms, only one has reverted to the Land Commission. The remaining four were bought by neighbors from nephews and nieces who had no interest in the property.

Of the 1857 landholders, in Townland A, three were women and their names are no longer on the land. There are four names not represented in the Valuation Report, two of these from recent sales. Two houses that bore names listed in the 1857 survey have been torn down; one of these was built on a plot that contained only

TABLE 4.2
Comparison of Townlands, Land Ownership 1857-1970

Townland A	1857 Griffith Valuation Report	1940 (informant's youth)	1970
English-speaking area 247 acres, total			
Mixed soils, good to marginal	12 tenants, 3 of them female	12 landholdings	7 landholdings,
Outmigration rate: 16%			
			5 houses "die off" with 1 farm reverting to Land Commission; 4 bought by neighbors
		population: 50+*	
			population: 13+

* The first population number given refers to year-round occupants; the + refers to elder sons who returned to the land during heavy work seasons, cutting turf, saving the hay, etc.

Townland B	1857 Griffith Valuation Report	1940 (informant's youth)	1970
Gaelic-speaking area 800 acres, total			
Poor soils, reclaimed marginal land	3 tenants	3 landholdings	2 landholdings, 1 "new" house
Outmigration rate: 45%			

Acquisition of land as of 1970:

Townland A		Townland B		Townland B, environs	
Bought	2	Bought	1	Bought	0
Eldest	0	Relative	1	Eldest	4
Youngest	2	Eldest with		Youngest	2
Middle	1	youngest	1	Eldest with	
Unknown	1	Total	3	youngest	3
Brother				Younger	5
& sister	1			Nephew	2
Total	7			Only son	1
				Only child	2
				Unknown	6
				Brother	
				& sister	3
				Brother (of	
				landowner)	1
				2 sisters	2
				Total	31

three acres and yet sustained a family of eleven children, and the other is the plot that has reverted to the Land Commission. This last is very isolated and no one in the townland deemed it desirable.

The second townland, deep in a Gaelic-speaking area, had only three tenants in 1857, despite its eight hundred acres. There are now two inhabited houses and the land of the third tenant has passed to a direct descendant who bears his name, but whose house is located slightly beyond the townland boundary. There are two new names, one of them acquired through a woman who inherited the land and passed it on to her son, and the other through a family that bought in but has since abandoned the land, returning only to collect the rent.

Here my informants estimated for me the landholders in the surrounding townlands and their means of acquisition. The transfers, including my informants' land, are given in Table 4.2.

Of the participants in these land transfers, only nine married, twenty-five remained single, and three were unknown. (No more than eight of the twenty-five are considered marriageable at present.)

Given these outcomes, the system of late marriage can be understood as an adaptive response to the problem of impartible inheritance, but the response has maladaptive consequences, in that it fosters celibacy. In the formal system, there is little room for variation; in the informal system, many such variations occur. The land tenure system is by no means a "traditional" one, but for the sake of keeping the name on the land, a number of extra-formal devices are used and these are sanctified by the label "traditional."

LIVESTOCK PRODUCTION

The aims of the study of livestock production methods were to compare production strategies pertaining to two kinds of domestic animals, cattle and sheep, and to provide comparative information about a specific means of environmental exploitation, the production of domestic animal biomass. Hypotheses to be tested were formulated around a central issue: what are the direct and indirect consequences for the human population of keeping certain kinds of domestic animals?

I considered four aspects of the keeping of different kinds of domestic animals: economic, ecological, nutritional and social consequences. The following variables were pertinent to the study of production strategies: actual and potential productivity of resources; ecological and growth efficiencies of different kinds of animals in a given environment; means of marketing livestock; family and group relationships hinged on production unit necessities; livestock as a form of capital asset; consumption patterns and energy expenditures required for tasks related to the care of domestic animals.

The overall findings from the sample were, first, that cattle are considered the prestige crop of the area, with sheep the cash crop of little prestige consequence; second, that production strategies reflect these convictions and are predicated on prestige considerations, rather than on short-term economic gains; and third, that the environmental resources available are replenished or conserved by the existing exploitation procedures. The three points — to do with production strategies and resources — were discovered by setting up testable hypotheses, some of which were disproved but all of which were helpful in illuminating the realities of the area's production system. Data were gathered with an interview schedule (Appendix B) designed as a general guide, from which specific questions could be addressed. I will outline the results and indicate the data in several sections, including livestock numbers, social aspects of livestock-keeping, livestock production strategies, and marketing procedures. (Animal health and husbandry methods data will be found in Appendix C.) In some instances, I have used government statistics, and in others, I have used data collected by intensive interviews and participant observation to reveal the many twists and turns within the production systems and to specify some of the hidden variables that emerged in investigating what seemed to be straightforward matters.

LIVESTOCK NUMBERS: CATTLE, SHEEP AND PIGS

Numbers of the major types of livestock produced in Donegal have fluctuated greatly since the turn of the century. Sheep numbers have more than doubled, pig numbers fell off sharply and were then partially restored, and cattle numbers have declined. The fluctuations can be seen from the livestock census reports in Table 4.3.

TABLE 4.3 Livestock Census Reports for County Donegal

	Cattle	Sheep	Pigs
1970	161,800	299,800	
1965			20,000
1950	152,000	157,538	8,000
1918	170,917	147,062	
1900			26,500

More specific breakdowns appear in Tables 4.4 and 4.5 and the dramatic changes in hay, pasturage, and rough grazing are apparent in Table 4.5.

Before interpreting these trends, some cautions are necessary. The punch line of the story about statistics should be recalled, i.e., "Those statistics were gathered for a different purpose."

The introduction of cattle and sheep subsidies has changed the purposes of gathering statistics; my informants were agreed that accuracy in numbers was greater in recent years owing to the sheep subsidy. It is nonetheless a relative accuracy and my suspicion is that figures prior to the subsidy may have been 50-75% accurate, whereas figures since the subsidy are no more than 85-90% accurate. This is based on the discrepancies between figures recorded on dipping certificates and information given me by informants, the latter number tending always to be somewhat higher than the former. For sheep, my own counts and comparisons with dipping certificate figures revealed the same discrepancies; before the introduction of the subsidy, everyone underestimated the number of animals and since the subsidy, everyone overestimates the number of animals.

Other difficulties are involved in the interpretation of statistical trends, e.g., the acreage of improved pasture seems to have risen spectacularly. "Improved pasture" is often defined as pasture to which lime has been added but while this additive distinguishes it from rough grazing statistically, it makes only a marginal difference to the grazing animals. The use of artificial fertilizers has increased greatly since World War II but the degree of improvement leaves much to be desired.

Absolute numbers of cattle have fallen off, doubtless in proportion to the number of abandoned farms, while hay acreage

DONEGAL'S CHANGING TRADITIONS

TABLE 4.4

Changes in Human and Pig Populations compared to Potato Crop

Year	Human Pop.	Pigs	Potatoes	Pig/Potato Ratio
1900*	100%	26,500 (100%)	40,000 Ac. (100%)	1:1.51
1910		25,500 (96%)	36,000 (90%)	1:1.41
1911	97%			
1918		25,500 (96%)	39,000 (97.5%)	1:1.53
1926	88%			
1930		18,000 (68%)	31,000 (77.5%)	1:1.72
1936	82%			
1940		10,000 (38%)	28,000 (70%)	1:2.8
1946	78%			
1950		8,000 (30%)	29,000 (72.5%)	1:3.63
1956	76%			
1960		13,000 (49%)	26,000 (65%)	1:2.00
1961	66%			
1965		20,000 (76%)	22,000 (55%)	1:1.1
1966	62%			

* base line year

TABLE 4.5

Changes in Numbers/Average of Cattle, Sheep, Hay and Pasture

GLENTIES RURAL DISTRICT

Year	Cattle	Sheep	Hay	Pasture	Other
1949*	22,147	46,719	11,929	245,188	
	(100%)	(100%)	(100%)		
1955	20,447	45,586	14,611	242,682	
	(90%)	(98%)	(125%)		
1960	18,074	52,130	12,455	24,689	224,362
	(82%)	(110%)	(100%)	(100%)	(100%)
1965	17,141	57,249	12,863	49,834	197,871
	(77%)	(121%)	(115%)	(200%)	(88%)

COUNTY DONEGAL

Year	Cattle	Sheep	Hay	Pasture	Other
1918*	170,917	147,062	62,057	not available	
	(100%)	(100%)	(100%)		
1939-40	144,628	164,830	58,175	263,552	
	(85%)	(112%)	(94%)	(100%)	
1949-50	152,000	157,538	59,645	not available	
	(89%)	(107%)	(97%)		
1959-60	164,400	309,800	61,000	248,500	
	(96%)	(211%)	(98%)	(94%)	
1969-70	161,800	299,800	71,700	324,100	
	(95%)	(204%)	(116%)	(123%)	

From: Annual Reports, Co. Donegal Committee of Agriculture, 1961 & 1969-70
West Donegal Resource Survey, Part 3, 2-3.

* base line year

has increased with the advent of tractors. The hidden factor in all this is that cattle now have more "condition" on them when they are sold, according to my informants. Cattle prices have gone steadily upwards, as has the demand for cattle in good condition. Tractors, another post-war innovation that took some time to become established, have facilitated this trend.

With these cautions in mind, we can review the changes in each population of animals.

CATTLE

From Table 4.5, it is clear that the numbers of cattle have declined in the Glenties Rural District; the human population since 1918 has also declined but not by the same proportion. There has been a twenty percent drop in human population and a much greater drop in the cattle population, and at the same time, an increase in sheep numbers. These changes seem to reflect changes in the human population — the population of men in the 20-39 age brackets has dropped off considerably since 1926, as can be seen in the population pyramid (Figure 4.1.). The human labor force available is an important factor in the decision to keep cattle or sheep, and in the opinion of all my informants, cattle were the more desirable animals to keep. The realities were otherwise, however, as shown in the tables. There were fewer young men available to care for cattle, and sheep, the less desirable but less demanding animals, have increased in numbers.

Herd composition in cattle has changed very little over the last fifty years. In former times, there were "scrub" bulls available to service cows; the Artificial Insemination Service provided by the government has taken the place of the scrub bulls and made little difference in the livestock production system.

Artificial insemination, however, has made a difference in the breeds of livestock; there has been a general upgrading in this respect, as farmers may now choose the breed they want, whereas the scrub bulls were of no particular breed. A few farmers told me that milk yields had declined with the advent of the Artificial Insemination Service, a perception that is borne out by the information available on milk yield heritability (20-30% is due to heredity, according to Campbell and Lasley 1969: 107). Most farmers pronounced themselves satisfied with the Artificial Insemination Service.

There was general agreement, too, that cattle were better and heavier and more marketable than in previous years, all factors encapsulated in the phrase, "the cattle have more 'condition' on them now than before." It cannot be stressed too often that the primary beneficiaries of new pasturage techniques and of improved land are cattle, not sheep. This point will emerge again in the discussions of animal health and marketing strategies.

SHEEP

Two factors are important in the dramatic rise in sheep numbers. First, the rise may be more apparent than real, for reasons discussed above, i.e., the subsidy on ewes may have increased the accuracy of the reporting. Second, between 1900 and 1970, there was a changeover in breed, from the former, nondescript breed that required better care to the present Scottish Blackface breed. The Blackface is a hardy breed, requires little care, and is, unlike most sheep, territorial. This territoriality further reduces the care given, for the sheep must be sought out by a farmer, often over vast stretches of bogland. One disadvantage of territoriality is increased vulnerability to predation; the "killer dogs" that roam in packs at night are unhampered by a herd organization, and a single ewe that attempts to "defend" her territory or her lamb against five or six dogs is helpless.

The number of sheep kept has increased but the means of keeping them, i.e., rough pasture, has not changed greatly since the Blackface was adopted. A major factor in the decision to keep sheep is the kind of land available; as one of my informants put it, "Well, [the decision] depends on the type of land. Some land is good enough for cows all year around and some land is so poor that only the sheep can make a living on it."

The effect of the ewe subsidy can be more precisely calculated. For this purpose I recorded the figures for sheep from each townland in the region over a period of years, both prior to and after the introduction of the subsidy in 1968. The number of owners and the number of sheep are given for 1967, 1969, and 1970.

TABLE 4.6 Number of Owners and Number of Sheep
Before and After the 1968 Ewe Subsidy

District	1967	1969	1970
Glenleheen	48–1973	44–3022	58–3534
Graffy	35–2166	61–4104	65–4633
Doochary	24–952	25–1340	25–1252
Fintown	34–1326	39–2014	37–2230
Glenties[a]	8–1326	none	3–146
Totals	149–6783	169–10480	188–13765

The rise in the number of owners, as well as in the number of
sheep, is of interest. While the number of sheep may be highly
suspect, the number of owners reporting sheep is probably
accurate, and it is clear that the subsidy has had an impact on the
number of farmers who keep sheep.

Another trend of interest may be found by comparing the
districts themselves. If they are rated according to the native view
of each district's potential, the rating would be as follows:

District	Native Rating	WDRS Rating	% of Increase
Glenleheen	good to poor	moderate to poor	175%
Graffy	excellent	moderately good	209%
Doochary	very poor	very poor	130%
Fintown	good to poor	moderate to poor	170%

It seems certain that the increases follow the area's potential.
A better understanding of the dynamics of the subsidy may be
gained from analysis of response within my sample. Of sixteen
farmers who kept sheep, the response to the question, "Are you
keeping more sheep since the subsidy began?" was in four cases
positive, in three cases positive but qualified, and in nine cases
negative. Of the four positives, three had land suitable for
development and one responded that he was keeping only a few
more, as he had not the "scope" necessary for sheep. Of the three

positive but qualified answers, all were engaged in development programs which included reclamation of land. Of the nine negative responses, three noted that their herd composition had changed; two felt that they were already sufficiently stocked and that their land would not take more sheep (in my own classification, the land belonging to both these men was "dismal" and would have necessitated heavy capital investment for reclamation); two kept sheep for other than financial reasons; one was an elderly man who had no one to help him, and the last of the nine had had bad luck with killer dogs which nearly destroyed his herd two years in succession.

All but one of those who responded positively to the subsidy had made improvements in pasture to accommodate the increase in numbers; the exception was the man who had added a few more but who had insufficient "scope".

I believe it is safe to conclude that the keeping of different kinds of domestic animals has had a decisive effect on land use patterns. The correlation between sheep numbers and improvement of land is not so close as I would have liked but if one assumes, as most Donegal farmers do, that one sheep needs two to four acres, then it is close enough. Although the increases show a positive trend, they fall below the government's expectations.

Though it may be little comfort to government officials, it is clear that the principles of economic rationality are followed in the production of different kinds of domestic animals. Cattle prices, especially for good cattle in excellent condition, are higher and more stable than sheep prices, and the proportion of hay to cattle indicates that a more favorable ratio prevails than ever before in the region. Sheep are increasing in numbers but not in value and marginal lands are being improved to accommodate them. The farmers are maximizing their production from cattle and minimizing their losses from sheep, and this pattern — quick response to innovation in the cattle trade, slow response to innovation in the sheep trade — emerges in every aspect of livestock production systems in the region. In the context of economic rationality, pig production figures also lend support to the farmers' judgments.

PIGS

In 1900, there were more than 26,000 pigs in Donegal. They were fed on a diet of skim milk and potatoes, a diet that gives a very poor conversion ratio. Pig-keeping became an uneconomic proposition when southern dairying interests came into competition with the small farmer in Donegal. In the South of Ireland, pigs could be fed year round on skim milk and prepared meals and, after 1920, the southern pig producers led the field. Table 4.4 gives the ratios between pig production, potato production, and human population; all have declined since 1900 but the decline in pig numbers follows a more erratic pattern. If the figures for the Glenties Rural District alone were available, I believe the correlation between pig production and potato acreage would be closer, since reliance on dairy produce has kept pig numbers in County Donegal as a whole higher than they probably are in Southwest Donegal, where dairying has never been a viable industry.

The lowest pig numbers were recorded in 1940; since that time, there has been an increase in pig numbers but the production techniques have changed considerably and in my sample reliance on purchased food for pigs was near 100 percent. Only one farmer in the sample allowed his pigs to root, for example; the others kept their animals confined all the time.

Animal population numbers, then, incomplete as they often are and inaccurate as they may be, nonetheless reveal interesting trends. Another way of looking at this is by considering these trends in relation to the human labor force.

HUMAN POPULATION NUMBERS

Here my primary concern was with the labor force and those factors that affected it, e.g., marriage and age-sex population pyramids. It was noted in the foregoing that a high rate of out-migration has prevailed in Donegal since the 1920's; the effect this has on the labor force and in turn on farm productivity is tremendous, as will be seen.

For County Donegal as a whole, there were 12,957 persons (11,436 males and 1,521 females) listed as farmers in 1961; additionally, 8,618 males and 630 females were listed as being engaged in farming occupations. The more specific breakdown is given in Table 4.7.

TABLE 4.7 Males Engaged in Agriculture, 1961

	Numbers	-as % of total males gainfully employed
Farmers	11,436	33
Farmers relatives assisting	5,968	17
Farm laborers	2,650	8
Total males engaged in farming	20,054	58
Total males engaged in all occupations	34,925	100

(Data drawn from P. Bolger, n.d., Land Use and Agriculture, mimeo.)

In the Glenties Rural District, there were 3,978 men engaged in farm work in 1960. By 1965, there were only 3,486. The numerical and percentage breakdowns are as follows:

	Males 14 to 18 years		Males 18 years and over	
	Family Members	Others	Family Members	Others
1960	447	2	3,352	29
%	11.2	0.1	84.3	0.7
1965	438	15	2,826	26
%	12.6	0.4	81.1	0.7

These figures indicate the extent to which the population is dependent on agriculture for employment and livelihood, and further, the extent to which farming is a family pursuit. Outside labor is almost never utilized. In my sample of thirty farmers, only two regularly employed outsiders. Both these men were dairy farmers and one only employed men "when he could get them." Neither had children old enough to help and both complained bitterly of the present shortage of good workers, but the situation apparently differs little from that of previous decades, Donegal agriculture having always been a family concern.

However, the figures are deceptive in one sense. Although a man's occupation may be listed as "farmer," many engage in seasonal occupations as well and may not pursue farming on a year-round basis. Odd jobs such as road building, hauling turf, or regular but seasonal occupations such as turf-cutting at the local *Bord na Mona* (Turf Board) installation or weaving would not change a man's classification as "farmer." Most able-bodied men will have engaged in these pursuits at one time or another in their lives.

Changes in the population structure are indicated in the following age-sex pyramid. The percentage distribution in age groups is as follows:

	0-14 years	15-34 years	35-64 years	65+
1926	31.2	27.8	28.3	12.8
1966	27.3	20.4	36.0	16.3

(W.D.R.S. Vol. 3:35.)

The decline in the younger age segments and the increase in the older age groups indicates the trends clearly.

The male-female sex ratio is generally more favorable in Donegal than in other parts of the country, and even more favorable in West Donegal than elsewhere in the County. Marriage rates, however, are the lowest in all of Ireland. The percentages of all females married (over the age of 15) is 46.1 in the Glenties Rural District, as opposed to 49.2% for the country as a whole. For males over the age of 15, 42% in the Glenties Rural District are married, as opposed to 48.2% in the rest of the country. Those in the older age groups, 55-64, who have remained single are 38.4% of men and 29.5% of women, in contrast to the national percentages of 27.6% and 24.3% respectively (W.D.R.S. Vol. 3:38).

The population decline affects various age groups differently. The West Donegal Resource Survey workers found that it was "not possible" to measure emigration from the Glenties Rural District, but they noted that as children pass into adulthood, they are lost from the area. "Over two-thirds of the children have left the area by the time they reach their 30s. In the Dispensary Districts of Carrick, Doocharry, Dunglow and Ardara the relative declines are even higher" (W.D.R.S. Vol. 3:40).

While it is clear that the population composition is shifting in the direction of a predominance of older age groups, it is not so clear from the data on land holdings that consolidation of farms is a countertrend. Some indication of this is provided by the

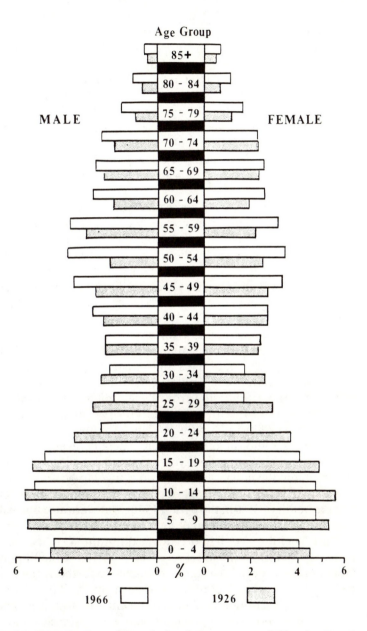

Figure 4.1 Distribution of Population by age group of Glenties Rural
District.
(source: West Donegal Resource Survey.)

experience of the W.D.R.S. workers. For their sample, two electoral divisions were chosen and 96 names in each of five size categories were selected at random from lists of landholders. 480 holdings were therefore to be sampled, slightly more than 10% of all holdings in the Glenties Rural District. 7.8% of the landholders had emigrated abroad, 2.9% had settled elsewhere in the country, 13.5% were incapacitated by old age or infirmity, while 4.0% were deceased and 12% worked full time at some occupation other than farming. Among the holdings of the non-participants in the sample, 9% had been let, 3.5% had been sold, 11.4% was unused, 18.6% was being farmed, and 1.9% was categorized as "other" (Vol. 3: 50-53).

The picture presented by these tabulations is a grim one, perhaps a distorted one. While it is certainly true that much of the land seems to be unused, it should also be borne in mind that much of the land was classified by the soil survey workers as "unusable." In fact, in view of the classification of 75% of the land (Vol. 3: 1) in the Glenties Rural District as "other" land, i.e., non-agricultural land, it is surprising that only 11.4% of the land in the total sample went unused.

Two more points might be inferred from this sample. First, it must be observed that the statistical recording of land ownership is often wildly inaccurate. This is not a fault that need be attributed to the Land Commission employees; it is more likely the outcome of the Donegal attitude towards officialdom and the result of the government's policy of basing eligibility for unemployment benefits on taxable valuation of land holdings. Several of my informants had holdings which were officially owned by relatives dead more than twenty-five years. Second, and more tenuously, the question of whether the labor force *ought* to be replacing itself remains. Those electoral districts in which population decrease was greater than 35% in the period 1946-1966 were also the districts containing the poorest lands.

Rural sociologists often debate the question of rural exodus vs. rural depopulation, the latter term referring to the inability of the labor force to reproduce itself adequately and the former to the refusal of the young people to remain on the land. Both are unquestionable trends in Southwest Donegal; young people are trained in school for employment elsewhere, giving impetus to the rural exodus pattern (see Hannan's excellent study of this phenomenon in Ireland, 1970). Another factor that contributes to rural exodus is the division of labor that presently exists among farm families.

DIVISION OF LABOR

The output per labor unit employed is lower in Southwest Donegal than in other parts of the country; this has to do with the nature of the terrain and the impossibility, beyond a certain point, of employing mechanical devices in most of the area. But apart from the statistics on labor unit output, there are sociological questions concerning the division of labor — recruitment, sex roles, and the influence of the population structure itself on production units. Most farm labor is also family labor and recruitment, therefore, is largely a function of reproduction.

Reproduction in turn is governed by marriage and the Irish system of late marriages is a peculiar one in anthropological annals. It is worthwhile to digress here to discuss the practice of late marriage and its place in the system as a whole. Two points must be made at the outset: illegitimate children do not inherit, and the ideal is to retain the name on the land, i.e., to pass the land on to a son. Had my data been more conclusive and shown definite trends, including the invariable retention of the name on the land, I would be reluctant to offer an uncommon interpretation of the practice of late marriage, but it is precisely the inconclusiveness of the data that tempts me to speculate.

My data on land transfers are set out above in the section on settlement patterns and land tenure. The commonest pattern of land inheritance is transfer to a younger son. In ecological terms this is an eminently sensible strategy because a farmer then has the benefit of all his sons' labor over the years. When his own energies are declining (as are the needs of his family), his replacement will be entering his prime. So, too, with reproduction — a younger son will be capable of raising his family after his father dies and the cycle will repeat itself until an heir fails to marry or to produce children. Thus, in production terms, late marriages and inheritance by a younger son insure that the land produces more at a time when it is most necessary (see Figure 4.2).

The system of late marriages, then, has advantages in both the ecological and reproductive senses. Ecologically, it allows a "fallow" period that follows the human life cycle; reproductively, it serves as a natural birth control device in a country in which artificial limitation of family size is forbidden. The generation cycle provides a natural fallow period for the land since there will be a peak productivity time about two-thirds of the way through a thirty-year cycle; the rest of the time the land will not be utilized to its full productive capacity.

Low fertility is a natural concomitant of late marriage, but infertility is another concomitant of that same system and infertility has brought about a periodic reshuffling of the land, thus facilitating a kind of "upward mobility" and opening up the possibility of land ownership for those who otherwise would not have had the opportunity to become farmers themselves.

The problem of late marriage might therefore be considered in terms of its positive features, as well as the negative ones that are customarily ascribed to it. It could be seen as a pattern which has served remarkably well in an area heavily dependent on human labor for subsistence. Though the Irish themselves rail against the system as an unjust and burdensome one, it probably has facilitated the population's survival. While my informants bemoan the number of old bachelors now on the land, and I share their concern for the region's future, it seems to me likely that there were always a number of old bachelors on the land and that their failure to reproduce ensured that land would change hands. The ideal pattern, of course, is to keep the name on the land but the actual pattern, as it appears in my data, is one of periodic reshuffling of land. It is my view that late marriage was a highly "functional" adaptation, given the external constraints imposed upon the population because 1) it provided the farmer with a continuing labor supply, and, 2) with infertility as one of its concomitants, it provided the population with some degree of mobility and opportunities to increase landholdings.

In the past, when early marriages were the rule and the land was divided into ever-smaller plots, population growth was inevitable, and inevitably disastrous. After the Great Famine and in the face of a ban on land division, late marriage served very well as a means of ensuring the labor supply and limiting population growth, but the by-product was infertility and a number of old bachelors on the land.

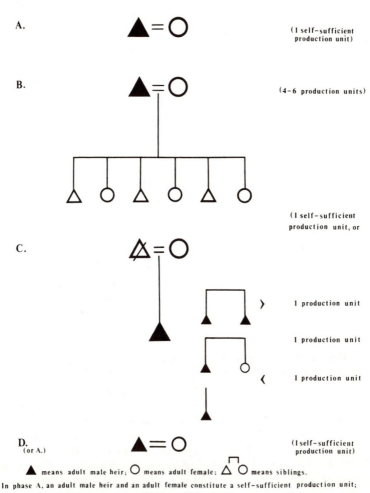

A.   (1 self-sufficient
                                                        production unit)

B.   (4-6 production units)

                                                      (1 self-sufficient
                                                        production unit, or

C.   > 1 production unit

                                                        1 production unit

                                                      < 1 production unit

D.   (1 self-sufficient
(or A.)   production unit)

▲ means adult male heir; ○ means adult female; △ ○ means siblings.
In phase A, an adult male heir and an adult female constitute a self-sufficient production unit;
in phase B. their children constitute, with them, additional production units, which are necessary
to support all members of the family; in phase C. the adult male heir is the son and the production
unit consists of mother and son or the alternates listed.

Figure 4.2 Production units and land transfers.

The problem now is not with the system nor with the number of old bachelors clinging tenaciously to the land; it is an external factor which has slowly penetrated even this remote area. Throughout most of Ireland since the 1920's, there has been a dramatic increase in the standard of living but in those parts of Donegal where out-migration has been heaviest, little has changed. There is no running water, no electricity, no paved roads; there is simply a hard life and a monotonous diet, and all are factors which older people may tolerate but which their children reject — having been taught to reject these standards by the improved schooling which the government provides. In 1971, the Comprehensive School in Glenties, a brand new facility with more than thirty teachers, had no course offerings in agriculture or farm management. Children are educated in subjects that will enable them to find jobs elsewhere and, there being no local employment, they leave with no intention of returning.

I suspect that the rise in the standard of living, the increase in the level of expectations, has brought about the difficulties, not the system of late marriages. Government officials customarily blame the latter for most of the area's difficulties and offer it as proof of the backwardness of the natives. But infertility is not a problem so long as there are willing heirs whose help can be relied upon, and it is only within recent times that there has been a dearth of willing heirs.

This digression covers the most important facts about recruitment of the labor force, but I will add one observation. I have here equated marriage with reproduction because this is what the system does and illegitimate children do not inherit property. In former times, I am told, unwed mothers were banished to England, usually at the priest's insistence. While this is no longer the case invariably, illegitimate children still do not inherit property. The fact that girls now remain at home and bear their children was often pointed out to me with some degree of vicarious satisfaction at this defiance of priestly authority, but no informant would agree that an illegitimate child had a right to inherit property. Such children, of course, bear their mother's name.

With the circumstances I have described, one would expect that labor patterns would develop around the authority of the father, whose decision as to the next heir is crucial. If the foregoing explanation of late marriage as a factor in high production levels is correct, it then follows that it would be advantageous to the farmer if the name of the future heir remains a secret.

Given these premises, one would expect a "stern father" pattern to be in operation and I anticipated, wrongly, as it happens, finding this. Most of my informants had what seemed to be good relationships with their fathers and seldom hesitated to interrupt or contradict a paternal declaration. The only times I saw the "stern father" stereotype in operation were, curiously, two cases in which the father-son relationship was absent; in one case, the authority figure was an employer, and in the other, it was a paternal uncle. While it is generally true that Irish children and young adults maintain silence in the presence of older people, this happens mostly when there are many adults present. The impression I garnered from being the only other adult (besides the parents) present is quite different, and I believe that within the family circle, there is much more interchange than one would assume from the classic literary descriptions of the patriarchal Irish family. However, one of the things my informants often volunteered information about was the decline of physical punishment in the schools and the subsequent lack of fear in the children, and it might be that adult-child relationships have changed somewhat in the past generation.

I did no interviewing on this topic of paternal authority but the subject of "fathers" arose naturally as a result of my questions about changes in herd composition or in kinds of domestic animals kept in the past. Most informants expressed admiration for their fathers' ability to "scratch a living from the bare ground" or recounted with glee a story or two about bargaining at the fair where their fathers had come out ahead. Admiration and respect were among the sentiments most often expressed, mingled in some — but only some — cases with affection. Several informants never mentioned their fathers, others did so very circumspectly.

I mention this only in passing because it bears on the question of paternal authority but such casual observations establish little. I did observe, both casually and otherwise, the patterns of displacement that existed in different kinds of households, and, surprisingly, I found that the most elaborate displacement behavior occurs in cases where two brothers hold the land jointly, and neither had married. In these cases, the younger brother assumed the role of the female in the household as far as chores were concerned and, oddly enough, also played a passive role in decision-making, in conversation with outsiders, and the like. The analogy that springs to mind is that of the *berdache* among certain American Indian groups (though in Donegal these younger brothers are not transvestites), in which the female role is caricatured by the male actor who plays it almost to perfection. The hierarchy in these dyads is readily apparent to any outsider, and the elder brother is usually more at ease socially while the younger seems to live in a state of constant tension, always anticipating interruption or interference, and taking on a sort of nervous deference which Irish women do not generally display.

In order to study displacement, I chose a simple measure and one common to all Irish households — who sits where. The place of honor in Ireland is the seat closest to the fire, and it is always offered to the visitor or, if there is more than one visitor, to the eldest male. In some households, the father may have a special chair which is his alone but this is unusual. Given the typical patriarchal family arrangement, one would expect that in the absence of visitors the father would customarily occupy the honored place. In the families I observed, where there were grown sons who had not succeeded the father as landowner, the seat closest to the fire was occupied by father and sons alike with occupance varying throughout the day. So, too, with seating positions at the table during meals; no particular order or "head" of the table attaches to this arrangement, and the men are fed first, then the children, then the women who have served the meal.

On this admittedly impressionistic basis, I would suggest that authority attaching to the Irish father is much more fluid than that generally ascribed. Daughters, too, participate in the game of musical chairs when they are not otherwise engaged but since most Irish women lead peripatetic lives, the issue does not often arise. (It was because I could participate in household chores and eliminate myself from the role of visitor that I could make these observations.) One might infer from the extreme deference shown by those in precarious or peripheral positions that the strong authority figure image has broken down or never fully penetrated the family norms of Donegal.

Contrariwise, few young Irishmen argue outright with their fathers, though they may interrupt or contradict a statement. When they disagree, it is done in mild tones and is usually answered in kind. Authority, though not unquestioned, is never disregarded and most younger men listen respectfully when explanations are given, as they generally are. This was one of the mixed blessings of my fieldwork; my questions often afforded unexpected opportunities for sons to extract further information from their fathers, or, in some cases, for sons to explain modern methods to their fathers. In the one case in my sample where I was able to observe three generations, the father treated his son with great respect and praised him for his good sense while the son listened sympathetically and with interest as the father related stories of the difficulties of the past. The grandson in this family was in his teens and he, too, was listened to with respect and assumed a great deal of responsibility for the herd.

To summarize, then, the male-male division of labor within the family is loosely organized around the father's authority. Young fully adult men tend to take on heavy work for longer periods, but this is not obvious, as most men and boys share out the work load and alternate tasks. There is no strict adult-child division of labor, though some chores are too dangerous or too difficult for children. It is taken for granted that children will help their parents and they participate willingly, often making a considerable contribution even at an early age. One of the advantages of growing up in a society that has few mechanical devices is that children can emulate their parents in their chores and are seldom banished to the sidelines to be kept from harm. Boys are "given" animals to care for, and they take special pride and interest in these. Often there is a considerable sentimental attachment to certain animals and these are given names and their personality characteristics outlined for any willing listener. Adult men tend to generalize about their animals and will call attention to one only if it happens to be an exceptionally difficult beast; the boys in the family name each animal and keep track of its offspring and its misadventures. This sentimental attachment must facilitate the learning process and lead eventually to a capacity I often marvelled at: the ability to recognize one's own sheep and to know where a particular animal is likely to be found.

The male-female division of labor is more sharp than stringent, that is, while there are boundaries within which each set of tasks is defined, these are freely crossed by members of the society who are in "special" categories, i.e., widows, spinsters, bachelors and widowers, and those who live alone. As I have said, there develops a special sort of relationship between two men wherein one brother assumes the responsibility for the household chores and the other assumes responsibility along more traditionally masculine lines. (I have often wondered whether or not these younger brothers contribute as much to the decision making process as do the Irish wives I met, since the latter tend to be quite vociferous in their expression of opinions.)

In my sample, the women's lives revolved, quite literally, around their stoves. The household stove — more than any other household item — indicates the family's economic status. No newborn infant ever demanded or received as much attention as these stoves require daily; approximately fifteen minutes of every waking hour in a woman's day is spent in adjusting, coaxing, replenishing or otherwise tending the stove. I must estimate this time, because it is impossible to count the number of trips to the stove made in a day when one includes cooking, heating water, drying clothes, and the like. Over and above the energy expenditure, there is an art to operating a turf stove smoothly and the art is a subtle one, not easily learned. Irish women do not think about the art involved — they simply make the appropriate adjustments and instruct their daughters accordingly by asking them to make minor adjustments.

The stove is the center of the household and the area around it serves as living quarters for the entire family throughout the day. Most farm houses have (only) one other room, a bedroom in which the whole family sleeps. Some houses have parlors, and others may have two bedrooms, but all activities center around the stove under normal circumstances. Throughout most of the day, the central passage of the room is kept clear of furniture and chairs are placed around the stove. At meal times, tables are moved from their positions against the walls; when the meal has been served, the central area is cleared once again. (This may happen four or five times in one day.) The primary occupation of an adult Irish woman, whether she is married or single, is cooking and even child care seems to be largely a matter of feeding the children. If there are two women in the house, both cook and care for the stove, but if the relationship is a mother-daughter one, the mother directs the daughter's activities almost silently and with very subtle cues. From late infancy, little girls are encouraged to imitate their mothers and praised for their efforts; at about four years of age, they are assigned regular tasks of a simple sort. These increase in complexity until, by the time they are ten or so, they are fully competent at most household chores and some are quite accomplished cooks. Between ten and twelve, most children seem to have mastered the basic skills necessary to the performance of their sex roles but aptitude varies widely. I knew only one boy, age fourteen, who actively disliked farming and he was away at boarding school most of the year. He participated fully, however, in family chores when at home on vacation. I knew two girls who disliked housework; one of these preferred to join her brothers at herding and the other had a decided intellectual bent, preferring her studies to household tasks. All these children were nevertheless fully competent, if uninterested, workers.

Girls are also taught to sew and to knit. Though parents are interested in seeing that their children do well in school, few encourage their children to read further than the school requires, and there is little distinction between boys and girls in this respect. Parents seem to be equally proud of boys or girls who do well in school but job opportunities are structured in such a way that it is more likely to be to a young man's advantage to continue his education than it is for a young woman to continue her education. A woman who gets a job locally may be employed in a knitting factory or some other type of expanded cottage industry, while a young man will be eligible, if he leaves the immediate area, for a government post or other civil service occupations. A young woman who leaves the area may find employment as a domestic or in a minor clerical position.

The study of the division of labor, then, suggests that the system of land inheritance and the custom of late marriage are intertwined with the division of labor in such a way as to ensure maximum productivity at the peak of need in the domestic cycle. This allows for fallow, or rest periods, for the land and the low fertility or infertility that may result from the system of late marriages ensures that the system will provide some measure of upward mobility for aspiring farmers. Perceptions of the lives of farmers as hard and unrewarding, however, lead many young people to choose other careers and the educational system supports this choice.

There is undoubtedly more variety in the life of a farmer than in the life of a housewife. Both work hard but the woman of the house has fewer positively sanctioned opportunities for leisure, e.g., her husband can visit pubs freely whereas she may accompany him only on select, "special" occasions such as election night or holidays. The husband may attend fairs, while wives are expected to remain at home, supervising the children and assigning the absent husband's chores to other family members. Several of the wives in my sample visited towns only once a week, to attend mass and to do a bit of shopping in the stores that are open briefly after mass. The rest of the time they were dependent on their families for social life and on the occasional visitor. Given the knowledge that life can consist of more than tending the stove, the children, and the livestock, and, given an opportunity to escape into the world of electric stoves and running water, many young women leave the area, vowing not to return. Ironically, the division of labor that so favors males is nonetheless dependent on women for the sustaining chores. Many an old bachelor told me that he had to choose between looking after his animals properly and looking after himself properly; if he looked after his sheep during most of the day, he faced a series of cold meals. Bachelors who live alone often subsist on a diet of tea, store-bought bread, and butter.

PRODUCTION UNIT CHANGES

One of my research hypotheses was that if minimal production unit requirements for different kinds of domestic animals varied, there would be points in the family cycle at which a change from one type of domestic animal to another is more likely to occur, e.g., a loss of personnel through emigration or death may necessitate changes in the domestic animals kept. There were few examples of this type of shift in my sample, because the limiting factors are imposed by the type of land owned. Some land is too poor to support cattle in large numbers no matter what the available labor.

Nevertheless, the figures are worth reproducing. My informants were in various stages of the life cycle and most reported changes in the kinds or numbers of domestic animals kept, even those whose land would not support cattle. Young men reported an increase in their herds, middle-aged men reported increases of larger proportions, and older men almost invariably reported a decrease in herd size. Most cattle farmers reported that the use of artificial fertilizers had increased the carrying capacity of the land, whether or not they were utilizing it in full.

Shifts in the kinds and numbers of domestic animals kept are apt to occur either during the peak production period I mentioned earlier, or at the beginning of the cycle. At the peaks, more animals of whatever kind will be kept; at the beginning of the domestic cycle, the switch tends to be made in the direction of keeping more sheep or, in two sample instances, to keeping pigs. There is another instance in which the transition to sheep is likely to be made, that in which the heir to the farm has another occupation, such as weaver. In these cases, sheep — which require little daily care — are used as supplementary sources of income.

Table 4.8 summarizes my observations by instance and age group.

TABLE 4.8 Responses to the
questions: Since you began farming, have the number and kinds of domestic animals you keep changed? In what direction?

	More sheep, fewer cattle	More cattle, fewer/no sheep	More cattle, more sheep	Same or fewer	Pigs
Young, with eldest child less than 10	3	1	0		1
no children	0	1	0		
Middle, with eldest child more than 10	3	3	0		
no children	3	0	0	1	0
Elderly with eldest child more than 21	0	0	1	3	1
no children	1	0	0	6	0

These numbers exceed chance expectations, in that the null hypothesis states that there will be random distribution of sample members in each of the categories and the actual distribution is anything but random. The middle-aged population is making shifts in an upward direction, the elderly is remaining constant or shifting downwards. The middle-aged population, of course, is not the one which has suffered a loss of personnel through outmigration or death. There have been six shifts in the younger generation, nine in the middle group, and three in the elderly population. While this negates the hypothesis (which states that there will be a disproportionate number in the young and elderly categories), the information garnered is more interesting than that suggested by the original hypothesis.

MARKETING

I have already described the process of selling animals at a fair; here I will only review the findings of the West Donegal Resource Survey workers about the other options available for marketing and add some information from my sample.

As has been observed previously, farming is a family enterprise in Southwest Donegal and it is not surprising to find, therefore, that "about half the total value of agricultural output of the Glenties Rural District in 1965/66 was consumed on farms", in contrast to a fifth in the whole of Ulster and 15 per cent for the state as a whole. (WDRS Vol. 3:18) Donegal's isolation is the major factor responsible for this. Cattle and sheep are the major products of the area; milk, poultry, potatoes and most other vegetables are produced for home consumption.

A marketing survey was carried out with a sample population of 258 farmers. Of 258, 163 farmers sold cattle in 1965. 144 of these transactions were with dealers, 11 were with other farmers, and 5 with farmer/dealers (three were unaccounted for). 85 of the sales were made on the farm, 77 at the fair, and one on the buyer's premises. More than half of those selling on the farm preferred this method because it kept costs to a minimum, and a quarter did so because they liked the method of sale. Of those 65 who sold cattle to the dealers at the fair, 44 preferred this means because of the more active market.

Transport is an important consideration in selling, and those cattle sold on the farm were removed by the buyers' transport. If they were sold at the fair, most cattle were walked there from the farm, and only 4 of the 77 fair-sellers hired transport for their animals.

Seventy-six farmers in the survey sold sheep and wool during the sample year. Of these sales, twelve were made to another farmer and sixty-four to dealers. Twenty-seven sales took place on the farm, forty-nine at the fair. Those selling on the farm claimed to prefer this method because of the lower costs associated, while those selling at the fair preferred the more active market to be found there. Twenty-three of those selling on the farm used the buyer's transport; of those selling at the fair, twenty-four farmers walked their sheep in, and eighteen hired transport. More than 75 per cent of the farmers who sold their sheep at the fair took them to the nearest fair, while more than 15 per cent took them to a more distant fair.

Without benefit of survey data, the workers observe that, "Even producers of cattle and sheep place little emphasis on gearing production to market demands, e.g., having the right quality product at the right time" (*ibid.*, p. 21). My own data contrasts strongly with this assertion, and with the statement that, "the amounts to be marketed are small so marketing arrangements remain simple and straightforward. The survey indicates that this trend is not likely to change much in the near future" (*ibid.*, p. 19).

First, owing to the nature of my data collecting, I must offer some generalizations about marketing. I concentrated on the present and the future, but I was constantly told about the past; all information gathered in this casual way refutes the proposition that there is no attempt to produce the right animals at the right time. The marketing of wethers will serve as a case in point. Some years ago, two year old wethers, or castrated rams, were in heavy demand for the autumn market. In the last ten years, the market for mutton has diminished and wethers are not kept past the age of thirteen or fourteen months, the time when two permanent teeth erupt and mark the animal as a sheep. Wether lambs are sold in the early spring and summer and, in one informant's estimation, would sell for five pounds, whereas keeping the wether until the following year would only increase its value by one pound, providing there was some market for it. My informant continued, 'Up until five years ago, wethers went to Antrim (Northern Ireland) and were sold in September and October. All this trade has now stopped. I remember the time when you couldn't sell a year-old wether at all but now there's a complete somersault and the older he gets, the less demand there is for him." The structure of the subsidy also has affected the keeping of wethers dramatically, since only lambs and ewes are eligible.

I offer this in contrast to the WDRS report, for this transition has taken place over the past five years and the right animals are being marketed at the right time. There may be a longer time period in Southwest Donegal than would be the case in a more commercially-oriented area, but then information diffusion about market trends is slower, too. Some individuals (two from my sample) still keep a few wethers; I witnessed the sale of six one day at a dipping. One of my informants sold the animals to a young neighbor, who planned to take them to the local fair the next day. The new owner believed he would make a huge profit and scoffed at the warnings of the older men present. I stood with him the next day as buyer after buyer walked past without a glance at his sheep. Later in the day, he returned home with them and they were eventually sold on the farm to a buyer who, it was said, probably offered to take them off his hands at a price far below what he had originally paid for them.

In order to get at marketing and production strategies, I asked each sample member who kept sheep to indicate how he would proceed, given 100 acres of good land. Only one of the sixteen indicated that keeping wethers would be a good strategy and even he no longer does this although the trade in wool and mutton was a flourishing one when he was young. Two sample members, as I mentioned, did keep wethers but even they kept very few and were constantly anticipating a rise in wool prices. Wool prices have dropped steadily since 1957 and show no signs of recovery. Cattle, too, are raised with market demands in mind and information diffusion seems more rapid among cattle farmers.

I would also take issue with the imputation of a stagnant market due to the small number of transactions, because although it is true that the amount of marketable goods is small, the arrangements are anything but simple and straightforward. The newest means of selling animals, the auction marts, is simple and straightforward; any other means calls out every ounce of Irish deviousness, for a sale is a public performance and one in which a man's honor, his allegiance, and his merit are tested.

For cattle, there are three options in marketing. Animals may be sold at auction in the marts, bought on the farm, or bid on at the fair. In the last two, transport problems are solved, since on-farm buyers provide their own transportation and farms are within walking distance of a fair. With marts, transport must be found or, if the mart provides it, the profit will be less shipping costs. On the other hand, prices at marts are apt to be higher because of the greater number of buyers and this may offset the transport costs.

Another dimension is time. Cattle farmers bring their animals to the fair in the morning, usually by 9 A.M. By noon, most animals are sold or, if they are not, they are penned up while prospective buyers continue to look for bargains. Ordinarily a man is free to return home shortly after noon, if he chooses, or to indulge in fair day convivialities. In contrast, mart sales are scheduled to begin as early as 8 A.M., although they seldom start this early, and they continue until all animals have been before the auctioneer. Some cattle are not bid on and in other cases the offering price is lower than the seller has specified as acceptable. In either of these events, the seller may return home with his cattle or make a private deal in which the buyer is aware that he has most of the advantages. The order of sale is determined by lot number and these are randomly assigned so that a man may spend a full day — until 6 P.M. — waiting for his cattle to be sold. Further, in order to provide ample parking, the marts are usually located some distance from the town, consequently at a distance from the pubs so conviviality is somewhat subdued. All attempts to transfer traditional fair sites — which are centrally located in towns — to the outskirts are met with firm resistance by the pub owners.

If selling cattle at the mart is an impersonal procedure with little room for individual control or initiative, selling animals at the fair is the opposite of this in every way. One of my informants likened it to a poker game and the simile is apt. The players are the farmers and the buyers, but judging from stories of past fairs, I suspect that until recently more of the buyers were locals and this must have made the game more interesting. Although there are some local buyers, most of the interaction is between the locals and the outsiders who come to buy on consignment.

At the time of my fieldwork, there were two ways of selling sheep, with an auxiliary third method still in the formative stages. Fairs were the most common method, and on-farm buying was increasingly popular. The third — and still uncertain — method was the "graded sale," the idea of an especially enterprising agricultural instructor working in the Glencolmcille area. Buyers interested in sheep were contacted before the graded sale and they specified their requirements and the price they were willing to pay, e.g., 60 lb. lambs at one shilling four pence a lb. The agricultural instructor then notified his farmers of the sale date and the lambs were brought in to be weighed. Those meeting the specifications (having been castrated early and free of obvious breeding defects) were accepted. This guaranteed minimum price of three pounds, fifteen shillings ($10.30) was better than the average fair price of two to three pounds, and the graded sale was preferred to the others.

But graded sales were infrequent because buyers who were willing to take seventy-five to a hundred lambs were hard to find

and still harder to convince that they could profit from
participation in the sale. The advantages of the graded sale were
that the very best lambs were offered and that a sixty lb. lamb will
gain weight quickly and thus be ready for the next year's sales
earlier. Buying at fairs entailed certain risks, which the graded
sale overcame, but the graded fairs also carried risks and these
seem not so easy to overcome. One buyer wrote of his experience
with the graded sale:

> We drew superb lambs, well bred, with excellent fleeces and
> averaging 67 lbs. Weather was kind to me and by mid-November
> I had saleable lambs, but no market! . . . there are willing people
> in the West and feeders in the East, but we must also develop
> the markets (Neville Chance 1971).

The problem with markets is an on-going one.

It remains to summarize my informants' marketing preferences.
For cattle, nine informants preferred selling at the mart and six
preferred selling at the fair. Only six of the nine sold exclusively
at the mart. Two preferred selling on the farm, and six gave on-
farm selling as a second choice. Five listed fairs and on-farm
selling as about equal, with no preference. No one thought that
transporting cattle to the fairs presented undue difficulties, and
most of those farmers who sold cattle at the marts nevertheless
attended eight to ten fairs a year.

For sheep, transport was often mentioned as a problem, but
seven informants nevertheless equated fairs and on-farm selling.
Four preferred the graded sale method, having actually sold sheep
this way, but few people outside the Glencolmcille area were aware
of these sales. Three men actively preferred the fair, and only two
chose on-farm selling above the fair. In the entire group, I had
only one informant who genuinely disliked livestock fairs and
refused to attend them or to sell animals in this way; he preferred
the graded sale or, if this failed, he sold his sheep on the farm. He
went only once a year to the fair in autumn to buy a ram and
otherwise avoided fairs entirely. He was widely hailed as the best
sheep farmer in the area so the buyers came to him and he managed
to avoid what may have been in his view the agonies of the public
performance.

Probably the most important point about fairs and sheep
marketing is that fairs indicate not just the quality of the offerings
but the quantities available. Each monthly fair has a more or less
"normal quota" of sheep and any excesses or insufficiencies will

be quickly noted by farmers. My town neighbors used to ask on the eve of the fair what I thought the fair would be like and how many animals there would be. To my astonishment (and theirs), I became quite adept at predicting the number and quality of animals, on the basis of my sample members' expectations. Farmers went to the fairs with certain expectations and when these were violated, a certain unease about market prices became apparent. It was difficult to document this because no one expressed it overtly except in such statements as, "There are too many sheep altogether now and that will bring the prices down." Some time later, the same informant might remark that he had sold his sheep to the first buyer who came to the door because he believed that prices were going down. And prices would indeed go down. Often, however, statement and action were not so clearly related, nor were motives for a particular sale so easily discernible.

Transmission of ecological information is less important for cattle rearing since supplementary feeding is so widely employed. Here comparative size and weight of animals and price information are more important than purely environmental matters.

The information presented on marketing, the division of labor, the human population, and on animal populations, is part of a more general heading, production strategies. With information on the production units, all production decisions can be summarized.

PRODUCTION STRATEGIES

In the following flow charts (Figures 4.3 to 4.5) I have indicated the decision points that bear on livestock production. The production unit is crucial to the number of animals kept, while the decision to keep sheep or cattle or both depends on the kind of land and labor available.

I have discussed above the parameters of all the decision points, except ecological consequences (which are as stated in the diagrams). Setting out the parameters clarifies the outcomes and indicates the possibilities available to each farmer. In the diagrams, Decision point A consists of the production units, that is the

Figure 4.3 Cattle production factors

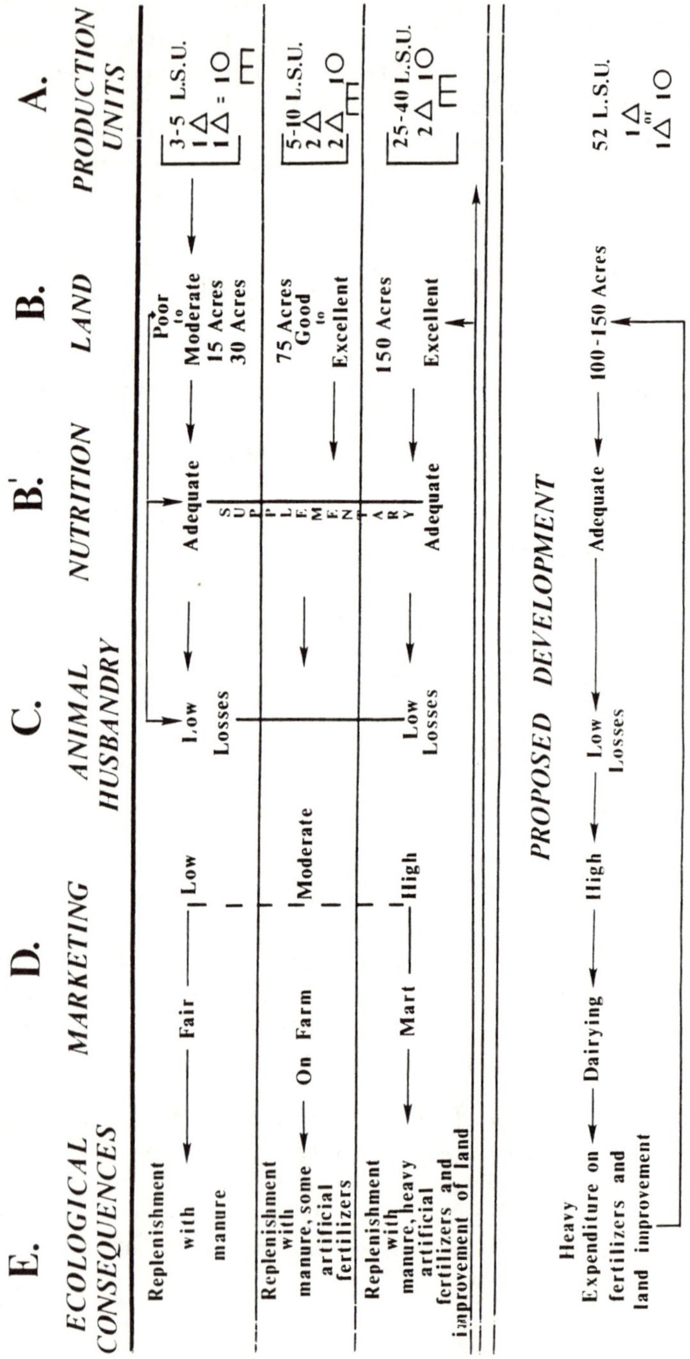

Figure 4.4 Sheep production factors

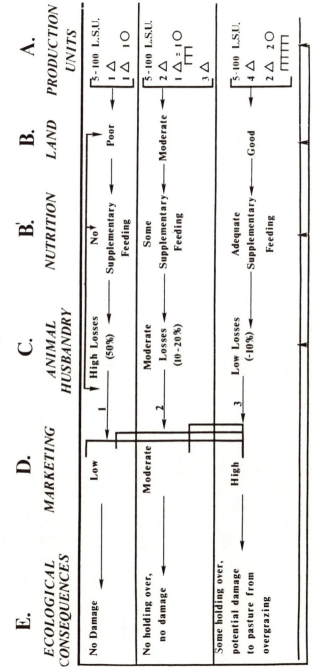

Figure 4.5 Mixed strategy production factors.

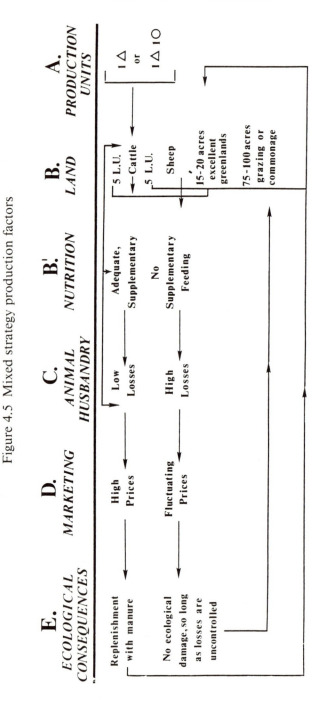

amount of labor available. Decision point B consists of two intertwined factors, land and nutrition. Decision point C is concerned with animal husbandry, the amount of time involved in the care of animals and the outcome of this. Decision point D lists several options for marketing and the range of prices available to each option. Decision point E indicates the outcome of each strategy as far as ecological consequences are concerned. There are further ramifications for point A from point E, and these will be discussed in turn.

Beginning with Figure 4.3, the all-cattle strategy, it is clear that the production unit and the kind of land available determine the number of livestock units which can be carried. (1 livestock unit = 1 cow or 5-6 ewes) Nutrition, as I have indicated, will be adequate for cattle, though at the lower end of the scale, it may be minimally adequate and at the higher end, it may be more than adequate. Despite charges of poor-quality hay of marginal nutritional value, losses in cattle are very low so it must be assumed that nutrition is adequate. (The point that the government would make in this regard is that cattle do not gain as quickly as they might, if they are wintered on minimal rations; Donegal farmers would not take issue with this, but they do maintain that cattle are smaller in Donegal, due to poor (comparatively speaking) rations throughout the year and they therefore feel that they are doing the best that can be expected under the circumstances.) Animal husbandry, therefore, involves high labor inputs and the outcome is low death risk for cattle. For point D, marketing, I have outlined the complexities of the choices available, but the crucial point is that cattle prices are steady and rising, though they may fluctuate to a limited extent. The market, in other words, is assured and cattle will not be held over to await a rise in prices. This generally ensures that point E, ecological consequences, will not be marked by devastating failure (in the sense that pastures will be overgrazed by animals kept too long). Pastures are replenished with manure (a minimally adequate measure), with some artificial fertilizers, or with heavy expenditure on artificial fertilizers, and perhaps on the improvement of land.

The differences between these strategies and the proposed one, involving 52 livestock units on 100-150 acres, are immense. As noted, in the proposed scheme, capital expenditure would be great and profit-making would depend on an established dairy industry. There are two further problems with this scheme, one of which is mentioned in the West Donegal Resource Survey plan itself:

". . . more information is needed on the effects of lime and fertilisers on sward composition and nutritional quality and on animal parasite build-up under improved conditions, in the local environment. Experience at the Peatland Experimental Station at Glenamoy under rather similar environmental conditions, has shown, all too clearly, that to confine grazing stock to limed and manured reseeded pastures on peatland leads to build-up of liver-fluke infestation of alarming dimensions" (WDRS Vol. 4:35).

Parasitic infestation is only one of the problems with the intensive grazing experiment; when I visited this station, I was told that there were two more difficulties with reclaimed peat. The dairy herd had to be kept indoors at all times, for the sward causes the top layer of soil to become very spongy and the cows sink into it to alarming depths. The other problem was that silage cut from reclaimed peat pasture was not palatable to the dairy cows, though its nutritional composition was judged excellent.

There is yet another problem, one that has arisen in the Southwest Donegal area in connection with intensive grazing. Dairy animals grazed on reclaimed peat will, at certain times of the year, produce "tainted" milk, milk with a strong taste unpalatable to humans, unsalable to dairies.

High production levels, then, present problems which so far are remote from the experience of the low-level Donegal producer. In the strategies that are presently used, the risks are minimized and the rewards almost certain; in the proposed strategies, the markets which would ensure that the high capital investment would be justified are not in evidence, and many of the pitfalls are not outlined. An all-cattle strategy can fail and lead to the breakup of the production unit, as illustrated in Figure 4.6.

The next strategy to be considered is the all-sheep production scheme (Figure 4.4). Most people keep a few cows to ensure milk for household consumption and these come closest to the pure sheep strategy but no one in my sample (or, for that matter, in the region) practiced this. The decision points are the same as for cattle, but their ramifications are different. In point A, production units, less labor is required for an equal number of livestock units and an individual may have outside employment to supplement his income. For sheep, there are three possible strategies, depending on the production unit and the land available. If land is poor and the production unit is small, the chances are very good that no supplementary feeding will be given. This produces

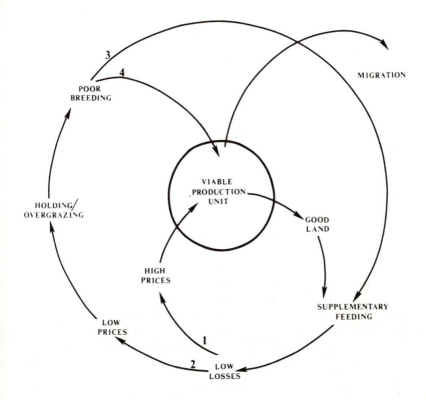

Figure 4.6   Beginning with 'viable production units':
Path 1 indicates an equilibrium state; good land + supplementary feeding + low losses + high prices.
Path 2 and 4 indicate the possibilities of imbalance; good land + supplementary feeding + low losses + low prices + holding and overgrazing + poor breeding, ultimately affecting the viability of the production unit, or leading to out-migration, as in Paths 2 and 3.

high losses, perhaps as much as 50% of the marketable herd, and the producer will get low prices for his sheep, as a general rule, since they will be smaller and of poorer quality than the usual range of salable animals. This producer, however, can afford to take low prices for his sheep because his investment in them is practically nil. And, of course, in a year when prices are high, he shows a nice profit — but even in a year when prices are low, his return to investment is high enough to justify the small labor inputs.

The producer with moderately good land who engages in some supplementary feeding and has moderate losses is usually in a position to realize his investment in supplementary feeding and labor, but he is restricted to a price range above that of the high-loss producer if he is to show any profit. In bad years, he has two choices: he may hold on to some sheep, in hope of a better market, or he may sell them "below cost," as it were, to avoid damage to pasture (and ultimately to the herd) from overgrazing. In a good year, of course, his return will be high but not so high as that of the high-loss producer.

The producer with good land, some of it improved specifically for the purpose of keeping sheep, takes the greatest risk. His investment, to ensure low losses, is greatest and he is therefore even more restricted as to price than the moderate or low-level producers. Should he fail to get his break-even price, he will be in serious difficulties and will have to choose between taking a loss on the sheep and holding them over until prices improve. If he chooses to hold them over, his investment in them becomes all the greater and he must invest far more than they may ultimately be worth in order to keep his pastures viable. This, in turn, creates additional health hazards and requires greater labor imputs, and I believe the increased incidence of footrot is a direct result of this strategy, for example. Greater parasitic infestation and a higher disease rate may also result in overcrowded pastures; the Blackface sheep is territorial and in unrestricted pastures spacing eliminates the risk of rapid spread of disease through a flock. Gathering animals together for supplementary feeding and restricting their natural spacing inclinations creates "unnatural" hazards and encourages the spread of infectious, but not necessarily fatal, diseases which can cause wasting, e.g., footrot, moon blindness, orf, etc. The pathways by which this production unit may break up are outlined in Figure 4.6.

By now the advantages of a mixed cattle-sheep strategy should be obvious. Cattle prices remain steady or rise; sheep prices fluctuate drastically and in some years, there may be a nice profit from them, while in others, the loss will not be great provided little investment has been made in them. Whatever investment in cattle is made will be returned through increased weight; the uncertainty of the return in investment in sheep makes farmers reluctant to invest in supplementary feeding. The response of the Glencolmcille farmers to an assured market is noteworthy in this respect; when they knew that prices would be good, they made the additional investment necessary, though some time was required for the transition. The marts, where cattle are sold by weight, will doubtless assure the production of heavier cattle in the future and this trend was beginning to show up in 1970-71.

One premise on which these diagrams are based should be stated: I have assumed that mortality and morbidity rates are closely tied to primary production, in the case of sheep, and that, *ceteris paribus*, more animals will die in a bad year than in a good one, thus adjusting, by natural means, the number of animals to the availability of pasture. This assumption is confirmed by my informants' qualification of their estimated losses. In a sense, the farmers of Southwest Donegal have two systems operating simultaneously, one a highly artificial and controlled population of domestic animals, i.e., cattle, and the other a semi-natural population subject to many of the same constraints in numbers as non-domesticated animals would be.

I have inquired into and discovered only some of the ways in which the nature of the domestic animal populations affects the human population. The indirect consequences of cattle keeping are social solidarity, in terms of labor required; ecological balance, in terms of replenishment of the soil; economic benefits, in terms of cash-cropping as a way of meeting those needs which cannot otherwise be satisfied; nutritional benefits in terms of animal by-products, and, finally, prestige which is directly associated with cattle as a form of capital asset. From the ecological point of view, the most crucial effects of keeping sheep are potential resource degradation and depopulation. Depopulation has already taken a severe toll, largely for reasons having to do with rising expectations in the standard of living, and degradation of resources may set in for similar reasons. All this has taken place quite apart from the possibilities of long-term degradation, but the death blow will be struck by a change in productive techniques from the mixed strategies to the mono-cropping suggested by government agencies. Far from being the least socially disruptive activity, an increase in sheep production promises to be the most socially disruptive activity. One can only hope that the natural hazards of the environment will make it impossible to facilitate such schemes.

The system as it now stands retains some of the characteristics of the long-standing pastoral adaptation but these are under attack from all sides and modern economic conditions are antithetical to this adaptation. When considered against the difficulties encountered elsewhere by farmers who have managed to adapt to modern economic conditions, only to find their new production levels contributing to worldwide disaster, the prospects of abandoning the old-style adaptation in favor of modern economic conditions should give one pause.

CHAPTER FIVE

Voices of the Present:

Five Farmers and Two Historians

"It's only the young who can afford to try radical new ideas; when our young men go abroad, they take with them the future of the area."   "Edward"

Understanding the current attitudes of the people of Southwest Donegal requires an understanding of their history, their myths, and their lives, as all these are bound up with the land on which they live and from which they wrest a sometimes precarious living. To understand their notions about their means of livelihood, I will here present the views of five farmers, whose ideas about tradition and modernity differ enormously. All five were members of my sample; I have changed some of their names and circumstances slightly to protect their identities but I have been careful to present their views on the past, present, and future of their area fully and accurately. Where possible, I have presented their views in their own words so that the reader may appreciate the differences in their outlooks.

Not one of these men is typical, it should be emphasized. While it is possible to average out certain aspects of production techniques — the number of acres of land devoted to hay, or the productivity of soil types — there is no way to average the farmers' attitudes to what they see around them. There is a true story about an earnest Irish official whose interest in economic development led him to suggest an innovative economic program based on many months of study and a determination of the "average" income and propensities of the small farmer. His superior questioned these averages and then, bewildered by the array of figures spread before him in support of the "average," replied, "No, Seamus, I don't think we can do this. They might all be different, you know." With which judgment I heartily concur. The following sketches will indicate some of that diversity but while Charlie, Ned, Seamus, Edward, and Francie are all real people, each with idiosyncrasies of his own, they and their farms typify many features of production techniques in the area. In fact, their production strategies are far more similar than their personalities.

Charlie is an innovative leader and a politician; Ned is a "mountainy man," an individualist who cares little for the opinions of others; Seamus is a shy man but renowned for his hospitality and good nature; and Edward is an active, good farmer whose intellectual curiosity extends far beyond his townland. It is hard to assign the labels, traditional and modern, to their farming methods because, like their attitudes, their strategies are mixed. Charlie is the most innovative and also most respectful of the "traditional" way of life, never having lived it; Ned and Seamus are ambivalent about traditional ways but Ned uses whatever innovation he thinks worthwhile; Edward, for all his keen interest in innovation, has actually maintained a rather conservative stance toward it in his own farming. All these men are "traditional" in some ways, and "modern" in others; none is fully committed in either direction, and in that respect alone are they like all but one of the other farmers — Francie — in my sample of thirty. Francie, the fifth farmer presented in this chapter, is an atypical man committed to wholly "modern" ways of raising sheep.

Before letting them speak for themselves, it is necessary to spell out a few of the similarities and differences in their life styles, as well as some things they take for granted. The reader will note that the proportion of those whose first language is Gaelic (three out of five) conforms closely to the present estimates of numbers of Gaelic speakers in the area (see Introduction, p. 5 *et seq.* for a fuller description). It should be noted, however, that all these farmers were born before 1936, that is at a time when the proportion of Gaelic speakers in the district was eighty percent or more. Thus, instead of three out of five Gaelic speakers, my five farmers should include four out of five Gaelic speakers. But the sample members I chose for inclusion in this chapter were selected because they represented different, sometimes extreme, views, not because they matched all the characteristics of the sample itself.

Many of the similarities in the ways of keeping livestock result from environmental constraints; all the farmers must deal with harsh environmental conditions and with poor soils. Even farmers like Charlie, who has good land, usually have some poor land as well. Most Donegal soil is bogland, suitable in its virgin state only for rough pasture. If all available land were reclaimed, that is, the 81,000 acres of bogland with less than two percent rock outcrop, the carrying capacity for sheep would be raised from approximately

20,000 animals to sixteen times that number — in a good year, when drains and seeding and fertilizing could be handled mechanically. But in a bad year, even a doubling or tripling of the current carrying capacity for sheep would jeopardize the resources normally available for cattle; in a bad market year, if sheep were kept because prices were low, overgrazing would also cause environmental degradation.

Other hazards for the sheep population include the "killer" dogs that ravage herds and an increase in parasite infestation, caused by the reclamation process, which creates the ideal conditions for the flourishing of liver fluke. Fluke is a problem in Donegal, but the magnitude of fluke infestation would increase proportionally with reclamation.

Given these hazards,the difficulties with sheepherding can be seen in perspective. Charlie's and Seamus's experiences with killer dogs are not unusual. The profit Charlie might have realized from his sheep was destroyed in one night, and he disposed of the remaining animals shortly after this slaughter. Seamus hopes that the rest of his flock will survive; he has not made the investment Charlie has — in seed, fertilizer, fences — and he has lost some of his sheep. Charlie has lost the money he invested and more than a third of his sheep.

Ned's way of keeping sheep seems quite reasonable, in contrast. He devotes much of his time to the herd and, although his losses are considerable, he has invested little money in the animals and is therefore unlikely to make either a great profit or loss. Like Ned's, Edward's calculation of the odds is shrewd: both men adjust their herd composition according to the market and the government subsidies. Edward, like Charlie, is primarily concerned with his cattle, where profits are sure and losses are few. The market for cattle, too, is more secure.

The physical resources available to farmers in Southwest Donegal are very limited: geography, topography, geology and climate all seem to conspire against high resource productivity. The high percentage of rock outcrop and the roughness of the terrain make the use of modern machinery difficult and inefficient. The vagaries of the climate and the scarcity of well-drained soils make intensive production of all but a few sturdy crops uncertain. A great deal of courage is required to risk all the natural hazards and to take a "fully modern" stance. With these constraints firmly in mind, then, we can listen sympathetically while these farmers explain their circumstances and strategies.

CHARLIE

The best cattle farmer in Southwest Donegal is Charlie, who describes himself as semi-retired but who nonetheless manages a herd of beef cattle more than a hundred strong. In 1968, after a subsidy was introduced, he began buying sheep for the first time in 25 years and improving marginal land to accommodate them. His land is among the best in the area; he has several hundred acres of rich soil set aside for cattle and another hundred acres of poor bog land, scattered in small plots within a few miles of his home. The poor land he has fenced and fertilized for the benefit of his hundred ewes and, when the ewe subsidy was raised to £2 a head, he expected to make a goodly profit. Speculation and innovation are habits with him and despite his semi-retirement his activities are still closely watched and widely discussed. It was rumored that he would soon give up his beef cattle entirely in favor of sheep.

The youngest son in a family of ten, Charlie was educated in a school that still stands on his property, a school built by his father with the express purpose of fitting his children for life outside Donegal. In consequence, the family is far-flung; brothers who became lawyers and doctors or professors now live in England or on the Continent. Distinguished clergymen were plentiful in the family and one brother, a lawyer, seems to have devoted his life to alcoholism. After he had disgraced the family for the third time this brother was given passage money to America. The fact that he was never heard from again apparently disturbed no one unduly. Only one sibling, a sister, married locally, and her son, Charlie's nephew, is said to be the most progressive farmer in Southwest Donegal. He keeps a large dairy herd and his sheep win prizes at all the local shows, even so far away as Stranorlar (32 miles). Charlie confides that, despite the acclaim, his nephew makes no profit on his sheep and supposes that he lacks a real "feeling" for them since the family tradition has always been cattle keeping. Charlie's nearest neighbor, his first cousin, was the first to import Herefords into the region and the breed has thrived; the family has always been able to turn a profit in cattle.

For many years, Charlie was chairman of the County Committee of Agriculture and so responsible for introducing new developments in agriculture to the farmers of his region. Unlike most, he does not keep his cattle in a byre (barn) over the winter.

His stock are outwintered, an innovation that has caught on slowly in the surrounding area. He uses chemical fertilizers as well as manure and can raise cattle almost to slaughter time while most farmers must sell before the animals are two years old, lacking the grass to fatten them. He sees the introduction of new husbandry practices as a discouraging task and believes that the government failed in its responsibility to the people of Donegal. He recalls the many trips he made to Dublin during his chairmanship, the pleas he made for funds to support true innovation in Donegal, the refusals by the fledgling government busy developing richer counties in the hope of building an export market.

Charlie has always been and continues to be politically active; he is the area chairman for the major political party. During the "trouble" times he was commander of the local IRA forces and casually points out the shells of buildings he was responsible for burning or the scenes of ambushes he planned. He speaks no Gaelic but he has a romantic and nostalgic view of the old way of life and misses the storytellers and the dances.

He is one of the few local men who buy cattle in quantity at nearby fairs; these he fattens and sends to the Stranorlar mart for sale. His best land has mineral soil, the best in the area for tillage or for grazing. He made silage for the first time 20 years ago, an innovation that is just now beginning to take hold in other parts of the region. In the 'thirties, during the Economic War against England, he produced an abundant wheat crop from this land and persuaded many farmers to follow his example. Through the years he has experimented with new types of drainage systems and created new fields out of sandy soils. With advancing age he has not been able to repair and clean these drains as often as is necessary and rushes now encroach on good pasture. Some of his land consists of coastal sand dunes, and Charlie has recently been persuaded by the Tourist Board to rent campsites to holidaymakers during the summer. Conscious of the blight on the landscape that the "caravans" (trailers) produce, Charlie remains aloof from the campers and observes that some pretty ugly things are being done in the name of progress.

His worst land is bog, located on steep slopes with protruding rocks, barren but picturesque from a distance because the white rocks resemble the sheep which move among them. When he began speculating in sheep he fenced his land, broadcast seed and fertilizer, and hoped that something other than the native vegetation would take hold. He has been well rewarded for his efforts insofar as the vegetation is concerned but not for the sheep. The unfortunate epilogue to Charlie's speculation in sheep is that "killer" dogs, in two separate raids, slaughtered 35 of the hundred. Charlie sold the rest and allowed the land to return to the native vegetation. His cattle are too heavy to graze this land during much of the year and the terrain is such that it would be dangerous for them.

Charlie's marriage was childless. A widower for many years, he lives alone in a magnificent eight-bedroom stone house and when he dies his land will most likely go to his nephew. He is pessimistic about the future of the area and believes that unless drastic steps are taken by the government to improve marginal land and to provide economic security for the farmer the way of life of the Irish small farmer will disappear in Donegal within a generation.

NED

The best sheep farmer in the area is also pessimistic about the future of the area, but for different reasons. Ned's farm is located at the head of an almost deserted valley. To get there one drives many miles without seeing signs of recent habitation. The skeletons of cottages along the roadside add to the feeling of desolation and, farther from the road, abandoned cottages blend into the landscape, noticeable now only because someone long ago decided to plant a tree in front of his house and his neighbors followed suit. Here the first wave of outmigration came after the Famine, during the Land Wars, when the landlord burned the cottages of those who refused to pay their rents. After most of the cottages had been burnt some "unknown" assailants killed the landlord. Those farmers who remained built new cottages closer to the hills where they had camped during the wars. Outmigration continued, however, and Ned points out with a chuckle that there is only one married man within five miles on any side of his property. He volunteers the information that he is himself uneasy around women and never married because "women are always too interested in conquering." He lives with his younger brother, a man in his fifties who has the uncertainty of an adolescent and the nervous mannerisms of a man who never expects to finish a sentence. In absolute contrast Ned is direct and self-assured, almost courtly in manner.

Both Ned and his brother are keen sheepmen and they spend their lives looking after a flock of about 500 ewes. Between them they once owned more than 2,000 acres of deep blanket peat but the younger brother recently sold several hundred acres to the Forestry Department.

Ned is known as a man with a "feeling" for sheep and is spoken of by most farmers as one of the best sheepmen in the area. He admits that he and his brother together can probably recognize most, if not all, of their ewes and they know where to look for a lost one. On a typical summer day they leave the house after "second breakfast," about 10:00 A.M., and go to the hill to see to the herd. They perform minor surgery on sick animals, rescue or search for lost sheep, examine carcasses for cause of death. At seven or eight in the evening they return after a walk of ten or fifteen miles, much of it involving negotiation of steep granitic slopes that bound their land. Ned is one of the last of the "mountainy" men, as the Irish call them, individuals known for their ruggedness and their refusal to be swayed by anyone else's opinion. He is outspoken, even caustic, on the subject of his (two) neighbors' deficiencies. Both of them, he says, left their hay too long on the ground this year and it rotted. Ned cut his hay earlier than they did and saved most of it, but then his needs are less than most for he keeps only two cows.

He owns a van in which to get around and goes to most of the fairs in the immediate area. His assessment of fairs, price ranges, and quality of animals — either before or after the event — is apt to be more accurate than anyone else's. He knows the preferences of Northern buyers in detail, as well as the quality of sheep likely to be supplied by any farmer for miles around. He believes strongly in luck and will not purchase rams from certain people no matter what the reported excellence of their animals. Some men, he says, have "unlucky" sheep; he cites the case of a neighbor whom he warned against buying from a certain man. The neighbor disregarded Ned's advice and brought home two rams only to find both dead before the week was out. Ned has a good eye for conformation in sheep and in minutes can pick out the best ram at a fair. His standards are similar to those a show judge would use but, in buying, the primary considerations for him are where the animal was reared, whether it has been hand-fed, whether it can survive the rigors of his land.

He has good luck with his rams, not so much with his lambs. Last year he lost more than half of them "to the ticks," that is, from tick pyemia *, and is determined that this will not happen again. After questioning the agricultural agent and the dipping inspector, and getting little satisfaction from either, he discovered in the national farmer's journal an article on ticks that mentioned a new sheep-dipping compound used in the North but outlawed in the Republic because of some ingredients which pollute waterways. Ned went immediately to the North to purchase this dip and has used it on his ewes already and plans to dip the lambs when they are old enough. He follows a regular dipping schedule, almost his only concession to generally accepted principles of sheep husbandry, and has little interest in most innovations. While he knows that his animals sometimes die of starvation he believes that the best way to combat this is to breed tougher sheep. He makes fun of a neighbor who feeds the weaker animals in his flock, saying that he treats them almost like pets. He and his brother, he believes, are among the last of the good sheepmen in the region and, when they are gone, the forest will take over because "young people have gone soft; they have no stamina at all any more, no taste for anything except easy living."

The outmigration rate in West Donegal is estimated at thirty percent but the statistic can be misleading. Most emigrants are young people — between 15 and 34 — and ultimately seven out of ten children born in Southwest Donegal will leave to find jobs elsewhere (W.D.R.S. Vol. III:40). They leave not because they lack stamina, as Ned would have it, but because they want a better standard of living than their parents had. Expectations, not physical capacities, have changed and young people's hopes for the future cannot be met in Southwest Donegal. Opportunities in the outside world drain off the area's youth; those who are left must adjust to the vicissitudes of the environment and, worse, to the loneliness of a once well-populated land.

SEAMUS

Seamus, the owner of a poor farm, is known to all his neighbors for his reliability and hospitality. He and his wife are native Gaelic

* Tick pyemia is a bacterial disease usually fatal to lambs.

speakers and have reared their children as such. The government pays a subsidy to those who speak Gaelic in the home but Seamus and his wife regret their decision and are not sentimental about the language they speak. As they watch their children preparing for emigration they reflect that it would have been best to train them in English, for Gaelic speakers will inevitably be disadvantaged in the English-speaking world where they must earn a living.

Seamus and his wife live in a remote townland three miles from the nearest church and shop, and seven miles from the nearest town. To get to a main road they must travel two miles on the dirt road in front of their cottage. They live much as Seamus's grandfather (who built the house) and father must have: they have no electricity and no prospects of it, and they carry their water up from a well at the foot of the hill. Their cottage is of a sort almost gone from Donegal, with the human quarters centered between a byre on one end and a milking shed on the other. The thatched roof of the cottage is supported by beams of "bog oak," petrified wood dug out of bogs.

The house commands a good view overlooking a quiet lake, the only obvious boundary marker on the property. Beyond are rugged hills covered with shallow blanket bog and impassable for much of the year due to moisture retention. The land Seamus occupies today was once the same as these hills and his farm was created by human hands out of bog. Immediately below his house on a steep rocky slope is the main hayfield, still rough ground despite two centuries of cultivation. A smaller, better hayfield is located beside the lake, a field that can be cut by tractor when the roads are good enough for the tractor to make the journey. There are no fences; Seamus believes the County should assume the responsibility for fencing the land but doubts that "they" will ever get around to it. Most of his land was reclaimed from bog land and the reclamation began more than a century ago. The land requires heavy manuring and good management, including drainage.

At the bottom of the hill near the lake is the cottage of Seamus's unmarried elder brother. Next to it there is a sizable vegetable garden, mostly of potatoes and cabbages, both of which do well in most soils. A small plot of "corn" (wheat) has been put in; some years it will reach maturity and others not.

During the growing season from March to August the cows must be driven to pasture on the commonage south of the lake.

Mainly composed of eroded deep peat this land is a hazard to cattle and one of the sons is assigned to watch the herd each day. There are four cows, three yearlings, and two calves, one of them a breed new to the area, called Charolais. No one in Seamus's area has kept a bull for ten years or more; the Artificial Insemination Service is prompt and efficient, and has enjoyed great success in introducing new breeds into the area.

Seamus's flock includes about 25 to 30 ewes. These are kept for most of the year on "the hill," a large mountain about three miles away where Seamus has rights in commonage. On St. Patrick's Day the sheep are brought from the hill and allowed to graze the hayfield until lambing time in early May. Loss of lambs is high because of the rough terrain but his most serious losses of late have come from the depredations of "killer" dogs, usually sheepdogs that are allowed to wander at night and appear to herd sheep by day and to kill them by night. Six years ago Seamus lost 16 ewes to these dogs; last year he lost eleven. He is grateful that he did not lose more either time as some of his neighbors did. There is a law against allowing dogs to run loose at night but no one to enforce it since the *Gardai* (police) have other things to do at night than visit remote mountain tops. Dogs found covered in blood after these raids are shot or, if an owner proves recalcitrant, poisoned by a neighbor at the earliest opportunity.

The ewes and lambs will go back to the hill after being dipped for ticks to prevent tick pyemia (see note, p. 136). Seamus does not know the technical term; in his view ticks cause "wasting" in a lamb and eventual death. He knows that, apart from natural hazards such as drowning, many of his lambs die of starvation but he feels powerless to prevent this.

The hay grows undisturbed from May until harvest time, usually sometime in August or early September, as weather permits. Seamus and his neighbors will consult several times about the best time for cutting hay and, when the time comes, all the people of the townland will begin on the same day. Seamus has the help of his own family for this task — his two sons who live at home, his youngest daughter and his wife, as well as his brother. If the "midges" (tiny biting gnats that seem to come in swarms) aren't too bad they can work until ten or eleven o'clock on a summer evening, when daylight lingers until nearly midnight.

Summer evenings demand hard work but winter nights offer entertainment. Those neighbors whom Seamus helps in the summer and who will help him put up his haystack in winter often give him a ride to a town 20 miles away where there is a flourishing Bingo game. Other times neighbors and kin come to visit, to gossip, and to tell stories. One neighbor, an old bachelor, sings from his repertoire of faintly ribald songs when he visits.

Although the surrounding district has suffered heavy losses from outmigration the sense of community in the townland is still very strong. Seamus's neighbors rely on him and on his sons for extra help when needed, and he freely gives his time and his sons'. He is always available for consultation if a cow has difficulty in calving, or for help in physically demanding work. If he needs help he calls first on his relatives, then on his neighbors. Outmigration has affected him only slightly, but he misses his immediate neighbors, a musically talented family away in Scotland. He rents their land as supplementary grazing for his cows but observes that, since no one in his family "has music," he would prefer his neighbors' company to their land.

He is unsure of himself in English and has not heard the names of many livestock diseases that have no Gaelic equivalents. He notes wryly that there were fewer diseases when everyone spoke Gaelic. (In Gaelic, a general descriptive term is often used for a variety of diseases having similar symptoms.) If he has serious trouble with a cow, he sends a son to telephone the veterinarian. For treating sheep he relies on knowledge acquired from his father and from his neighbors. The latest developments in animal husbandry are usually published in English, hence meaningless to him. He has never met the agricultural agent in his district and does not believe, in any case, that he needs advice.

The farm does not provide much of a living but he manages and is philosophical about his losses. He sells his sheep on the farm or occasionally at the fair, when a relative with a lorry provides transportation. The two sons at home may inherit the land together, as he and his brother did, and one may marry and raise a family as Seamus has done, while the other remains a bachelor. Perhaps by that time there won't be enough to support a family but the name will still be on the land. He doubts that he will ever make much profit from his land but that is not his aim — his goal is to survive. He knows that there will be good years and there will be bad years but he has raised his family to survive both good and bad.

EDWARD

Edward, the owner of a good farm, was my most astute informant. Though he is well informed and displays considerable intellectual curiosity, he was by no means the most successful farmer in my sample. He and his wife and their youngest child, a daughter, live in a well-kept cottage tucked under the crest of a hill, a measure taken to protect the house against high winds. By local standards the house is a new one; it was built by Edward's father. It has undergone several changes since his time: a new slate roof, electricity, a stove in place of the old open hearth. Prominently displayed are the television set and an untidy bookcase filled with books on diverse topics.

The view from his front door takes in a broad alluvial valley and Edward's best land includes about 20 fenced acres on the slope reaching down to the valley floor. The slope is gentle enough to allow the use of a tractor for cutting hay, a practice he has recently adopted. Unlike some of his neighbors he has not taken the next step and used hay balers; he still prefers the old-fashioned method of saving the hay once cut, that is, stacking it into bundles and turning it over with a pitchfork. At harvest time his two sons, both of whom live and work away from home, return to help with this heavy work.

At one side of the house he maintains a large vegetable garden and, on the other side, a well-kept byre attests his reputation as a good farmer. The number of cattle he keeps varies through the year but seldom goes below ten, including six cows and their followers. His wife boasts that they have a good milk supply all year round, unlike most of their neighbors. She churns her own butter and dislikes offering guests anything except homemade bread and jam. She is a thin energetic woman who shares her husband's interests in the outside world but whose household chores occupy most of her day. She works while talking to visitors, inviting any female guests to help at the churn, and in the odd moments when she sits down she knits sweaters for a firm in the good-sized town some three miles distant. The hayfields are the only part of Edward's 60 acres free from rocks. These are mineral soils with moderate productive capacity. They are easily worked and with the addition of manure will produce an abundant hay crop each year. They require close management but Edward is luckier than most in that his soil is on a slope that provides good natural drainage. His neighbors nearby have similar soil but with imperfect drainage, so that use-range is severely limited. The valley soils are even more restricted, being comprised of peaty-gleys and subject to frequent flooding.

Above the house the soils are of extremely poor quality and, because they occur on steep slopes with rock outcrops, cultivation is almost impossible. On the hill and beyond it, to the commonage on the other side, some 50 sheep, bearing Edward's "brand" (a paint mark, with colors and placement varying according to owner) wander for most of the year. The good land and the hay it produces are reserved for the cattle, except during two short seasons: just before lambing and at mating time.

A native English speaker, Edward is aware of all the latest developments in cattle and sheep production. His interest is more intellectual than practical, however, and his responses to questions about livestock are succinct, almost impatient. When asked carefully phrased non-technical questions he responds with the technical term. The sheep subsidy has changed his herd composition, he says, but not the size of the herd. He once kept wethers (castrated male sheep) for market but these now have little value after the age of one or two years so he keeps more ewes and hoggets (yearling female sheep) instead. To raise more sheep would involve far more work than he feels they are worth and, since he gets by on the earnings from his cattle, he would rather not put extra labor toward an uncertain return. Innovations in livestock keeping interest him, as do other innovations, but he is cautious about adopting any program that could harm his cattle, should it fail, and he prefers to leave experiments in sheep keeping to those who have more interest in sheep.

Although he is widely regarded as an excellent farmer he became a farmer because he was the youngest son, not by choice. Had there been money to educate him he would have become a lawyer or doctor instead. He is more interested in national and international politics than he is in livestock and he devotes much of his time to the local development committee, which he chairs. He believes he is doing better than his ancestors before him and that one of his sons (whichever inherits his land) may do better yet. But he observes sadly that only young men can afford to adopt radical ideas and, when the young men leave, they take with them the future of the area.

FRANCIE

Francie was the best small farmer in my sample and, incidentally, my best informant. He is almost an impossibly good farmer in the sense that he has defied all the odds, including his mother's disapproval (a risk not lightly undertaken by many Irishmen), and still managed to show a profit. Francie owns land that is unusual in its uniformity and it is uniformly poor — deep blanket bog which can only be reclaimed with considerable effort. He has made this effort and more; so far, the results have been exceptional.

Francie is a small, shy man, a bachelor in his early fifties; his features could be reproduced on souvenir portraits of the Irish leprechaun. He is reluctant to speak Gaelic with strangers for he believes that his townland "hasn't the good Gaelic." This, he says, can be found in the next townland over and in another up the Glen (valley), but where he lives he believes they speak an inferior form of the language. (This is a common assessment; "good Gaelic" means there are few English loanwords and a great many proverbs.)

Francie believes in answering questions fully. In response to any query he gives his own experience, his neighbors' experiences, the agricultural agent's experience, and the latest County statistics. To this list he has recently added a further contrast, the American experience, for he insists (the only member of my sample to do this systematically) on receiving information about America in return for that given about Ireland. He knew more about breeds of livestock than any other member of my sample, going back to the last owners of the breed of sheep that preceded the present Blackface and forward to the latest experiments (unpublished) from Glenamoy.

When asked what he believes causes people to undertake drastic innovations of the sort he has adopted, Francie replies after a moment's interval, "I think it's in the brain." It is possible to reconstruct more tangible causes: Francie is a shy and diffident man whose farm has always been a poor one. His mother raised Francie and his nine brothers and sisters by selling butter; she was widowed when Francie, the youngest, was an infant and her husband left her ten children and a few cows. She sent all the children through school until they reached the age of sixteen, relying on the cows to support the family. Francie, as her favorite, inherited the land but, while she is proud of his success with his sheep, she does not approve his decision to raise them and believes that he will ultimately be forced to return to cattle rearing. Her conservatism is based on her own experience; she recalls farmers who did well in sheep farming for several years, until market conditions changed, and who were then forced to return to cattle. No amount of hard work, she believes, will change the bad luck that eventually overtakes the sheep farmer.

So far Francie's luck has been good and his labor input high. He began his improvements to the land in 1966; he fenced, fertilized, and seeded it. In 1967, after fertilizer was added, he grazed 20 ewes with lambs for 23 weeks, and sold 15 lambs, with a total weight of 813 pounds, for £36 (about $86). In 1968, with the same amount of fertilizer added once more, he grazed 26 ewes with lambs for 28 weeks, and sold 23 lambs, with a total weight of 1,400 pounds, for £81 (about $195) (Co. Donegal Committee of Agriculture, unpublished).

Apart from the difference in prices (from $86 to $195, 1971 exchange rates) and in pounds (from 813 to 1,400), the most remarkable increase is in carrying or grazing capacity. As of 1971, the four acres required to support one ewe (in 1966) supported sixteen. Lambs weighing on average 65 pounds were ready for sale much earlier in the year. Mortality rates are low due to Francie's almost constant attention; the few lambs he lost in 1971 were killed on the road.

Though he has developed a "feeling" for sheep, Francie is himself skeptical of the ultimate rewards of raising sheep. While he was one of the first to undertake the improvement of bogland, he believes that the government is too optimistic about the possibilities: "They believe that a farm [that is, productivity] can just go up and up and up; I believe that if there are three good years, there'll be two bad ones then." The bad years, in Francie's conception, can be brought on by low prices, bad weather, epidemic disease, and a host of other unpredictable variables.

A whole value system is encapsulated in Francie's beliefs, and it is a value system with far-reaching implications for economic development in Southwest Donegal. Two attitudes commonly attributed to the farmers of the area are a belief in the "image of the limited good" (Foster 1965) and fatalism. In Foster's view, peasants all around the world believe that desirable commodities exist in limited number and supply and that if one person obtains any of these goods, the chances of everyone else obtaining them are thereby reduced. Fatalism implies a belief that nothing can be done to lessen the odds of failure; Francie's mother is a fatalist about sheep keeping but Francie himself is not. Nor is he a believer in the "image of the limited good."

Francie's cautious attitude toward production methods is an accurate reflection of the environmental hazards he has coped with all his life; I have quoted his beliefs because Francie is such an uncommonly good farmer and because he devotes some 280 days a year to beating the odds. To paraphrase Foster's statement, the sheep farmers in my sample believe that desirable conditions — weather, markets, freedom from diseases, good luck, and the like — exist in limited quantities and that if one year brings some of these, the chance of their appearance in the next is lessened.

I saw no evidence of belief in the image of the limited good among the farmers generally. One man's good pasture does not decrease another's chances for a good pasture of his own, nor do another man's good prices mean that someone else will get less. The general attitude toward these accomplishments is positive: "If Francie can do so well with his lambs, maybe I could, too," or, "If Charlie got that much for his bullocks, then I may ask that for mine."

Cattle farmers do not display as much anxiety about fluctuations in weather, markets, and disease incidence. The cattle farmers are, in their own terms, already operating at near maximum productivity and they can expect stable markets and a more or less assured hay crop. Cattle prices fluctuate within a narrower range than sheep prices; the hay may not be of the highest nutritional value but it can be supplemented with other feed, including potatoes and purchased grain.

Because the sheep are dependent on grass alone, the variability of the climate is a major element in the forebodings of the sheep farmers. One could call this fatalism or realism. Fatalism is seen as an enormous impediment to economic development but the extent to which such an attitude prevails is difficult to ascertain. The year 1971 was a bad one for Francie, for example, and in recounting his woes — which included setbacks in spreading fertilizer because the ground was too wet to accommodate the tractor, and the weather too bad to permit the assiduous care of drains necessary to keep them operating well — Francie observed that "some years you went up, in others you were lucky to be able to stand still."

In sum, I find it impossible to categorize the farmers' attitudes as fatalistic or as indicative of a belief in the limited good. This is due, not just to the differences between the farmers, but to their willingness to try innovations, where these seem feasible or practicable. Of the five, only Francie has devoted his labors wholly to innovative methods and only Seamus has been practically untouched by them. Ned, Charlie, and Edward, each in his own way, have all experimented with those new production methods that interested them, and I would characterize their attitudes toward innovation as flexible and realistic not as bound by tradition or fatalism or notions about the limited good.

All are aware, however, that the major constraint on improved production methods is the rigorous climate, and a primary notion held by farmers is that there is a cycle in agricultural production and that this cycle over the long run will eliminate both peaks and valleys in production. While the farmers understand the government's attempt at introducing continuous progress in an upward direction, so as to upgrade the standard of living, they do not accept it as a plausible goal within their environment. This attitude should not be seen as fatalistic; it is based on experience and a realistic assessment of the uncertainties. Francie knows very well that there will be wet springs when the tractor cannot negotiate his land but there is no provision for variations in weather within the potential production schemes.

Francie's commitment to wholly modern production methods is unusual; but his attitude toward eventual success more closely resembles Ned's or Seamus's. All believe that, given the odds against them, they are doing well enough.

Here a brief mention of the category of economic rationality is pertinent, for it is commonly said that "traditional" farmers make irrational choices and "modern" farmers make rational ones. It should be clear that the individuals in my sample exhibit wide variation in their choices and that it is nearly impossible to say which decisions are the more rational. Francie, the most modern of the farmers, may be making the least rational choice, in deciding to defy the odds against success. Seamus, the most traditional of the farmers, may be making the most rational decisions, given the constraints of the environment. If survival were the goal, then Seamus's strategy is the most rational, at least for the recent past; if profit making is the goal, as it has been for only a few decades, then Francie's strategy is the most likely to succeed, at least in the short term.

Francie, with his insistence on recounting all the experiences he had had or heard of, pointed up another aspect of my sample that puzzled me. As part of my interview schedule (Appendix B), I included questions on kinds of livestock, breeds, and practices that were prevalent during the informant's youth and I had wondered about the contradictions between what my informants believed to be "traditional," what Francie told me, and what I had read about the history of the region.

For example, in Donegal at the turn of the century, nearly every household kept at least one pig (Micks 1925). Francie knew this and discussed it with me; none of the other sample members mentioned it. A few, when questioned again, remembered that the family had kept a pig, which used to be called the "savings bank" because it was the family's savings. The pig was carefully reared, then slaughtered at the end of the year; the money it brought was used to pay the rent. One of the folk historians of the village recalled that he and a boyhood friend had spent much time in their youth anticipating the annual slaughter of the pig and speculating about whether a person could "ever get his fill of bacon," that is, eat as much bacon as he wanted. Bacon is now a staple in most households, although pigs are no longer kept on small farms and bacon is purchased from the shops. At the beginning of the twentieth century, however, bacon was available only once a year and was considered a great delicacy.

Why had most people "forgotten" their pigs? I discarded the dismaying thought that I had somehow managed to find the only farmers in Southwest Donegal who had grown up in households without pigs, and began investigating other forgotten aspects of production strategies. In part pigs may have been forgotten because they were associated with poverty; to forget the symbols of poverty in times of plenty seemed a normal reaction. But there were other aspects of production strategies that did not yield to such explanations and for these, I had to go outside my sample of active farmers to the folk historians of the region and learn more about their ideas of the "traditional" past. In seeking the views of the two local "historians" (or ethnohistorians as anthropologists term them), I learned a great deal about both production strategies and renderings of the "traditional" past. Both these historians were older men and both were schoolmasters; neither was any longer involved in farming as a way of life. Both grew up on small farms, however, and both had been involved in caring for

livestock. They had another characteristic in common as well —
they have the same name, and since it is necessary to distinguish
them, I shall call them by their nicknames, "Wee Paddy" and
"Big Paddy."

Wee Paddy is the historian whose published works I have drawn
on above. His memory, he says, is good for sixty years back (to
1910) and in his youth he spent a great deal of time talking to the
older people in the community, acquiring the information that
has made him a noted folklorist and historian. He remembers the
introduction of the Blackface sheep, the difficulties with landlords,
and the splitting up of the *clachans*. Big Paddy, the younger of the
two, grew up in the twenties and remembers when fairs and
markets were in full swing. He has witnessed the events of the
last four decades with a different sort of interest than Wee Paddy's,
and has been a leader in local development committees for many
years. Although his primary interest is in modernization and
change, he is not pleased by a great many of the changes he has
seen.

Wee Paddy was brought up in a mountain townland that
"belonged" to Loughros Point, that is, a townland that in former
years was the summer grazing area for the lowland community.
Dowries were common and Wee Paddy's father was a respected
matchmaker. "Cattle, as you know, were the wealth of the people
at that time and if you tried to take away their cattle, you took
away their means of livelihood. When a girl was married, that
always formed part of her dowry. She got so many, or maybe she
got only one — but that was a springer, one that was going to
calve shortly — and whatever else she got, she got that and she
got so many sheep. Then no matter whose were sold, she stuck
onto hers."

The "grass of a cow," in Wee Paddy's early 20th century youth,
was more than the two-acre standard common in the rest of
Ireland. He describes the system as follows:

> Where I was reared, we had about fifty acres. That was for sheep
> and cattle. Ours would be from three to four cows; I know
> neighboring people had 57 acres (I remember these from old
> maps) and they would have four to five. People were very proud
> in those days of an extra cow and those who had a thirty-acre
> farm would have about two cows. A cow's grass was often a
> dowry. In the days before land division, a girl from the farm
> that I was reared on was married to another man in the townland

and her dowry was the grass of one cow. As the land was not
divided, she got that cow's grass in so many little plots. When
the land was divided into farms, that cow's grass went with their
farm, which was four or five farms removed from us. I always
remember my mother used to grudge that cow's grass, saying
that we should have it — and it was away for a hundred years
at the time — and we could have another cow if we had it, if
those generations that went before us didn't part with their land
so easily.

The dowry system described here differs from that described
by Arensberg and Kimball (1968:140-51). At the time (1930's) of
their investigations in County Clare, dowries were paid in money.
I can find no reference to dowries ever having been paid in money
in Donegal, perhaps because money was not much used, except
for rents. The landlords' agents constantly complain of the
difficulty in getting the people to pay their rents in money rather
than in kine (McGill n.d.). In Donegal, dowries were paid in
cattle, in sheep, or in land. The dowry system no longer survives,
but poultry are commonly given as wedding gifts, and it is usual
for guests to turn up for a wedding with a number of chickens or
geese in hand.

Not only is the dowry system not remembered, it is never cited
as a reason for land passing through females in past generations,
though some people can trace the history of the land back further
than the time of which Wee Paddy is speaking. It may be that the
dowry system was not a commonplace in the area, or that my
research into land transfers, being largely confined to poor
communities, was not sufficiently broad.

The system of land use which Wee Paddy describes, four or
five cows (and a dozen or so sheep), continued in form until about
1940, when emigration and the dole (unemployment benefits)
among other things, helped to break the pattern. Cattle and sheep
breeds began to change much earlier, about the turn of the century,
and the "native" breeds had been almost completely supplanted
by the mid-twenties.

Scottish Blackface Mountain sheep were introduced to Donegal
late in the nineteenth century and immediately became a source
of discord. Wee Paddy says of this:

Scotch sheep were first brought in by what we call now the
'planter' type of people, those English and Scotch people who
got great tracts of our land. They built big houses here and then

had maybe thousands of acres; they got it into their heads that they were going to make fortunes on farming this kind of sheep. Well, they didn't always understand the climate of Donegal and they didn't understand looking after sheep or the kind of care that they needed in various ways and then when they lost those sheep or those sheep died of hardships on the hillside, they accused the neighbors of killing them and doing various things with them and that caused a lot of trouble.

The introduction of the Blackface sheep coincided with the height of the difficulties between landlords and tenants, and the new breed which died "mysteriously" must have had an exacerbating effect. According to Wee Paddy, the new breed did not reach the Southwest Donegal area until the early years of this century.

The native sheep had a much finer fleece than the Blackface and it was on this wool that the native weaving industry had been based:

> They were very fine wooled sheep with a kind of white rusty-colored face and if they had horns at all, they were only little stubs...They had these kind of sheep with very fine, knitted little wool on them and silver grey (a type of homespun) was white and black wool mixed together. They dyed some black, very black, and then this fine wool came out in little dots of black and white, just like a shower of hail.

Opinions differ about this wool; many people believe that it was of the poorest quality and had little value in any but a local market. The Congested Districts Board imported better quality wool (mostly from England), and in 1925 a commission assigned to investigate local industry reported that goods valued at £700 were sold in the monthly markets at Ardara and Carrick (*Coimisiun na Gaeltachta* 1925:18).

Of the native sheep it was said that "they were not at all so hardy as the black-faced. They required better housing in the winter and even in the summer time but their wool was better" (*Coimisiun na Gaeltachta* 1925:18). The Blackface breed originated in Scotland, in highland country not unlike the Donegal highlands, and is widely known as "one of the hardiest breeds of sheep. It is seldom provided with shelter or supplemental feed in the highland country of its origin" (Ensminger 1964:77).

Despite this reputed hardiness there has been persistent trouble with sheep imported from Scotland, especially with the first

generation, which dies off quickly. The second establishes itself
and thrives.

The wool of the Blackface is of carpet grade, too coarse for
better uses. Although the world drop in market prices for wool
has not left Donegal unaffected, the most severe price change has
come over the last five to seven years. Prior to this time wool had
good value by local standards and was widely marketed.

The second historian, Big Paddy, believes that sheep husbandry
standards have been considerably elevated during his lifetime and
that the major improvement is probably in the grasslands which
are now fertilized. As late as ten to fifteen years ago, he says, sheep
were not fed on the lowlands in the winter at all. Improved
grasslands also provide them with trace minerals, such as cobalt,
which the highland grazing lacks.

Another change has been the introduction of sheep dogs. As he
puts it, "fifty years ago, if they had a dog, they'd be much better
without him." Ill-trained mongrels probably damaged the sheep
herds — but most people did not have sheep dogs at all. In 1945
sheep dog trials were instituted at the Southwest Donegal
Agricultural Show held annually in Ardara. Well-bred dogs were
exhibited and bred in the area for the first time, and most of my
informants point to the introduction of good sheep dogs as a
major improvement in sheep husbandry, one that eliminated a
great deal of the labor involved in herding sheep. The dogs
presently in use are much abused by outsiders as being poor,
inefficient animals, and this is certainly true when one compares
them with the excellent breeds developed in other countries.
Despite their bad reputation, however, the present dogs serve
their purpose and some are admirably well trained.

Big Paddy believes that 30 to 40 years ago lamb losses were
tremendous because of a lack of feed, poor breeding, lack of
information as to proper care, bad climate, and lack of shelter. At
the same time, cattle were well fed and attended to, so that losses
were never so high.

The history of cattle breeds in the area is more difficult to work
out. Many different breeds — such as Friesians and Herefords —
came in only within the last 20 years and, as noted above, both
Angus and Shorthorn bulls were distributed by the Congested
Districts Board. The native animals were referred to as "roan" or
"brindle" cattle, and according to Big Paddy, milk production
from these animals was low, no more than an average of 300
gallons of milk per year.

Butter was a cash crop in the early years of the century and continued as such until about 1940. Since butter was very valuable, some calf mortality may have been due to the making of butter at the expense of the calf. The breed most suitable for milking would have been the Shorthorn; indeed, one wonders if the "native" breed might not have been a kind of Shorthorn. Other informants recall that the Shorthorn of previous years was a better milker, an observation borne out by critics of the government's attempt to produce a hybrid beef-and-dairy Shorthorn.

Among recent introductions the Friesians were judged too heavy and too big to feed, and Herefords, which put on weight rapidly, are not as acceptable to butchers as are the Aberdeen Angus. Herefords and Angus gain at about the same rate, but the latter have smaller bones. Other breeds have been tried; one attempt was made at raising Galloways and another at raising Kerry cattle but neither breed was acceptable, though both have a reputation for hardiness. None of my informants could say why these animals didn't work out, but I will hazard a guess, that it is because hardiness is not the supreme consideration. Quite apart from market preferences, hardy animals have very poor conversion rates and tend to be "slow-growers," as they say. Because cattle are well cared for in the area, hardiness need not be the supreme consideration. Both the Galloway and the Kerry are small animals and the experimental group may have been too small to be considered salable. Somewhere between the midget Kerrys and the giant Friesians there is a mean for cattle. If they are too large they will eat too much; if they are too small they will have to be kept too long.

Big Paddy says that economic self-sufficiency was the norm up until about 1940, and each family kept three or four cows, relying on butter as a cash crop and buttermilk as a dietary staple. Potatoes were the other major staple of the diet, and a surplus of potatoes was produced and marketed each month in Ardara. Changes began in the late '20s and early '30s, the Depression in the States affecting both emigration and foreign money sent to Ireland. After 1940 the number of cows kept had dropped from an average of four to an average of two per household, unemployment compensation being a major determinant of this change because eligibility was determined by a "means" test and livestock holdings were an important measure. Big Paddy regards the dole (unemployment compensation) as a menace, observing that it has ruined the "social fabric of the community" by replacing the economic self-sufficiency of former times with dependence on the government. As an example he cites Loughros Point where, of 147 farms previously operating, there are now only four farms "really" operating.

Both of these men remember the fairs and markets once held in Ardara, the big fairs that were social occasions as well, and the monthly markets, at which produce of all kinds was sold. Both remember the pig fairs that were held on the first of November, and the times when most families kept a pig or two as the savings bank of the family. Both believe that the quality of life has degenerated in modern times, that the "social fabric" has been disrupted by fluctuating economic conditions and emigration, though they arrive at this conclusion from very different starting points. Wee Paddy regrets the passing of the close-knit Irish community, with its Gaelic-speaking storytellers, while Big Paddy bemoans the loss of the self-sufficient small farmer.

According to the folk historians, then, the history of Southwest Donegal over the last fifty years has been one of slow change, but not for the better. There are two constants — the pastoral subsistence base and the care given to cattle — while all other factors have been subject to endless revision according to changing economic and political circumstances.

CHAPTER SIX

Conclusions

Tradition — which sometimes brings down truth that history
has let slip, but is oftener the wild babble of the time, such as
was formerly spoken at the fireside and now congeals in
newspapers — ...
Nathaniel Hawthorne, *The House of the Seven Gables*

Livestock production strategies, traced out in terms of current
decision-making and the historical record, have been my jumping-
off point for a closer look at traditions and at the interactions
between recorded history, tradition, and current practice. I chose
this way from the many available to document what consistency
there is in Southwest Donegal between views of the distant past,
the recent past, the present, and present ideas about the
"traditional" past. I have been at pains to show how the verifiable
present relates to the recorded past; in the process I have shown
how often and in how many contexts "traditions" or customs are
changed or inverted to meet current needs. On the basis of my
findings, it is clear that much of what people "remember" has to
do with what presently is, not with a reliable assessment of what
has gone before and I have indicated my profound distrust of
"unselected" but selective informant memory.

I have also said that I believe the most important use made of
tradition in Southwest Donegal is as a predicate for ethnic identity,
the "we" in the statement "We've always done it that way," and
I have outlined the reasons for the on-going formulations of ethnic
identity in the area. In this way, I have carried out what I believe
to be the task of the social anthropologist: "to find out what a
society was trying, either consciously or unconsciously, to
'say'"(Maybury-Lewis 1970:134). The formulation of ethnic
identity is an on-going process of "saying," whether or not what
is being said is accounted for by Centuries Of British Oppression,
or whether the process is conscious or unconscious. It calls for a
close understanding of different kinds of history, of different ways
of understanding the present. The question of ethnic identity is a
particularly complicated one in Donegal, but it is neither

153

indecipherable nor inexplicable. I believe, however, that nothing is gained by an *a priori* assumption that the culture or the traditions are moribund and I have urged my colleagues to speak not of the death of Irish traditions but of the birth of a new variant of Irish tradition, of the ethnic identity of those we study. Anthropology gains not by assisting at the wake but by understanding the circumstances in which a new variant of tradition may be born.

There are other ways of approaching the questions of tradition and history; I have mentioned the small shopkeepers of Ireland as a worthy object of study and I will add that kinship also repays careful analysis, as Eileen Kane has demonstrated. Were I designing this study now, I would stress the need for a more detailed analysis of the concepts of space and time, as these are understood in Donegal. And I certainly would include more about the women of Southwest Donegal, the wives, sisters and mothers of the farmers I have concentrated on here. My focus on production strategies all but eliminated the women from consideration but they are nonetheless worthy of the most careful study, particularly as their decisions about emigration will probably determine the future viability of Southwest Donegal as a farming region. I have given the details of a ritual, the cattle sale/fair, that was fast disappearing from the region in 1975, but I am willing to bet that by now those ritual details have found their way into other contexts; in any case, a thorough study of rituals in the area has not been and should be done.

The study of symbolic themes in Irish life is a direction I believe to be both illuminating and useful. One such theme might be the revenant in Irish oral traditions, another the careful documentation of the tendency in oral literature to elevate those who conquered Ireland to the stature of giants, to reduce those whom the Irish conquered to dwarfs. These studies would add considerably to our understanding of the "combinations or clusters of modes of consciousness and life," and they would allow anthropologists to study people from the inside out, as Glassie says, "from the place where people are articulate to the place where they are not, from the place where they are in control of their destinies to the place where they are not."

Such studies demand a different understanding of history than that anthropologists have been accustomed to, and they are far more difficult tasks than declaring that Irish traditions are dead. The view of history I have taken is close to Lévi-Strauss's, for whom history is not developmental and progressive but diverse and contextual: "history is a series of combinations or clusters of modes of consciousness and life, individual and social, spread out in time. These different clusters represent the different contents or events that 'fill in' the structures of 'Mind-As-Such' in different historical epochs" (Zimmerman 1970:230). In order to stress my own view of tradition as an active, creative force in societies, I have taken Levi-Strauss's idea of history as a suggestion, not as a blueprint for an interpretive study (which it is not, in any case).

I want to carry the implications of my findings on history, tradition, and informant memory a step or two further and discuss the implications of my essentially structuralist position for future studies of tradition and change, particularly as these relate to Ireland. I have mentioned the "genesis" of anthropological studies of Ireland in the capable hands of Arensberg and Kimball; I should also outline what seem to me the necessary and logical next steps in Irish studies fifty years after Arensberg and Kimball. Indeed these are logical steps in any studies made of societies that have historical records, against which conceptions of history, tradition, and living memory may be tested and compared. To do so, I will again take up the question of why those who have worked in Ireland maintain that Irish traditions or culture are dead.

I have said that this premature declaration may result from an anthropological (or more broadly social scientific) view of tradition as a passive, stultifying force, and from an overly romantic view of Irish culture, a view often espoused by the Irish themselves. In the West of Ireland, particularly, people seem inclined to believe that American students spend most of their time awaiting opportunities to descend on the West, to probe its vital signs for imminent failure, and to sit the wake. I have mentioned that people in Southwest Donegal do not consider their area a part of the "West," and it may be for this reason that they have not yet caught on to this necrophiliac custom. Not that I think they would be unwilling to try it. I never noticed any objection to a good wake; all the better if the supposed corpse isn't dead and outsiders are providing the drink.

There is a more serious point to be made, however, and that concerns a failure on the part of ethnographers to come to terms with the differences between history and tradition. Anthropologists have seldom dealt well with history, probably because they considered that their subjects had none that a historian would deem worthy of the name. There were two approaches to history within anthropology, roughly the British school of social anthropology and the American school of cultural anthropology, each of which dealt differently with questions of history and tradition.

In the British school, Malinowski did not eliminate history from consideration in formulating his functionalist precepts, but he did deal with it rather haphazardly, drawing history in where it suited and ignoring it where it did not. His students, notably Leach and Vansina, dealt with history more systematically and to better effect, asserting that history was vital for the understanding of the shifts in politics, or for understanding oral traditions and myth. Thus when Lévi-Strauss advanced his ideas about the relation of structuralism to various forms of history, social anthropologists were able to move toward the consideration of various kinds of history without great (conceptual) difficulty.

The American school of cultural anthropology had a different view of history, a result of the teachings of Franz Boas. American anthropologists investigated and recorded a past that they called the "ethnographic present," a record of the past made from the memories of living informants. Those who wrote of the ethnographic present usually prefaced their monographs with a statement such as, "I am writing as if the pre-conquest times I am describing were still in effect, as if the social structure of the past were extant."

In Boas's time at Columbia University, recording of the past of American Indian groups whose few surviving members were dying out was regarded as an important mission. In their haste to make these records of the ethnographic present, however, the ethnographers sometimes failed to notice the real present that confronted them and their informants. Among Boas's collection of artifacts, art, and crafts from the Northwest Coast is an unforgettable photograph: in the right-hand corner, there is seated an Indian woman, spinning thread in what was presumably the indigenous manner. The woman and her craft are the focus of the picture; the background is dark and reveals nothing of the surroundings. However, owing to the nature of photography in 1894, the plate as a whole (of which the Indian subject was only part) shows far more than the Indian woman. In the left-hand corner stands Boas, holding up a blanket that serves as backdrop for the subject; behind him is a picket fence and the roof of a well-built, modern house.

To me this woman represents what anthropologists call the ethnographic present, i.e., the presumed pre-conquest period; but the "real" present consists of the woman, the house and the ethnographer. Boas's subject is being photographed in this ethnographic present, as if she were living in the past; the reality that surrounds her is obscured, blotted out by the ethnographer. Hence, two pasts were lost: the events of the past that were known to the informants and the circumstances of the past that was present in 1894, when the informants were being interviewed. To Boas, it was urgent to capture, before they were irretrievably lost, the memories of those who remembered times past, those who had witnessed and survived the coming of a new civilization and the changes it brought. We cannot know what that past was like — we can only know what Boas's informants told him it was like and, from that, what he chose to record. Boas's was a valid goal, but it is not the goal of anthropological research today.

Anthropological goals and techniques have changed, as have the subjects of their inquiry. As anthropology has turned away from the purely functional viewpoint, where the metaphor was the living organism and its vital processes, toward more dynamic, processual analyses, where the metaphor is the birth, life, and death of an organism, an emphasis on death was in some ways inevitable. The theoretical shift was from function to dysfunction. Certainly anthropologists have witnessed the "death" of cultures, when individuals who were the last bearers of a particular culture, the last speakers of a particular language, died. But in the Irish case, there is no corpse; a visitor to Donegal sees not glass-coffined relics of a past that never was but living, breathing, often Gaelic-speaking human beings who are concerned with adapting themselves to the "modern" world, just as their ancestors before them had to adapt to the latest version of modernity. What Boas and his contemporaries did is lent validity in our own time because it gives to the present generation of American Indians a record of the history and traditions of their people. But if, as Evans-Pritchard said, anthropology is history, then the history that was recorded using the ethnographic present as a key concept was scientifically invalid, because it relied on the selective memories of the informants and because the present circumstances under which the ethnographer worked were lost or ignored.

We risk a similar loss today, but the urgency of our own mission springs from a different source, a need to understand the mechanics of integration into the modern world, and for this we need different interpretations, drawn from different perspectives. We must go from the assumption of the dysfunction of tradition to a study of the structures that govern present understandings of tradition. What was gained by the declaration that Irish traditions were dying, perhaps, was to bring Irish society into the realm of legitimate anthropological inquiry; but what is lost by that declaration, that a priori assumption, was a perspective on the real present, the present in which people were coping with the modern world, not being swamped by it. I need not reiterate my objections to the reliance on memory, especially without benefit of comparison with other sources and I have commented elsewhere (Shanklin 1981) on the pernicious effects of the anthropological habit of reconstructing a homogeneous and idealized past. In this book I have pointed out that a far more interesting study may be done of the revisions and reformulations of those same traditions, and I believe it is appropriate that Irish studies be the field in which this is done, for it was in Ireland that anthropology made one of its earliest steps toward the investigation of "modern, civilized societies."

After this necessary revision of the anthropological view of traditions should come a second step, a careful investigation of the memories on which traditions are based, particularly when dealing as in Ireland with a world view that reformulates and recasts innovations as traditions. And I must warn anthropologists to be very careful with the assumptions they make about what is "reality" in that world view. If, as anthropologists, we are socialized by our informants and thus influenced by their world view, we must examine all the predicates of that world view. To be influenced is one thing but to be blinded by our informants' perceptions is another, more dangerous matter. It is the habit of old people the world over to deplore the present and the changes that have come during their lifetimes but, rather than being caught up in this habit, anthropologists ought to be aware of it and prepared to deal with it.

To carry out the second step in the continuation of studies of modern civilized societies must also involve a careful assessment of what I have called the "Context of forgetting" in another work (Gemima's Children: An Oral History of an Appalachian Family, in preparation). This assessment necessarily involves the study of the present action, for the context of forgetting is primarily but not entirely present action; what is considered history and what is considered tradition is dependent on the present and it is neither fully conscious nor fully unconscious, but a product of the point-counterpoint relationship between the present, the traditional past, and history. In Donegal, to return to an earlier example, hereditary leadership was replaced by a "tradition" of intermediaries or go-betweens; the hereditary leadership probably gained somewhat in the affections of the people as a consequence of the dislike and distrust of go-betweens. It is the task of anthropologists (along with historians and folklorists) to assess those gains realistically.

Another example is found in the lament of Ferflatha O'Gnive, court poet in the time of Elizabeth I. I cited his opinion of the decline of Gaelic customs but I also indicated that those same customs were replaced by different customs. Five hundred years after O'Gnive, in the reign of Elizabeth II, we find Millman speaking on the same subject in much the same terms: "This island has fulfilled the geographical destiny of 'the West.' It has become a landscape of death, and to walk on it today is to know the myriad shapes of death" (1977:202). The point of departure here ought not to be the chorus of death rattles but the observation that the "tradition" itself is to declare the death of traditions, or the death of the West.

Thus traditions are best treated as symbolic forms, not as realities; in this way their adaptive significance can be revealed, as can their political significance or their consequences for the formation of ethnic identity. These need not be and should not be taken as unicausal factors, but rather as factors that interact in the formulation of the Irish world view. I believe that the study of the "context of forgetting" is the most promising direction Irish ethnography could take. Its subjects are the descendants of people who, in order to revise and remake their world, have produced a revolution each century, have produced giants who stood on the shoulders of giants, to borrow a phrase from Umberto Eco.

Arensberg and Kimball were pioneers in a then uncharted field, i.e., Irish studies, but those who have followed in their footsteps have rendered them not the homage of innovation or the restructuring of understandings from that field, but the more pallid compliment of imitation. Arensberg, Kimball, their Irish subjects and even "Mother Ireland" herself deserve better from those of us who are hitching a ride on the shoulders of giants and we must begin by joining our informants in proclaiming "Irish tradition is dead — long live Irish tradition."

Fieldwork in a Western Society

> We are a different people. We admire personality and look coldly
> on character. It may come from being a conquered people obliged
> to develop secret weapons against our rulers — men of character,
> probity, will, discipline, uprightness and stern justice. The catch
> comes once the foreigner has adapted to all this gay Irish
> volatility, and enters on the grim adventure of buying a horse
> from the enthusiastic visionary before him.
> Sean O'Faolain, 1977:502-503.

It is commonly observed by anthropologists that fieldwork in
a Western society is more difficult than in a non-Western society,
because in a non-Western society many things are startlingly new
and thus noticeable for a Westerner. Doing good fieldwork in a
Western society, however, is more difficult because so much is
(apparently) familiar and so many things seem to be shared.

But things that seem "familiar" are often not so and they may
be quite different in their uses and meanings. These are what
Ernestine Friedl calls the "unexpected mental hazards" of
fieldwork in a Western society and after I have discussed some of
those, I want to describe the order in which I learned the lessons
that are the substance of this book.

Anthropologists usually categorize the information they gather
about a society in neat, formal chapters with headings like
"Ecology; economy; kinship; religion ..." These categories are
convenient for organizing material, and they help in writing what
Leach (1976:1) calls "potted ethnographies." But fieldwork itself
does not yield neat categories of this or any other sort. Data comes
in globs and bits, rather like an unintelligible Morse Code. With
luck and patience, the globs begin to be intelligible, and each bit
that is illuminated hints at what its surrounding components might
be. After discussing the unexpected mental hazards and the
problem of preconceptions, I will try to illuminate the globs of
informal data in something of the same order in which the
information I gathered became intelligible to me.

The first thing an ethnographer must learn before beginning to
examine specific problems is how to cope with the "natives" and

how the "natives" may cope with the ethnographer. In this learning process I encountered the first obstacles to my research — my own preconceptions. These preconceptions included my impression that Ireland was much like other Western nations and that I should behave as I would in dealing with citizens of any modern agrarian state. I was prepared to learn Gaelic and to deal with officials whose function it was to oversee the implementation of modern agricultural practices. I was not prepared for the nuances of English as spoken by the Irish, nor for the elaborate etiquette and different value system that pervade Irish business dealings.

In the recent past it was a matter of some pride and considerable frustration that anthropology professors did not tell their students what to expect in the field. Laura Bohannan says of her professors that they advised her always to walk in cheap tennis shoes and to remember that she would need more writing tables than she thought (Bowen 1964:4), both doubtless sound bits of advice, but neither very helpful in dealing either with preconceptions or with the "natives." Even now, with volumes on fieldwork issuing hourly from the presses, I doubt that students are much better prepared than they were in the past. Fieldwork remains a personal experience, not because one wasn't warned about possible hardships but because a major hazard of fieldwork is learning about oneself and one's preconceptions. Restudies clutter the libraries but each trauma and unfamiliar sensation is experienced differently by every fieldworker.

The traumas and unfamiliar sensations are learning experiences. This is especially so if one is working in a Western society in which the outward forms are seemingly familiar. Ernestine Friedl (1962) cites the instance of shoes as one of the "unexpected mental hazards" of doing fieldwork in a society akin to one's own:

> The shoes, pumps, and slippers are within the range of styles for such items available in the United States. But the contexts in which the Greek villagers wear their shoes and slippers provide surprises. Men in Vasilika wear ordinary oxfords for work in the fields, for walking in mud, rain, and even snow during the winter — with no other foot protection. When the fields are flooded for irrigation, men remove their shoes and work barefoot. Within their houses, men do not change into slippers; they do not own any. Women, on the other hand, wear cloth slippers both indoors and outdoors, around the house and in the fields, in all weathers and in all seasons. Their leather pumps are saved

for church, for holidays, and for journeys. On such occasions
women wear pumps regardless of the weather. They daintily
pick their way through muddy, unpaved village paths and stand
for hours in unsubstantial pumps on the stone floor of the
unheated church each Sunday throughout the cold, rainy winter
(1962:5).

Ireland looks much like most Western countries at first glimpse,
but the "unexpected mental hazards" appear in the process of
what seems to be an easy adjustment; the customs are apparently
those of a rural country, not of a distinctively Irish countryside,
and Irish "culture" looks much like a direct transplant of modern
American culture, complete with television reruns of American
gangster shows. The Irish appear to be familiar with American
customs and well informed about them; they also seem to be
amazingly tolerant of transatlantic oddities.

Most of this modernity is superficial, and it vanishes like the
proverbial Irish mist when tested. In its place there are implacably
Irish attitudes, immovably Irish convictions. I have often thought
that this resolute core of what, for want of a better term, I will
call "Irishness" may account for the harsh behavior of the English
toward the Irish. The English offered the Irish their (English)
language, their (English) titles, their (English) notions about central
government and urban living, as well as a cultural heritage to be
part of — and the Irish remained Irish, turning the English
language into poetry about fairies and anarchy, mocking the British
nobility, and beginning at least one revolution per century
predicated on the glories of Irish rural life and the Irish language,
Gaelic. All — perhaps not calculated but guaranteed — to infuriate
the English, who had probably believed that the Irish would put
their "gifts" to proper use and become proto-English. It may be
that there was something about the appearance of similar customs
that incited the English to fury; when they dealt with other
colonials, it was easy to conclude that those with bizarre customs
did not and could not understand the ways of the English, that
racial differences, if nothing else, made them incapable of
understanding. The Irish looked sufficiently English, but they
perversely, willfully, refused to become English.

All this has considerable bearing on the initial view of the Irish
gained by unwary visitors and unsuspecting anthropologists. The
Irish seem to be sensible, provincial people with a strong regional
accent — until one encounters an incident that is not explicable

in the terms of another country. A trivial example will illustrate. In a Dublin hotel one day I witnessed the following exchange between a man with a Cork accent and a waiter:

Guest:	I'd like some tea and sandwiches.
Waiter:	What kind of sandwiches would you like, sir?
Guest:	Ham and tomato.
Waiter:	Sorry, sir, we're all out of ham.
Guest:	Chicken, then, and tomato.
Waiter:	Sorry, but we're all out of chicken as well.
Guest:	Beef?
Waiter:	Sorry, sir, but we're out of beef.
Guest:	Tongue?
Waiter:	Sorry, sir, but there's no tongue.
Guest:	Cheese?
Waiter:	Yes, sir, cheese and tomato sandwiches. We're out of everything but cheese and tomato today.

I know of no way in which a professor could prepare a student to deal with this conversation, much less to explain it to the rest of the anthropological world. It is an Irish conversation; it would not have happened in New York or London. An American or an English guest might have inquired at once as to what kinds of sandwiches were available, or the waiter would have immediately told the guest what was available. In Dublin this did not happen; both parties were Irish and both understood that to admit the restaurant was lacking vital sandwich ingredients would be to admit failure.

There are many possible explanations for this small scene: the most likely one is that if the guest had chosen cheese at once, there would have been no need for the waiter to reveal the deficiencies of the kitchen. Yet the waiter is not reluctant to do this though he makes the announcement at the end of the conversation, not at the beginning. Other possible explanations are that both parties to the conversation are insane, that they are indulging in verbal games, that neither has anything better to do than attempt to carry out an afternoon's conversation with a stranger. The incident need not be explained in these ways, however; it illustrates a single point: that the Irish do not treasure efficiency in verbal exchanges.

Efficiency is an accidental concomitant of certain processes; although there is no objection to efficiency in other contexts, efficiency in conversation is deplorable and rude. Coming straight to the point would indicate to the other party that his company was unwelcome. The guest would have thought the waiter surly and the waiter would have thought the guest ill mannered if, in the interests of efficiency, the waiter had immediately volunteered that the sandwiches available included only cheese and tomato or if the guest had demanded this information. As it turned out, both honor and appetite were satisfied.

Because each fieldworker must come to terms with her own preconceptions, professors are not able to prepare students for the challenges to those preconceptions; nevertheless, they are able to prepare them for ecological research. The choice of production strategies as a focus for my study was an especially pertinent one, for they are a source of major difficulties between the people of Southwest Donegal and the Irish Government. Agricultural policy in the Irish Republic is directed toward bringing the population up to a "modern" standard of production and many efforts in this direction have met with an extraordinary lack of success. The reasons for the farmers' decision to forego modern methods have not been dealt with extensively by the agricultural policy makers; it has been easier for them to assign the failures of modernization policies to the "prehistoric mental outlook" of the people.

But barriers to communication work both ways. The government in Dublin has manifested an ambivalence toward the people of Donegal in its attempt to preserve what the sentimentalists call the "Gaelic way of life," and in its determination to upgrade the standard of living. Most of the advocates of the Gaelic way of life never lived it; in its less colorful aspects it included all the trappings of desperate poverty: a monotonous, substandard diet; dirt floors; a high infant-mortality rate, coupled with severe overpopulation in the west of Ireland. There are few advocates of Gaelicism in Donegal, but there are a number of people who grew up in one-room cottages, in families that included more than ten children.

Many Irish politicians hoped to preserve the colorful aspects of the Gaelic way of life — the storytellers, the *ceilidh* (cottage dances), and the language itself — while upgrading the material circumstances of the people. The Irish Republic was designed to better its citizens' welfare, but it was hampered in these efforts by sentimentalism about the Gaelic way of life, on the one hand, and by the remoteness and intransigency of Donegal, on the other.

With only a vague understanding of the political divisions that set Donegal off and kept it a remote, exotic part of the Irish

Republic, I began my fieldwork by requesting interviews with officials in Dublin and promptly encountered another obstacle, my own preconceptions about government officials and their "appropriate" concerns. When I tried to explain my aims to the Dublin officials, I had great difficulty in making my purposes clear. All seemed to want to cooperate and some were very helpful, but most were bemused. A typical conversation went:

E.S.:	I've come to study livestock production methods in the west of Ireland.
Official:	There are no livestock in the west.
E.S.:	Oh? According to your agency's report . . .
Official:	Well, there may be a few but there's none worth talking of. Now if you're interested in livestock and agriculture then you'd be better to go to the Midlands where they have fine animals altogether.
E.S:	As a matter of fact, I'm interested in the people's ideas about livestock keeping, not so much in the animals they keep.
Official:	Ideas, is it? In that case, you'll find that the people of the West have some pretty strange ones, but they're nothing to do with livestock . . .

One official advised me to take up fishing since I was determined to go to a part of the country where the fishing was especially good; another assured me (quite mistakenly, as it happens) that the people of Donegal were entirely taken up with the I.R.A. and their revolutionary activities and would have no time for me.

The real problem in communicating with officials was my preconception that I should come straight to the point of my visit and not make a social visit out of an interview. Long before I arrived in Ireland, I had sent copies of my research proposal to the agencies I thought likely to be concerned with similar matters. Most of the people I talked to in Dublin undoubtedly knew as much as they cared to know about my research plans; their interest was in finding out what kind of person I was and the exchange of an hour's worth of pleasantries was an appropriate prelude to assessing my character. In some cases, too, officials wished to dissuade me from going anywhere in the west of Ireland, in their view the country's most underdeveloped region. A number of regions have completely modern, fully mechanized agricultural techniques; that this was not so in Donegal had been a factor in my choice of the area for study. The natural pride of these officials in their country's very real accomplishments undoubtedly led them to urge me to visit the highly developed regions and may have caused them to speak harshly about the west.

By the time I got to Donegal, I was better prepared to deal with officials than I had been when I first got to Dublin. I had a fairly good idea of the social requirements and could hide my dismay when what I thought was a straightforward question triggered the recitation of a long Yeats poem, and I was prepared to point to quite objective and real-looking cows nearby in case I was informed that there were no cattle in Donegal.

In Donegal my interviews with officials went smoothly and I had time to reflect on my mistakes in Dublin. A classic Irish story involves a man who goes to visit a neighbor, spends most of the evening talking, and as he starts out the door remarks, "Oh, and by the way, I was wondering if I could borrow your donkey tomorrow." I had assumed that because officials were busy people I should come straight to the point of my visit, so as not to waste their time.

The Irish are seldom pressed for time; the saying is, "When God made time, He made plenty of it." There was no hurry in getting to the purpose of my visit. It was more important to be polite and to allow the person I was talking with to form his own opinion of me. After that — assuming that the conversation had gone well and I had expressed reasonable opinions on the Irish weather, the traffic, the Kennedy family, the situation in the North of Ireland, the Common Market, and Yeats — it was possible for me to ask my questions and get helpful answers to them.

On this basis my interviews in Donegal were very productive; the study called for the selection of a sample of farmers whose production strategies could be studied in detail, and the officials provided me with a list of farmers who might agree to cooperate.

During my first two weeks, while I was learning about Southwest Donegal from the officials' point of view, I lived in a hotel in a village I am calling Banagh. I learned enough about the region to isolate those factors that would be most important to my study: an active livestock fair; a central location in a region of diverse resources, from which I could make daily trips to a wide sample of farmers whose production techniques would provide illustrations of both modern and traditional methods of keeping livestock. Two villages, each with a population of about 500, suited these needs and I had to choose between them.

Julian Pitt-Rivers says that he chose the Andalusian village he studied after visiting the local pubs in a number of villages; he settled in the village where he was first offered a drink in the pub (1961:2). My decision about where to live was nearly as arbitrary; having determined that either of two villages would suit the requirements of my study, I chose Banagh. The other village had won the Tidy Town competition in Ireland the previous year, and part of the credit for that prize went to a flock of geese that patrolled the main street, gobbling up stray morsels that otherwise would have made the town look untidy. I happen to have a particular dislike for domesticated birds and, in those early days, I also had to deal with a heightened level of frustration. Knowing that rapport with informants might be damaged if the local anthropologist were seen kicking a goose down the main street, I chose to live in Banagh, the less tidy but goose-free village.

Once settled, I could begin to find informants, and it was clear that I was going to have to come rapidly to terms with people as people, as human beings, as farmers — not as sources of information or as research subjects — and that they would have to come to terms with me, if I were to carry out the research I had planned. Happily, the people of Southwest Donegal were better able to deal with me than I was with them in the beginning. They sorted out the social roles I could occupy almost at once, and some of these roles took directions I had not foreseen. My own preconceptions were again obstacles to understanding the useful social roles that could be occupied by outsiders.

I had overcome a few obstacles; I knew better than to begin a discussion by coming straight to the point, and I had grappled with some preconceptions, in the process of acquainting myself with Irish officials. I had also learned something about the formal apparatus of Irish government bureaucracy and the informal rules of etiquette in Irish social life. Official permission to carry out my study was a formality; the informal circumstances — pub interviews and denunciations of Donegal, and of Donegal livestock in particular — had taught me to be cautious about assuming that what I perceived as similarities between Irish rural life and rural life elsewhere were in fact similar phenomena.

After compiling a tentative list of farmers who were actively involved in livestock production, I set out to find them. I believed that I was well prepared to carry out my study, at least as well prepared as an ecological trainee who cannot read road maps can ever expect to be.

There is an enormous advantage in being unable to read road maps — at least as long as you are traveling in a well-populated country. While you may not be certain where you are geographically, you are always quite certain where you are in human terms. Whether people are friendly, how they react to slightly daft tourists, what they want to know about you — all this information is immediately available.

It is safe to say, to use the Irish phrase, that I was lost on every road in Southwest Donegal during my first few months of fieldwork, and that, for all my planning and elaborate field techniques, being lost taught me more about the countryside than I would have learned any other way. To map readers and other efficient travelers, the reasons for this will not be immediately apparent and will need elaboration.

The first thing one learns in asking directions in Ireland is that notions of spatial distance depend on one's means of transport. In an automobile, a short distance is about a mile; on foot, a short distance is a few hundred yards. "Just a little way out of the town" probably means that a visitor will not be able to distinguish the house that sits on what looks like the town's boundary, and will drive several miles beyond before discovering the mistake. "It would be the third cottage on the left" seems a fairly specific direction until one learns that the first two cottages were destroyed in the Land Wars a hundred years ago and only their foundations remain but they still count as the first two cottages. "Turn to your left after you've passed the second crossroads" is explicit only after one knows that a "crossroads" is anything that meets the road; cow paths qualify for this designation, as do roads that do not cross the main road.

The second thing one learns in asking directions is that there are two naming systems. If you are proceeding toward a certain townland and stop to ask where you might find Mr. Boyle, the response is apt to be, "We're all Boyles here." So, consulting notes, the right Boyle is Francis. "Francis B. or Francis X?" is the reply. At this point it becomes necessary to describe the object of the visit, and to learn the respective merits of the two Francie Boyles who live in that townland and how, by tortuous genealogical calculation, both are related to the direction giver. Almost invariably the conversation ends with, "You might find the other one better at telling you what you want to know," a recommendation unsolicited, unwelcome, and, sometimes infuriating.

A fieldworker with a good sense of direction and a very detailed map could probably sort out these difficulties without going through the laborious processes I have described. But to do so would be to fail utterly to grasp the significance of what is being pointed out, to miss the informal system that goes along with the formal, recorded system. In the case of directions, there are superficial directions which include "obvious" landmarks, and there is an informal system (informal in the sense that it is unrecorded, except in folktales) of boundary markers. The people see their landscape according to the informal system but, in giving directions, they mix the two systems freely, thus indicating to the bemused visitor that "landmarks" are in the eyes of the beholder. In the case of names, too, there is a formal system and an informal one. Where, as in many townlands, all families have the same surname and a few Christian names, middle initials may be important to a census taker, but more important to the residents is the nickname given at birth.

It is said that God tempers the wind to the shorn lamb; in place of a sense of direction and map-reading abilities, I was given a very good visual memory and that memory enabled me to learn the townland boundaries quickly because I could easily recall the sequence of natural features. At the same time I learned what those boundary markers meant to the people who lived their lives in and around them. A willingness to learn the native system of names indicated that I was not on an official mission; when I turned up at a door and asked whether I had found Francie Johnny or Francie Con, I was almost automatically guaranteed welcome. Such are the fortuitous beginnings of participant observation.

It was clear from my early forays that the formal systems of land division, as recorded on maps, would not suffice to understand the land boundaries used by the people. It was also clear that the formal system of surnames was not an adequate key to understanding group loyalties. There are a few villages in Southwest Donegal, and many townlands; the traditional and modern systems, the village and townland systems, intermingle freely. There are a few surnames and given names (the most common given names are John, James, Colm, Francis, Edward, and Patrick; among the common surnames are Boyle, Feeney, Cannon, McGill, Gallagher) and many kin groups; the informal and formal naming systems also intermingle freely, but residence is the final identifying marker.

To identify a person, the formal name is first mentioned; I will use the name Francis Boyle as an example and to identify him, Francis X. Boyle is the next distinction. These are formal distinctions, used by census takers and mail carriers, but there are easily twenty individuals by this name in Southwest Donegal. For the outsider, the true distinction is the townland plus the middle initial, thus Francie X. Boyle of Croveenananta. For the Boyle family or families living in Croveenananta, Francie will be known by his own and his father's given names, thus Francie Con or Francie Johnny. Sometimes individuals are given nicknames according to their distinctive features, such as hair color or stature or occupation, thus, Red Francie, Wee Francie, Lame Francie, Francie the Fiddler. During his lifetime a man is identified by his informal name, and after his death identified formally as Francis X. Boyle, Croveenananta, Banagh.

Putting this in American terms renders the contrast more clearly. In Donegal town, one gravestone reads, "Here lies James Feeney, 14 Charles Street, Boston, Mass., U.S.A., died on holiday in Donegal, August, 1950, R.I.P." Because Americans do not usually indicate mailing addresses on gravestones, this identification may seem strange but it is an appropriate extension of the Irish principle that individuals should be formally identified by their place of residence. Mr. Feeney's permanent residence was thus given, along with a clear indication of his activities and the fact that he was an outsider to the area at the time of his death.

This was but the beginning of my understanding of the differences between the formal and the informal systems in operation; I was to learn more about kin groups and neighborhood loyalties in the process of carrying out my participant observations. A member of one's kin group is referred to in Donegal as a "friend," and friends and neighbors are the most important categories of relationship. To some extent, the categories overlap; a close "friend" who lives far away may be asked for help only after a neighbor has been unable to render the necessary aid. Friends and neighbors are people; beyond these categories are outsiders who are mostly non-people with no individual identities beyond that of outsiders. When I began my fieldwork I often had the feeling that I was invisible, a feeling common to anthropologists working in exotic areas; as my identity as neighbor became established I lost my invisibility and also my marginal status.

When I eventually found the people I was looking for, I knew better than to begin a discussion by announcing the point of my visit. Like the officials in Dublin, the people of Southwest Donegal were aware of my purposes; what was left to determine was whether specific farmers and their families would cooperate. That depended on their judgment of my ability to contribute something to their lives, not on my convincing them of the worthiness of my research efforts. I used the first interview to get to know the people I was visiting, and they used it to get to know me. At the end of the visit, I announced casually that I was interested in livestock production and would like to come back and ask them some questions about cattle and sheep. Only a few refused; those who agreed, however, did so for reasons I had not begun to suspect.

Before I understood the apparent ease with which people accepted me and tolerated my presence, I had to divest myself of two preconceptions — that I could remain aloof from the active gossip network and that I could remain an innocent bystander.

Having done fieldwork in New York City I assumed that I could as readily join a group in rural Ireland as I could in an urban environment. Early in my fieldwork I did so as I went from cattle fair to political gathering to ram show. I was never excluded nor made to feel unwelcome nor — being female — was I expected to help out in any of the tasks at hand, whether loading cattle, buying drinks, or grooming animals. I imagined that since I had no Irish ancestors, it would be easy to avoid allegiances and retain my marginal role. Two incidents made me aware, however, that though I might think of myself as a free agent and an innocent bystander, the people of Donegal had no intention of allowing me to remain apart from the proceedings.

Because I was engaged in the study of livestock production, I attended all events having to do with cattle and sheep. The first incident took place at a ram show; one of my informants invited me to attend the show, which was held in a town some thirty miles away. I accepted the invitation eagerly since I had planned to attend in any case and welcomed the prospect of learning his impressions of the show firsthand. When I arrived at his house I was neatly put into a situation that culminated in my volunteering to drive. Thus began my loss of innocence; rather than going to the show as an independent onlooker, I was attending it in the company of a local man, a situation that established my identity as his "neighbor."

When we arrived at the ram show he became involved in what seemed an interminable conversation with someone he knew and

I wandered off to look at the animals, hoping to gather information on perceptions of "good breeding" in animals before the actual judging began. There was a good-sized crowd in attendance, maybe two or three hundred people in all. As I gazed at the penned sheep and walked around to see the exhibits, several people spoke to me, initiating conversations with evaluative comments about the sheep I was looking at and offering to show me better sheep nearby. When they encountered acquaintances I drifted away, only to have the experience repeated. No introductions were made and none seemed appropriate; no one asked where I was from or what my business was.

I was very pleased at having chosen a field site where everyone was so open and friendly and I congratulated myself on my abilities as a fieldworker. By the time the man I had come with announced that we should go for lunch, I had talked to more than 12 people. Outside the arena he introduced me to the people we were joining and I discovered that all of them were people I had spoken with earlier; they were "friends" (as noted, meaning relatives) or neighbors of my informant. While I had not recognized them, they knew of my presence in the area and had assimilated me into their rather loose "group" as a neighbor. As the experience of the afternoon proved, what I had taken for friendliness on their part was more likely a certain feeling of trepidation about a visit to a distant town and the consequent drawing together of the ties of neighborliness. I was adopted as a "neighbor," and expected to behave like one.

I returned to the arena after lunch and took a seat in the grandstand to watch the judging. People drifted in and out and a number of them spoke to me; I carefully memorized their features and outstanding characteristics in order to check with my informant about them later. In the afternoon there was less restraint about my duties as a neighbor: one man handed me his ram's lead to hold for a while; another demanded my opinion of which was the better of two rams offered for sale. My loss of status as innocent bystander was complete; I had little choice but to behave like a neighbor in this situation.

On the way home my informant identified all the people I had met. In an entire day, in a crowd of perhaps 250 people, I had met all but a few of the 35 people from Southwest Donegal who attended the ram show, and only one person who had spoken to me was a "stranger" from another part of the county. (The stranger had introduced himself and asked me my business.) In a border town miles from Southwest Donegal I was adopted as a member of the local group representing Southwest Donegal. The other members of this group, who would never have approached me in their own villages, decided that I as some sort of neighbor was someone to whom they could speak freely. I had listened to and been included in discussions of the judge's intelligence, criticisms of neighbors' sheep, complaints about smuggling, and the like.

Thus sensitized I started to analyze the process of group formation. I had marvelled at the cooperation of the bystanders whenever any task was to be carried out, had been amazed at the amicable relations that prevailed when cattle were sold and the seller was buying drinks for all and sundry, had wondered why, when a cattle buyer was loading his newly purchased animals onto his truck, only his assistant and the seller were available to help him. I began asking knowledgeable informants to identify for me all the participants in these groups. After a few such exercises, I could predict group composition.

If a man had a large family, all his kinsmen and many of his neighbors would help; if he had a small family, fewer kinsmen (of course) and fewer neighbors were available for assistance. One more correlation struck me forcibly; the more sons and nephews a man had to help him, the more help he received.

The explanation for these actions is very simple, though not apparent to someone socialized in a more anonymous setting. In the long process of selling cattle, a seller is advised at intervals by his kindred and his neighbors; they are therefore on hand for the redistributive ceremony in the pub that marks a successful transaction. The cattle buyers are comparative strangers to the area since they come mostly from Northern Ireland, and they are disliked in a general way. So, when they could use some willing hands, no one is around to offer assistance. The reverse is true for a local man; some members of his family are sure to be present and he is expected to assist them, will expect them to assist him in turn and, since neighborly relations are almost as important as kinship ties, his neighbors too will come to his assistance. A man with a large family who gets help without appearing to need it will also be in a position to lend several helping hands another day. He therefore gets unnecessary help from those who may someday be shorthanded themselves. None of this informal structuring of cooperation seems calculated; informants, when asked about it, thought it natural to help someone who needed help (thus rendering the outside buyers invisible or as non-persons) and referred their willingness to the tie involved — "He's a friend," or, "He's a neighbor."

A normal six-year-old knows a great deal about neighbors and kin but the distinctions between the two groups do not become important until adolescence. In childhood, all-male and all-female groups predominate and residence seems to be the dominant consideration. Although many children have close or best friends in the English sense of the term, these friendships are subsumed in larger groupings and the children form what, to an anthropologist, is reminiscent of an African age-set organization, with two or three-year intervals between groups. These friendships are based on residential ties but at adolescence the local groups break up into dyadic relations, that is, friendships between two people, and the word "friend" comes to mean what it means to adults, a close relative. In late adolescence, relationships between two people are re-formed, most often along kinship lines, sibling ties being the most noticeable instances with occasional local bonds persisting.

These are the basic rules for group formation in Southwest Donegal; kinship is the first consideration, then locality. There are two exceptions to this rule, however; the first appears in fighting and the second in political gatherings. In an area such as this, where animosities are handed down in families and fights are more ritual events than occasions of violence, a man who gets into an argument will be carefully attended by his kinsmen only; his neighbors (who may be related to his opponent) will either take their own kinsman's side or avoid the fight altogether. The other exception is group composition at political gatherings, where political affiliation is uppermost. Party membership, like traditional quarrels, is almost hereditary so the members of a family will usually be in the same general area. They do not feel obliged to remain together as a group; the group itself is a larger one, consisting of all the local members of the party.

During my stay there was a general election, hence many political speeches were made in the village. People stood in the main square randomly and wherever they could get a good view, at least so I thought at first. As I became aware of the political affiliations I realized that members of each of the three parties had a particular area in which they stood and at the front of this group always stood the local party official, the secretary. I never witnessed a political dispute but often wondered if the rules for group formation would be transcended on such an occasion and whether each party was not, in fact, marking out its territory. No informant could recall a political event that had ended in a fight.

This, a small-scale community of long standing, is a place in which events are predictable and, except for cattle and sheep sales, outcomes are known in advance — there will be no bloodshed if a fight occurs; an oversized work group will (usually) accomplish a task more quickly than an undersized one, and social relations with specific rules proceed smoothly. In rare and unprecedented instances, such as when an outsider becomes ill, a crowd gathers seemingly at random and there is a great deal of flux in such a group, almost as if people were checking to see if some neighbor or relative were involved. Their curiosity satisfied, they move off again.

I watched one day as a group of Irish hippies attempted to draw a crowd. They carefully set up a speaking platform in the center of the town, arranged their public address system, and began exhorting the villagers to accept their views on some parliamentary matter. No one watched for more than a few minutes; the effort to attract people was futile, in part because their appearance was an "unscheduled" event, and in part because they attracted no one of sufficient importance around whom a crowd might have gathered.

Questioned privately, informants are suspicious of the concept of an "innocent" bystander. When I suggested that children in Northern Ireland had been injured or killed by bombs and that the children certainly must have been innocent bystanders, I was told that the parents were negligent in allowing their children to be so close to the scene of the fighting. When I countered by suggesting that shoppers in department stores were not engaging in militant activities and they, too, were often injured or killed, the response was that they should have known better than to be out shopping in a strife-torn city like Belfast. To the people of Donegal (only some of whom are IRA sympathizers) there is no escaping the notion that each individual is responsible at all times for his or her place, however dreadful the consequences may prove.

There was a second instance that brought to my awareness the paucity of innocent bystanders; it was almost the reverse of the incident at the ram show. In the second instance I was again made a member of the group, albeit temporarily and probably for quite different reasons. A person of marginal status or questionable loyalties may become a threat under certain circumstances and the threat I posed was neutralized in two ways: by speaking Gaelic to me, thereby identifying me to outsiders as a "local," and by drawing me into whatever conversation might be going on as a way of ensuring that I gave away no privileged information.

This incident took place at the local fair. Sean, a man I knew from a nearby village, was selling sheep at the fair of the village in which I lived. Here I was the local resident and Sean was the outsider. When I saw him I went over and began a conversation on some pretext. A sheep buyer then came up and I was delighted at the opportunity to witness the proceedings firsthand. To my dismay, rather than devoting his attention to the buyer, Sean turned to me and began a conversation in Gaelic with "You remember that Gaelic proverb I quoted to you the other day?" He then went on to explain in excruciating detail the "meaning" of this essentially meaningless utterance which, as he had pointed out on the former occasion, was rather nonsensical. Sean knew perfectly well that my Gaelic was quite limited and that, while I could follow a conversation about livestock in Gaelic, I could not manage the nuances of literary allusions.

Sean stood there solemnly expounding while I frantically tried to think of some way of interrupting him (perhaps he had not seen), and to turn his attention to the buyer. He would not be interrupted and he ignored my astonished gaze. The buyer casually inquired of an employee of Sean what Sean might be thinking of asking for his animals. The employee shrugged his ignorance, then interrupted Sean who replied very offhandedly and launched once more into his "explanation." The employee again interrupted to say that another price had been offered; Sean considered it, then shook his head and turned back to me with, "About that health bill . . ." Not having made such an inquiry I was bewildered by his conduct and unable to understand why someone who had come to town intending to sell his sheep should display so little interest in a prospective sale. The buyer moved on and my friend's conversation became less intense while I stood by feeling slightly guilty about my part in the proceedings. Another buyer approached and I was about to depart when Sean, who had been standing quietly gazing into the middle distance, suddenly began, "There's another interesting Gaelic proverb . . ."

The entire scene was then repeated but this time brought to a successful commercial conclusion after several offers and counteroffers, made through the haze of our very intense conversation. I no longer felt guilty, and my suspicions about having been an accomplice were confirmed when, from a safe distance, I watched the entire scene reenacted with different players. Selling animals, like fighting, is a ritualized activity, and the more indifference the seller displays, the better the performance is considered. The we/they distinctions become quite apparent when a "foreign" buyer appears and, in this case, the distinction between the locals and the outsiders was underlined by a discussion conducted in Gaelic (by "us") and bargaining conducted in English (with "them"). As part of the process of neutralizing my presence and guaranteeing that my loyalties remained with the locality I was never allowed to stand by innocently when buyers approached. If a buyer spoke to me directly, as often happened, I was introduced as a relative or, if the seller were single, as a girlfriend.

Such are the dynamics of group formation in a small-scale community. One's position — physical, as well as mental — at any given moment depends on the event, on kinship ties, or residence affiliations. In a society in which affiliations are known to all and few secrets are kept for long, there can be no innocent bystanders.

Allied with my preconceptions about bystanding was my conviction that I could remain aloof from the area's gossip network. Before I could understand the functions of gossip in the region I had to give up the idea that gossip was necessarily a malevolent habit and one that I, as an anthropologist, ought not to practice. With "bystanding" I had quickly come to terms with the expectations of others; with gossip I confronted a major dilemma about those expectations, for they could have jeopardized my research.

My interviews were proceeding smoothly and I was getting good information in all but a few areas. I could not get informants to talk about livestock sales, however, and I was being offered information I did not want. When I inquired about fairs or marts or other ways of selling animals, I was told about the anticlericalism of some families, insanity in others, or the political activities of the neighbors. Not only was this information irrelevant; most of it was concerned with events that had taken place fifty years before. When informants — probably in exasperation — began pointing out what they knew of my activities, I made the appropriate connections between the gossip network, the irrelevant anecdotes, and their expectations of me.

The following conversation, condensed from several recorded early in my fieldwork, illustrates some of the difficulties. My informant and I began from the same premise: I wanted to know what he thought about the price of cattle at fairs and at marts, and he, knowing full well that I attended all the fairs and marts in the region, wanted to know what I thought about the price of cattle. As I refused to give answers to his subtle queries he refused to give answers to my straightforward demands for information, but his refusals are phrased as contradictions or irrelevant anecdotes, not as abrupt denials of knowledge.

> Informant: I understand there's no price in cattle at all these days.
>
> E.S.:   You may be right. What do they say about prices?
>
> Informant: They say the price of cattle at the Dunkineely mart yesterday was poor altogether.
>
> E.S.:   Did someone from around here go to the mart then?
>
> Informant: Ah, there's no one in this townland that goes to the marts at all.
>
> E.S.:   Where do they sell their cattle?
>
> Informant: Oh, well, they sell them all ways: at the fair, the marts, or on the farm . . . [a fifteen-minute discourse on the way cattle were sold by the informant's father, grandfather, and all his neighbors' ancestors] but I hear there's more price in the cattle sold at the mart.
>
> E.S.:   Have you ever sold at the mart?
>
> Informant: I have not but my brother in the house below [next door] has.
>
> E.S.:   And did he get a good price for his animals?
>
> Informant.   He did not. They've warbles . . . [a twenty-minute digression on warbles — a parasite that makes cowhides resemble sieves — and on government policy, agricultural inspectors, the North, and other topics].
>
> E.S.:   I thought you said no one here went to the marts.
>
> Informant.:   Right enough; we'd not go near them after what happened to my brother there. My nephew above, though, says that he might take his white bullocks to the next Dunkineely mart if the prices hold.

The contradictions in this conversation resulted from my informant's wish that I tell him about the Dunkineely mart I had attended the day before. My refusal to do so resulted from my fear that, since knowledge of mart prices might influence his decisions, I should not discuss them and interfere with the normal information exchanges. The conflict led to a near standoff.

As a result of many conversations like this one I learned the rules of gossip. First, those privileged to travel are obliged to provide information about what they have seen. Second, it is unnecessary for outsiders to provide names; recounting incidents will suffice (and it is likely that the local people already know who was involved). Third, some information exchange is vital to the process of interacting with informants, but this need not be important information. Fourth, most people hear the same stories several times, and usually compare notes on the versions they have heard (there is very little exaggeration). Finally, there are few secrets, although most people are secretive about their own activities.

Once I understood the rules I was able to play the game. As an anthropologist studying ways of selling livestock I did not want to bring information to those I was studying; I wanted to learn about their sources of information, not be one of the sources myself. The solution I chose was simple: when I attended a fair or mart in the northern part of the region I avoided visiting people in northern parts in the days following the event. I went instead to visit those who lived in the southern parts. This may have hampered my research because I could not collect impressions of an event from an informant before those impressions had been clarified by many visitors, but it kept me out of awkward situations with informants who believed it was their right to know what I had seen. When I did go back to the northern region, information about the fair or mart had been printed in the local papers and those who had attended had already passed judgment. I could then discuss the event without difficulties.

By resigning myself to the necessity of engaging in some gossip and by monitoring the information I gave, I could be reasonably sure of getting good information about fairs, marts, and on-farm sales. I was very careful not to give information that would not be available in the local papers within the week, and I never gave information about individuals who had attended the fairs or the price their animals had brought.

This solution was a satisfactory one; once I expressed willingness to discuss a fair or mart my informants could discuss with me what they had heard about the event: who was supposed to have received a fabulous price for his animals, and who returned home disappointed. If pressed for information about specific individuals I always replied with a general range of prices. If pressed further I put my fulsome and hard-won knowledge of the art of digression to work and talked on and on about whatever came to mind.

Personal gossip about people I knew was harder to handle; I decided to relay information about illness, deaths, formal, scheduled events at political meetings, and visitors — once again subjects the newspapers would cover. Statements to do with someone's reputation — who was beating his wife, who was thrown out of which pub — I omitted from my conversation, with two exceptions.

In the village where I lived, there were two people who were much discussed. One was the village drunk, whose antics were well known to all. Among the more outrageous antics were two especially interesting incidents: when the interior of the bank was being painted and the furniture had been removed and placed outside on the central square of the town, the village drunk proceeded to try to sell the bank furniture to the passersby. He had almost succeeded in selling a desk to a woman from Northern Ireland and just before they agreed on a price the negotiations were halted by one of the painters. The lady bought the village drunk a drink at the nearest pub anyway. Another time he rented a bulldozer for a day and instructed the driver to begin excavations for a swimming pool he wanted installed. This activity came to an end when a neighbor pointed out to the bulldozer operator that the village drunk did not own the land he had ordered plowed up. Because I lived only three doors away from him I could not deny knowledge of his activities, nor did I attempt to.

The other person was an elderly American woman who, among other eccentricities, had the habit of stopping people in the streets and engaging them in conversations that often lasted as much as four hours. So long as her targets were unsuspecting visitors, no one minded; however, anyone who came to the village with some purpose in mind dreaded meeting her. Her appearance in the village square cleared the streets faster than any natural disaster would have.

Because she was an American and understood the "body language" signals that indicate the end of a conversation, I was rather adept at getting rid of her, an ability that was widely admired. On occasion I helped others to get rid of her, much to their relief, and most people were very curious to know what I thought of her. Thus her name arose in many conversations, and her entrapment of a well-dressed visitor from the North of Ireland, accompanied by one of the regular "heart attacks" she had when she sensed that the attention of her victim was waning, provoked a good deal of hilarity.

Interestingly, the priest was the only other person in the village who could get rid of this lady smoothly and without fuss. Despite her senility she did understand that some people, among them the priest, had to be on their way, but most of the local people had no defenses against her endless, rambling conversations and they stood helplessly by, sometimes for several hours. If the Irish have nonverbal signals or other means of ending conversations, I never learned them — and neither did she, after 20 years of residence in the village.

I believed it was safe to discuss the activities of these two people because they were well known and because neither excessive drinking nor senility had anything to do with my research objectives. I did not initiate conversations about them; I did supply details of the latest anecdotes, if asked.

Personal gossip about individuals is difficult to handle in any field situation; rumors are widely circulated without the aid of an anthropologist. My impression was that information about fair prices traveled faster than gossip about individuals; I was able to document that the fair-prices information traveled further. Informants who had never visited the village in which I lived always knew a great deal about the monthly fair held there (information beyond that contained in the newspapers), though they might not know the village drunk or the (other) resident "Yank."

My unwillingness to engage in scurrilous gossip or to give information about the activities of others probably helped make me "trustworthy," and once my position was clear, informants volunteered recent anecdotes and a great deal of evaluative commentary about people I knew well. I concluded that there were two kinds of gossip, the first benign and the second malevolent. Benign gossip involves the exchange of information; in much the same way that American students exchange information about movies, restaurants, or college professors, the Irish exchange information about prices, crops, or other people's livestock. Benign gossip is evaluative in its function, and everyone is expected to engage in it. Malevolent gossip, too, is evaluative but its focus is on other people's social activities and many people are excluded from the "knowledge" that it brings. Malevolent gossip seems to me to function to evaluate the activities of those who violate the moral rules of the community, and while specific rumors may be groundless, those who are talked about usually are deviant in some readily observable way.

Contrary to American notions, a surprising amount of malevolent gossip is either accurate, or distorted in a predictable fashion. In Donegal the distortions are most often in the direction, not of exaggeration, but of sexual fantasy.

One man in my sample was widely disliked by his neighbors. He was an upstanding member of the community, very hard working, and had made a substantial profit from his endeavors. He was, however, rather neurotic about time; he insisted his employees arrive for work on time, and he had fired many of the young men in the vicinity because of their failure to be punctual, a failing that most people would not have noticed or taken seriously. In his surroundings he was nearly a complete misfit; his dour temperament and his perfectionism caused him to be isolated from the society in which he lived. In addition to being a Protestant (a "fault" the people of Southwest Donegal tolerate), he had one other failing that may have incited the animosity of his neighbors: his wife adored him.

Irish men treat their wives much like American men treat their mothers — cautiously, respectfully, and often with considerable ambivalence. Mothers in Donegal are treated like Americans treat their girlfriends or wives — affectionately, and as friends or confidantes. A wife who openly adores her husband provokes comment, and the comment most often made about this uxorious man was that he had only one testicle.

I do not know (nor do I believe that my informants knew) whether this man in fact had only one testicle. I suspect that if he had been of a different temperament his wife's adoration might have made him a figure of fun but not the target of malevolent rumors.

Malignant gossip seems to function to warn others about the possible deviance of some members of the community; in this way members of the community who are in any way "outstanding" may be prevented from realizing whatever ambitions they might have. By his own account the man "with one testicle" had tried and failed to enlist the aid of his neighbors, even though he was willing to pay for it. Much of the anthropological literature dealing with gossip focuses on the motives of those who start malevolent rumors, and little attention is paid to the social outcome of the rumors, that is, to the isolation or potential isolation of those who are the targets of the rumors. Malignant gossip serves as a form of social control; "what the neighbors think" is thus very important.

Before I could learn the Irish rules for gossiping and bystanding I had to give up my preconceptions about those activities. In doing so I learned a good deal about the informal workings of the social realm in which my informants lived. Little was told to me in so many words, for the Irish "teach" by example: recalcitrant children and bemused anthropologists will have the lessons repeated over and over until they are grasped.

APPENDIX B

Interview Schedule — Livestock

Interview date, time, special circumstances

Name of respondent

Townland

Post office

Family members present in household; approximate ages

Family or other household members — not in household at time
of interview

Approximate farm size

Dispersed acreage or altogether?

Other holdings or conacre land?

Rights in commonage?

Other, e.g., land worked for relatives.

Do you have a specific allocation for commonage or can you graze
as many animals as you choose?

Types of land and approximate acreage.

Yearly cycle:	Tillage	Pasture	Commonage
February			
March			
April			
May			
June			
July			
August			
September			
October			
November			
December			
January			

How many animals per acre?

Sheep
Cattle
Pigs
other

Labor force. How many people are required daily to look after your animals?

Are there special times when more people are required? When, how many?

Are there occasions when you and other members of your household help others? When, how many? Which friends (relatives), which neighbors?

Interview date _____

Livestock Sales

How do you sell animals?
Fair (which, how many?)
Mart (which, how many?)
Buyers (on farm; which, how many?)

Which method of sale do you like best? Why?

Do you attend fairs
_____ regularly, i.e., once a month
_____ often, once every three months
_____ only when you have animals to sell?

Can you tell what the value of each animal is likely to be
before you take it to the fair/mart?
_____ within 5 shillings
_____ within 5 pounds

How do you decide when to sell an animal?

How do you decide what an animal is worth? what about
the animal tells you its value — its weight, build,
market conditions (list in order of importance).

Special precautions when selling animals?

You prefer to sell your animals at _____ or at _____.
Do you think you get a better price for them than you
would if you sold them at _____? Why?

Special conditions relating to selling.
Respondent

Observer

Do you ever sell animals to neighbors?

      to friends?

Animal Disease   Interview date _____

    Of the common diseases in livestock, which are presently the biggest problem for you?

	Cattle	Sheep	Pigs	Chickens
1.				
2.				
3.				
4.				
5.				
6.				
7.				
8.				
9.				
10.				

Do you know which were the biggest problems in the past, say for your father or grandfather?

	Cattle	Sheep	Pigs	Chickens
1.				
2.				
3.				
4.				
5.				

Diseases:	Current Method of treatment	Past Method of treatment

Animal Disease   SHEEP

Louping Ill

Head staggers

Dullnamollog

Footrot

Galornagcat

Black leg

Braxy

Wool ball

Pains

Sheep   _____

Date   _____

How many per acre?

Does this vary at different times of the year?

How are they rotated?

What is the minimum number of sheep required to make any sort of profit from keeping them?

What is the maximum number of sheep a man might look after by himself?

   Two men?

Which diseases were the cause of most losses for your father or grandfather?

   In cattle?

   In sheep?

Causes of most losses for yourself?

   Cattle?

Have you in the past maintained different types of animals, e.g., more cattle and fewer sheep or vice versa than you do now?

   What made you decide to change?

How do you decide what an animal is worth?

   What do you use to judge the value of a ewe lamb?

   Wether?
   Ewe?
   Ram?

How much would it cost you to produce a ewe or wether lamb?

A ewe?
A ram?

How many sets of twins, say from 100 ewes mated?

Mortality rates: Wethers   Hoggets   Rams
Ewes

Which of these animals is most likely to survive a bad winter?

When are ewes put with the ram?

Do you give the ewes any extra feeding beforehand, do anything
    special for them?

Are rams raddled?

Do you make any special effort to feed the ewes that have twins?

Do you ever cull sheep?   Why?

What is the reproductive span of a ewe?
    At what age is she first bred?

What would you believe would be the best way to approach
    problems of economic development in the area with respect
    to cattle?

    to sheep?

How do you feel about the present structure of subsidies paid for
    cattle?

    for sheep?

Principal grazing locations

Type of sheep	Period Pasture	Hill or rough grazing	Commonage
Ewes			
Lambs			
Hoggets			
Wethers			
Rams			

Animal Health

Braxy

Louping ill

Pulpy kidney

Swayback

Fluke

Tick pyaemia

Galornagcat

Dullnamollog

Orf

Head staggers

Foxes

Subsidy

Cattle   _____

Date   _____

A. Breeding Preferences

1. Which animals do you prefer to keep, beef or dairy or mixed type?

2. Which do you actually keep?

    Why?

3. How do you choose — by weight gain, ability to withstand climatic rigors, by breed standard or . . .?

4. Which breed is best for milk?

5. Which breed is best for beef?

6. Which breed winters best?

    In versus out-wintered stock?

7. How many calves/cows/y.o.'s can one man care for?

    Can 2 men care for?
8. Is there a difference between heifers and bullocks in terms of hardiness?

9. Where does calving take place?

    Outside?

    Inside?

10. Do you get calves with birth defects often?

11. How long between calving and a new pregnancy?

12. At what age does a heifer come to the bull?

13. At what age do you sell off surplus animals?

During which season?

14. Where do these go?

How sold?

Where?

15. Would you prefer to have several light animals or a few heavy ones?

16. Is milk for the house or for the calf the most important consideration?

II. Labor, Production

1. How much time does it take daily to feed and care for the stock you keep?

2. Have you any idea what it costs (including vet. fees, feeding, etc.) to produce:

a milk cow

y.o. bullock

y.o. heifer

other

3. How many acres per cow? Do they still reckon a farm as being a "place of _____ cows" or whatever?

4. What sort of land do you have around here?

5. How much treatment with fertilizers, etc., does the land require?

6. During what months do animals require supplementary feeding?

7. Do bulls and heifers gain at different rates or about the same?

8. How much will a calf weigh at birth?

   At 3 mos.?

   At 6 mos.?

   At 1 year?

   At 2 years?

9. In producing hay or oats, how much help do you need to produce enough for all your stock?

10. How many hours/days are necessary for various operations involved in saving the hay?

11. At which points do you need extra help?

    How much?

    Who?

    Do you usually pay these people?

12. How much manure does a cow produce over a year? Does this fill most needs?

13. Who does the milking?

    The cleaning up?

14. How do you feel about subsidies paid for cattle at the present time?

    Could anything be done to improve this setup?

15. What would you believe would be the best way to approach
     the problem of economic development in the area?

     As far as cattle are concerned?

16. Do you think the area could keep more cattle?

     By what means?

APPENDIX C

Animal Husbandry and Health

Livestock production in Southwest Donegal involves four primary
factors: nutrition, parasites, disease, and husbandry practices.
Given proper nutrition, animals can withstand all but a few of
the diseases and parasites in the environment. Lacking appropriate
nutrition, they will be subject not only to diseases and parasites
but more prone to accidents and predators as well. In sheep, the
primary cause of loss is malnutrition, though its role is not always
recognized and the immediate precipitating factor may be taken
as cause instead. Lamb losses may be as high as 40 percent in a
bad year or 30 percent in a good one, while calf mortality never
goes above 5 percent, the lowest mortality rate in the whole of
Ireland (W.D.R.S., Vol. 2 and A.F.T. Rural Economy Division
Report, Series No. 13:26).
A major concomitant of nutrition is land use, and here the
distinctions between cattle and sheep are clear. Cattle are kept in
byres and fed on hay from November or December until May.
They are kept up at night by most farmers throughout the year
and are often given supplementary feeding at this time. (The
greater the proportion of unfenced land, the greater is the tendency
to keep cattle up at night; the animals are not being protected
from predators but from accidental injury.)
Cattle are the first beneficiaries of the rich "aftergrass," grass
remaining or growing after the hay has been cut. In most cases,
they are the only beneficiaries of the hay. The West Donegal
Resource Survey Workers analyzed the nutritional content of a
series of random samples; the official findings indicated that the
hay was substandard.

> Analyses of some 250 samples of hay, taken at random in the
> area, showed a crude protein range from 5 to 15.5 per cent in
> the dry matter with a mean value around 9 per cent. This hay
> would have a starch equivalent value of approximately 37 on a
> dry matter basis. As most of the hay comes from old meadows
> and is harvested late in the season the digestibility is low
> (W.D.R.S. Vol. 2:57).

This standard is hotly contested by most farmers: as one of my
informants put it, "We've heard about poor quality hay since

these people started coming here and maybe it is poor compared
to what they can make in other parts of the country. But what
they don't seem to understand is that the problem here is not
between poor quality hay and a slightly better quality; it is between
poor quality hay and none at all, as often as not, given our
weather." The speaker is one of the few farmers in the area who
owns his own tractor and he is therefore much less dependent on
external aid than most farmers. He still makes (and in good years,
sells) hay in the traditional way and sees the alternatives to this
as undesirable or risky, mainly the latter.

Quality of feed, then, is a relative matter but for some animals
it is more relative than for others. For cattle, it is relative to the
year's weather. At present, no matter how bad the year, some hay
will be saved but this has not always the been the case. In the
years before the advent of modern machinery, the hay crop was
sometimes destroyed, resulting in direct damage to cattle and
indirect damage to the human population which relied on cattle
products for sustenance. For cattle, therefore, nutrition is relative
to the many factors involved in hay production; in a good year,
this will be moderately good, and in a bad year, moderately bad.
For sheep, the relativity of the factors can be more devastating
since their sustenance depends almost entirely on the climate in
a given year.

For a more precise rendering of information on livestock
feeding, a random sample of hay was taken, as mentioned above,
and the averages estimated as follows. Assuming that purchased
feed is used, and that the average purchased per farm is 11.9 cwt
per annum, the feed reserves for livestock would be:

3.3 acres of hay @35 cwt DM/acre	
@37 per cent starch equiv.	= 4,786
0.3 acres oats @25 cwt DM/acre	
@60 per cent starch equiv.	= 504
11.9 cwt purchased concentrates	
@72 per cent starch equiv.	= 960
	6,250

Given approximately 5.4 livestock units wintered (an average
based on a sample of 250 farms of varying sizes and land types)
and a 150-day winter, the available feed would be distributed as
follows:

Maintenance @7 lb. starch equivalent/day/livestock unit   5,670
Balance for production (6,250-5,670)   580
Expected liveweight gain @2.25 lb. starch equivalent/lb gain
0.3/day. (W.D.R.S. *ibid*).

The report indicates further that, "The feed available, therefore, is sufficient for maintenance and small weight gains in the animals wintered "(*ibid.*). The survey goes on to point out that the above figures belong to cattle farms only; for cattle and sheep farms the figures would be:

4.4 acres of hay @35 cwt DM/acre
  @37 per cent starch equivalent   6,382
0.3 acres of oats @25 cwt DM/acre
  @60 per cent starch equivalent   504
16 cwt purchased concentrates
  #72 per cent starch equivalent   1,290
                        8,176

For the same number of cattle (5.4 livestock units) over the same period (150-day winter), the feed might be distributed in this way:

Maintenance of 5.4 l.u. of cattle @7 lb. starch
  equivalent/day/l.u.   5,670
Balance for production   2,506
                        = 3.1 per l.u./day
Expected liveweight gain @2.25 lb starch equivalent/lb gain = 1.4 lb/day

> This level of winter nutrition is more than adequate for the minimum nutritional requirements of dry cattle including dry cows and is almost sufficient for moderate fattening of dry stock. If the sheep on these farms were fed from the same reserves, then the nutritional requirements of the total live-stock would not be adequately satisfied. From the information available, the sheep in this area do not get supplementary winter feed in any form. Instead they are required to graze the hills during the winter (W.D.R.S. Vol. 2:61).

There is little one can add to these findings. The system as it stands is producing adequately for the cattle, as is borne out by the calf mortality statistics. It is not producing hay for the sheep, nor are other forms of feeding being used.

The other variable involved in nutrition, one which is not taken up in the W.D.R.S., is the kind of land available. For obvious reasons this is more important in the case of sheep than for cattle. A survey of my sample members indicates the relationships between the type of land available and the feeding practices. I asked each sample member to estimate his losses, were he to begin with 100 lambs. There is a clear correlation between these estimates and the sample characteristics and surprisingly, even feeding over the winter does not have the dramatic effect one would suppose it should. The only good correlation I found is between soil type and losses:

% of loss	Soil Type — Feeding	No.
1-2	Mineral-Regular Supp. Feeding	1
9 or less	Organic & Mineral-Casual Feeding	2
10 or less	Organic & Mineral-Regular Supp.	1
15	Gley & Organic Mineral-Casual	3
15-20	Reclaimed Peat & Mt. Peat-Regular Supp.	2
20	Reclaimed Peat & Hill Peats-Casual	2
25-30	Mt. Peat & Lowland Organic Mineral — No Feeding	1
30-35	Mt. Peats & Lowland Reclaimed Peats — No Feeding	2
35-40	Mt. Peats-No Feeding	2
		16

There are other factors involved in this correlation: rough, unfenced mountain pastures are common to all those with the highest loss estimates (25-40 per cent). Those who estimate their losses at 20 per cent or less have partially or completely fenced land and some good hill grazing. Those whose losses are 10 per cent or less have lowland pastures and the sheep are fed supplementary concentrates during some winters at least, or parts of winter.

There is experimental evidence to bear out what I have said about the influence of this factor. Further south, in Glenamoy, where experiments were performed on the feeding of ewes, the results show a rather undramatic change in losses. The lambing percentage of ewes fed on concentrates through the winter was 84.1, and the control group lambing percentage was 82.2 per cent. The percentage of lambs weaned was 82.5 with the ewes that were fed, and the percentage weaned in the control group was 76.4. That is to say that mortality decreased only by 6 per cent where ewes were regularly fed and all other conditions were held equal (Michael O'Toole, personal communication).

At Glenamoy, one of the government's most elaborate experimental stations, there is a saying which makes the rounds. The local farmers say of the sheep experiments that, "the government puts everything in and takes nothing out; we put damn all (very little or nothing) in and take everything out." As it happens, this may be an accurate assessment and it probably illustrates the advantage of being a peasant with a long-standing tradition from which to work. All the factors have been experimentally sorted out in ages past, and all the mistakes have been made. While each generation may be free to make new mistakes of its own, certain things are taken for granted and a production strategy which permits "everything" (an overstatement) to be taken out will be retained until a new strategy can be demonstrated to be better. Thus far, for the people of Southwest Donegal, none has been. Cattle are fed over the winter and sheep are not; it is that simple for most farmers. One would have to be "daft" to think otherwise, though of course most are aware that feeding would increase survival rates in lambs.

Given these findings, it does not seem unreasonable to suggest that a long time ago, the farmers learned that feeding the sheep regularly would reduce the hardiness of cattle population and that this had direct consequences for the human population. Left to themselves, some of the sheep would survive, but to feed them all would be to risk the family's livelihood and this risk is too great. The principle seems to them so obvious that it requires no comment, but its expression can seem bizarre to an untutored outsider.

One such expression appears in the legal code. During my stay, charges were brought by the County against a man who had been left in charge of a relative's cattle over the winter. The man was charged with cruelty to animals because he had allowed the cattle in his care to roam freely until the neighbors complained, whereupon he confined the herd to a field without adequate provision for feed. Several of the animals died and went unburied; the rest were found in an emaciated state by a County official, some so far debilitated that they had to be destroyed. The punishment for this offense was quite severe, and involved a heavy fine and suspended prison sentence. The judge expressed indignation at this treatment of animals and noted with some relief that it seldom happened in the County and that such a case had never come before him. It struck no one as odd that what was defined as cruel and unusual treatment for cattle is exactly that which is accorded to sheep every winter.

The varied treatment accorded sheep and cattle nutritionally is carried over to animal health measures as well. I mentioned earlier that the calf mortality rate in Donegal was the lowest in all Ireland; it is evident that the lamb mortality rate is one of the highest in

Ireland. According to the West Donegal Resource Survey, "In the more exposed areas cattle are often housed for six months of the year and frequently the only winter feed is poor quality hay. Nevertheless the health of the cattle which are indigenous to the area appears to be no worse than the norm for the country." (WDRS Vol. 2:63). The most important health problems for cattle are: 1) parasitic infestation; 2) mineral deficiencies; and, 3) bacterial diseases.

Of the parasites, liver fluke is most prevalent. All of my informants dosed for it regularly, and most were aware that improved pasture, especially peat soils, would aggravate the problem. Several mentioned that fluke could never be eliminated and that their precautions merely kept it under control.

A few informants were knowledgeable about other internal parasites such as roundworms, largely, I believe, because they read the worm medicine bottles very carefully, and noted that the medication was intended to destroy fluke and roundworms. Most, however, were not aware that roundworms could and often did cause economic loss. Hoose or lung worm infection was not recognized as a common parasite, despite its presence in the region. Most informants believed that it was treated for with the same medicine they used for fluke and roundworms.

Eleven informants reported that they regularly treated animals for roundworm (usually along with fluke dosing), and seven of these were convinced that the same treatment applied to lungworms, an erroneous conviction since lungworms are treated with injections. Five reported no incidence of roundworms and seven said the same of lungworms.

Dosing for fluke is commonplace but, according to the government reports, the dosage given is inadequate or too infrequent. The usual response to my question on dosing was, twice a year in spring and autumn. The government recommends dosing at least three times — "in October, December and April or May." (*An Roinn Talmhaiochta Agus Iascaigh* No. 138:4) No one reported this schedule to me, though several replied that they dosed for fluke all year round or according to the laboratory reports on dung samples. The most common response in the case of an animal which seems to be "low" is to dose it for fluke, providing there are no recognizable symptoms of any other disease. Since cattle are carefully watched, most owners would quickly become aware of the problem, should an animal fail to thrive or stop putting on weight. Insofar as inadequate dosing is concerned, I can only say that on those occasions when I participated in dosing, great caution was taken as to amount, and it was explained to me that overdosing might cause as much harm as the parasites. Even the standard dose seems to put animals off their food temporarily and an overdose could have serious side effects. Many informants explained, however, that the standard dose indicated on the label for a lactating cow, for example, would be too much since cattle in the area were smaller than most in the British Isles. I did not participate in this downward adjustment of doses but I was told that three-quarters of the 'normal' dose was usually enough for the smaller Donegal cattle.

Several kinds of mineral deficiencies occur in the area. Copper deficiency and cobalt deficiency ("swayback" and "pine") were unrecognized as such by only a few farmers but most reported no incidence of these deficiencies. In the few cases where a disease was diagnosed by the veterinarian, the farmers dosed their animals regularly thereafter and there had been no recurrence. I suspect that the incidence of these diseases is also lowered by the practice of feeding supplementary meals and calf nuts to cattle, since they usually contain trace minerals (as do salt licks). Once more, because cattle are cared for so assiduously, a deficiency disease will be recognized in its early stages and not allowed to progress much beyond the first symptoms.

The most serious deficiency disease in the area resulted from a lack of phosphorus. The Gaelic term for this was *crupan*, and it is my impression that this is the only deficiency disease for which there is a Gaelic term. Seventeenth century writers report *crupan* as a serious problem, as did most of my older informants. It has not been in evidence for many years, except in some few instances and areas, because of the use of artificial fertilizers. Three informants reported that they treated their cattle for it, and one reported that it was only an occasional problem. All of the members of my sample were aware that artificial fertilizers would cure the disease but, curiously, the veterinarian was amazed when I told him of this connection. The old cure for *crupan* was to transfer animals to a different — usually higher — pasture. Many informants were unaware of the cause or the reason for the cure; they simply knew that fertilizers took care of the problem. I never saw a case of it and the veterinarian reported that he had not seen one for several years. Its former widespread incidence was attested, however, by many of the women I spoke with because one of the symptoms is a depraved appetite and they recalled seeing cows devouring clothes off the line.

Not quite in the category of deficiency diseases since its origins are unclear is grass tetany or hypomagnasaemia. It is thought to result from a low magnesium level brought on by an imbalance in intake of other minerals. Animals which develop this disease often die rapidly and a very few informants reported having lost an animal with it. Only three sample members had treated animals for it and four others reported that they had had animals afflicted with it.

Bacterial diseases are not as much a problem in Southwest Donegal as in other parts of Ireland. Careful husbandry and small-scale production undoubtedly account for this; tuberculosis was eradicated in the region with ease in 1963, while it continued to present serious health hazards in the south up until 1966. Disease eradication programs are commonly begun in Donegal as a matter of policy.

Dysentery, trichomoniasis (a venereal disease) and ketosis are virtually unknown; mastitis, the plague of dairying areas, is rare but may be on the increase.

Scours, particularly in calves, were reported by six informants and cures ranged from home remedies to veterinary treatment with the emphasis on the former. Boiled water is one common cure, a remedy which indicates that scours are probably not a serious problem.

Two bacterial diseases account for most of the reported instances — blackleg and redwater. Blackleg was known to three informants from personal experience and redwater (*murrain*) was widely known and dreaded. Redwater is an especially virulent disease transmitted by cattle ticks and in Donegal it seems to occur only in "bought-in" cattle. Seven of my informants reported having lost cattle from it, and all these animals had been recently purchased. The West Donegal Resource Survey comments on this, "Cattle introduced into the area or transferred over a considerable distance within the area show acute symptoms of redwater. This is a good example of immunity in an indigenous cattle population" (Vol. 2:68). My informants disagree; animals brought from short distances are susceptible, they maintain. No one attributes this to ticks or to specific and highly localized immunities, I should add. It is one of the many dangers of transferring animals, and an especially inexplicable one since wasting and death are very rapid. In every reported case of redwater, however, I was able to establish that the animal had come from the immediate area (within a radius of fifteen miles) and had not been transferred over long distances.

The occurrence of redwater in conjuction with the transfer of animals raises an interesting point about folk beliefs associated with cattle. Transferring animals carries a certain hazard due to natural factors, e.g., diseases such as redwater in cattle or a change of diet in sheep. It was several times reported to me — always as a joke — that "some" people sprinkled "Protestant" cows with holy water after transfer, as a precaution. The danger associated with transfer was thus neutralized by ritual means.

Another of the dangers of transfer is that the animals will be seen by someone with the evil eye. Opinions about this vary but the evil eye seems to be held responsible for the unexplained dangers to which animals are susceptible. Cattle run wild (often due to warble fly attack) or fall into drains (ditches) for no apparent reason; sheep are found dead and the cause cannot be diagnosed. Before veterinary services were widely available, these events must have been explained by reference to supernatural agents and traces of these beliefs still linger. There are, after all, inexplicable accidents and strange afflictions even now, especially insofar as cattle are concerned.

One man was reputed to have the evil eye and his actions were widely discussed. Some people doubted that there was such a phenomenon; others seemed skeptical but remained cautious in the sense that they would identify others' cattle as their own if he inquired at a fair. A very few maintained that they refused to have anything to do with him and even these were careful to point out that he was not responsible for this power, that it was a faculty given at birth and perhaps inherited through the female line.

Data on this subject was difficult to gather and I do not know whether there was more than one man so endowed in the region. Knowledge of this man's possession of the evil eye was common in the glen (valley) in which he lived but outside it no one admitted to knowledge of the evil eye or its powers. Because the glen in which he lived was not a Gaelic-speaking area, I wonder how widespread this belief actually is. My Gaelic-speaking informants denied all knowledge of such a concept, while freely discussing spirits which wander through the bogs at night carrying torches and other supernatural phenomena not authorized by the Church.

Church doctrine may be important here. I was told (and Irish stories often mention) that priests used to make emergency calls to dispel the evil eye, but the clergy no longer honors such requests. The increase in veterinary services available may have something to do with the decline of the belief.

The man with the evil eye was a native, living in the house in which he was born and, like most of his neighbors, engaged in farming. He was a pleasant, innocuous-seeming person with no very striking physical characteristics or unusual habits. Although he was described to me as "always looking", I was unable to discern any extraordinary alertness in his demeanor. He was said to display avid curiosity about other people's livestock and to be relatively unsuccessful in his own livestock ventures. This curiosity may have set him apart for, as I learned, any unusual display of interest may be regarded with disdain. It was not until I knew most of my informants well that they volunteered to show me their livestock and even then they were not motivated by pride (as would be the case amongst American farmers, cf. Bennett 1969) but simply wished an outsider's opinion on the value of an animal or its condition.

In only one respect was the possessor of the evil eye unusual outwardly; he had for some years past supplemented his meager farm income by acting as a tourist guide for visiting fishermen, a job that was said to have paid very well. This may have earned him the enmity of his neighbors. His father was said to have been a good farmer, well-liked by his neighbors; his mother elicited little comment, favorable or unfavorable, though there seemed to be some reticence on this subject.

The evil eye and the ritual precautions taken to insure the safety of a newly-bought animal are two manifestations of "magical" beliefs associated with cattle; there is a third, a disease which is common to both men and cattle. Once again, none of my informants had actually participated in the cures for this; they were simply reporting what they had been told. Ringworm is common in cattle and is easily transmitted to humans. Most people believe that doctors have no effective cure for this disease and they consult folk "specialists" whose cure consists mostly of reading certain pages of the Bible in a prescribed order, odd prayers, and the like. Several informants named people who had undergone this treatment and who were now free of the disease. Local healers had formerly been available but at the present time all known healers lived out of the County.

There is one more "parasite" which afflicts cattle, though it does not feed directly on them. In spring and summer, the warble fly lays its eggs on the hair covering the lower parts of an animal's body. The eggs hatch and the larvae begin boring their way into the skin, eventually settling on the animal's back, where they pierce breathing holes. Upon reaching maturity, they force their way out of these breathing holes, damaging the hides irreparably.

This pest causes thousands of pounds worth of damage to hides each year and, while this is not generally known in Southwest

Donegal, heavy infestation also reduces milk production considerably. At the present time, animals showing signs of warbles are denied entry into Northern Ireland and in economic terms, this means that an otherwise healthy animal must be sold for a lower price to a local farmer, rather than commanding the full price a buyer from Northern Ireland might be willing to pay. Cattle sold at the mart are inspected prior to auction and warble infestation is reported before the bidding is begun. On several occasions, I have seen a buyer request further warble inspection and if the animal were infested, the price bid would drop ten pounds or more.

The government instituted a campaign to eradicate warbles in 1967 and specified that all animals would be treated at the time of tuberculin testing. Farmers were to pay 10/per head for treatment. When the scheme had been underway for 2 years, the National Farmer's Association protested that the charge per head was too high and asked the government to provide the service free of charge. The program was thus stalemated, for the government made no counter-offer, and mandatory treatment was discontinued. The loss on any animal with warbles might be as high as £15, ten or fifteen times the cost of treatment. Nor is the treatment complicated; it consists merely of pouring a small amount of liquid (derris wash) over the back of the animal.

Curiously, many farmers eschewed both government-supervised and home treatments and preferred to "take their chances", a gamble which must have cost them considerable sums. I estimated that three to four of every ten animals sold at the mart in Dunkineely had warbles while one in twenty sold in the Donegal mart might be so afflicted. I do not know the reasons for this seeming disregard of economic gain, nor do I understand the adamant position taken by the National Farmer's Association. Some farmers in my sample (four) treated their animals voluntarily and all those who customarily sold at the mart did so; others insisted (wrongly) that the campaign to eradicate warble flies had been entirely successful and that there was no need for further treatment. Gaelic-speaking farmers were generally unaware either of the controversy or the problem, a function of a more general lack of communication between Gaelic speakers and the government, but those who spoke English and understood the controversy roundly condemned both parties to the dispute.

Though I do not thoroughly understand the causes of this situation, I should point out that the Dunkineely mart was recently opened and that many farmers were selling there for the first time. It may have been a surprise to them to learn that warble infestation cost money; the contrast with the Donegal mart and my sample members may indicate that there is either a lack of information or a failure to take this information seriously. In any event, I would predict that the incidence of warble flies will diminish rapidly wherever marts are established, government policy and the NFA notwithstanding.

As grazing animals, cattle and sheep share many parasites and mineral deficiencies; animal health practices regarding sheep can be similarly divided into problems of parasites, mineral deficiencies and bacterial diseases but, for the most part, the similarities end there. Apart from malnutrition, a common problem with sheep, there is a range of minor diseases, such as photosensitization and opthalmia, which cause losses in sheep from secondary infection (as in photosensitization) or from accidents due to blindness.

Of the parasites, fluke is most common and is universally treated though the frequency of treatment varies. Three of my informants dosed for fluke once or twice in the year; six dosed twice or three times a year; one dosed four times in the year; five treated animals for fluke "constantly", and one dosed according to dung sample diagnosis. Like cattle, sheep should be dosed three times a year according to the government, but animals which do not seem to be thriving will occasionally be treated for fluke. The difficulty with sheep, of course, is that they often will not be seen to be suffering until the infestation has almost destroyed its host. A further point should be made here — sheep are often found dead in the fields and no cause of death is apparent. It may be the case that some of these deaths are caused by acute fluke (as opposed to the chronic form), in which large numbers of fluke migrate through the bowel wall to the liver. In small numbers, this migration will not be dangerous but if the fluke are present in large numbers, it can be fatal.

Another parasite which affects sheep is the tapeworm, and in its intermediate stage, this creature burrows through to the bloodstream where it may be carried to the brain and spinal cord. In these locations, they develop into cysts (up to two inches in diameter) and produce, by pressure on these organs, the symptoms of gid or head staggers. Two of my informants reported a high incidence of this disease, six reported some cases of it, and of this last group, only two were aware that the tapeworms are carried by dogs. This was the only disease affecting sheep which all my informants agreed should be referred to the veterinarian. Gid is treated with an operation usually performed by the veterinarian, an operation which requires boring a hole in the animal's skull and extracting the tapeworms. A few of my informants practiced this technique, after watching the veterinarian, and all knew about it. The chances of survival following the operation are about fifty-fifty and some people, knowing this, did not bother to have the operation carried out.

These two parasites are the only ones considered to have serious effects on sheep, though two of my informants regularly dosed lambs for worms. Most felt that worm-dosing was unnecessary.

The two major mineral deficiency diseases are pine (cobalt deficiency) and swayback (copper deficiency). Nine informants reported treating animals for cobalt deficiency, and eight treated for copper deficiency. (Some fluke remedies contain these trace elements, a course which the government ought to require by law.) Some informants reported odd cases, usually untreated, of these diseases, and all but one informant knew the symptoms associated with them.

Twin lamb disease or toxaemia is another deficiency disease brought on by the ewe's inability to sustain two lambs, but this is a rare condition doubtless because twins are also rare. Four informants treated against it.

Of the bacterial diseases, braxy is most common and farmers vaccinate against it almost universally. This is an especially virulent disease which kills sheep almost overnight and there is no known cure. The vaccine is highly effective and informants reported that their fathers and grandfathers lost more sheep from this than from any other cause before the vaccine was developed.

Pulpy kidney is a similar (clostridial) disease, fatal and with rapid onset of symptoms. Eight of my informants vaccinated against it regularly and two reported the occasional case of it. Lamb dysentery, another of the clostridial group, is rare but five of my informants treated against it, usually by means of a vaccine which immunized the ewe prior to lambing. Immunization is not passed through the placenta but is conferred by heavy doses of antitoxin in colostrum (Worden *et al.* 1963:580). There is on the market one vaccine which immunizes animals against seven diseases, including all the clostridial group and some that my informants had never heard of. Because it is more expensive than the vaccine against braxy, it is not so commonly used but several of my informants mentioned that they were considering it for the future. A large number of losses from "unknown" causes may be a contributing factor in this decision.

There are two diseases associated with ticks, louping ill and tick pyaemia. The former is a bacterial disease which affects animals of all ages. In past years, there was a vaccine against it but this was taken off the market due to production difficulties or irregularities. In its absence, dips that protect against ticks were recommended and, although these dipping compounds are efficacious and there are few deaths from louping ill now, most of the farmers in my sample expressed their indignation at the withdrawal of the vaccine.

The difference in attitudes toward vaccines and dipping compounds is striking and — apparently — grounded in fact. During one visit to an informant, I was shown a prize ram and I observed that the animal did not seem well. The next morning the ram and several ewes were found dead of braxy and my informant assured me that the sheep had been vaccinated. When I mentioned this to others, I was told that if the animals had indeed been vaccinated, they would not have died of braxy. The cause of death was indisputable, since it was diagnosed by the veterinarian but, I was told, the ram might have been missed during vaccination. On this all informants were agreed and my next visit confirmed their suppositions, for the man's wife remarked that she thought he'd learned a lesson and would vaccinate the sheep next year. Vaccines are as infallible as dipping compounds are fallible, it seems, and this was one of the major conversational topics during my stay.

Every man has his favorite dip, some travelling to Northern Ireland to obtain compounds with ingredients outlawed in the Republic. Several waxed eloquent about the "substandard" product used by the government in the County dipping pits. The margin of error in the dipping compounds may not be entirely at fault since — unlike the vaccines — a great deal of leeway is left for human error. By law, sheep must be dipped twice a year, the first time between June 1st and August 7th, and the second between September 15th and November 30th. This regulation is not always complied with. In addition, there are a number of dipping "styles" and some of these do not comply with the government's recommendations for the length of time animals should be kept in the pit. The official suggestion is one full minute in the tank (*An Roinn Talmhaiochta Agus Iascaigh Leaflet* No. 16) and the actual practice involves a time between thirty and forty-five seconds. It may be that the compound does not adequately penetrate matted wool in this short time or that the mixture is too diluted to be effective.

Whatever the reason, the failure of dipping as a procedure is attested by the high mortality rates in lambs from tick pyaemia, locally known as "pains". Lambs are normally dipped before they go "to the hill" or about a month after birth. Shortly thereafter they may contract "pains" and die. Heavy losses are thus incurred and this is not explained by my speculation above, since lambs at this age have only light 'sweater-like' wool and dips should penetrate this easily. Perhaps the dipping compounds are ineffective (many people believe that a dip which is too strong will do serious harm to a sheep) or that their efficacy is limited to short time spans. The few deaths from louping ill and the many from tick pyaemia render this a bit mysterious.

There remain three diseases which affect sheep, none of them necessarily fatal except through accidents or secondary infection. Orf is the ovine equivalent of ringworm, although it, unlike the latter, is a bacterial disease and it occurs primarily in young sheep and lambs. It is highly contagious among sheep and can be transmitted to human beings. In sheep, it has serious debilitating effects if the animal is unable to eat due to the sores around its mouth. According to the local doctor, there is no medical cure for it in humans but penicillin will clear up the secondary infection. In animals, as with ringworm, the disease will run its course and disappear without medical treatment. Only three of my informants treated animals for it, and two had seen the odd case. The old remedy was rubbing turf soot on the sores, a 'cure' that apparently did no harm. What is interesting about orf is that sheep farmers go to the doctor for treatment if they contract it, and there is no medical cure; there *is* a medical cure for ringworm, yet cattle farmers who develop this seek supernatural cures.

Another factor of interest is that partial immunity to the disease may be acquired through handling sheep. The doctor in Donegal reported that he had never seen a serious case of it, though sheep men did contract it occasionally. (Like ringworm, it is unsightly.) Further south in a government experimental station, two workers caught the disease and became seriously ill, one of them so much so that long hospitalization was required. The two were the only station workers who had no previous experience in handling sheep, a fact which suggests that immunities may be acquired early in life. There is a vaccine which immunizes sheep against orf and some of my sample members were aware of it, though none had used it.

A similar problem — debilitating but not fatal — is photosensitization, though this is not a word which is understood in the area. The local term for this syndrome is "*galornagcat*", the disease of the cat, as it is translated from the Gaelic. This term describes the effects: the sheep's ears wither and drop off, leaving stubs which resemble cats' ears. The connection with sunlight is unrecognized but the more knowledgeable farmers attribute the disease to consumption of a tiny plant called the "sun dew" plant. This disease is an old one and folk cures for it abound, as do theories about it. A common cure is to rub buttermilk on the ears but, in fact, the animals usually recover from it in any event unless their eyes are severely affected. Losses are probably due to secondary infection and the most highly recommended cure at present is penicillin, though neither the veterinarian nor the chemist understand why.

This disease is of interest because it offers a perfect test case of folk medicine and disease theories. Many people attribute its incidence to the wind or speculate about its relation to high mountains. As noted, the more knowledgeable attribute it to the sun dew plant and state that it is found on wet, marshy lands. Recent experiments performed at the Agricultural Institute's Sheep Research Station at Maam, Co. Galway, indicated that the sun dew plant is not palatable to lambs, even if they are starved for a while before it is introduced. The experiments were carried out in consequence of an article tracing the cause of the disease in Norway to bog asphodel, a plant also common in the West of Ireland and one found only on wet, acid moorlands. The experimental lambs found this plant highly palatable. Thus one aspect of the folk theories was proved correct; the syndrome results from the ingestion of plants found in the areas predicted.

Contagious opthalmia is another disease with a long history in the area and it is called by a Gaelic name, *dullnamollog*, or moon blind. This disease causes a white film to appear over one or both the eyes of the affected sheep, and again, it is treated in many different ways. Some sheep farmers are skilled in removing this film by snipping away a small piece of it, then using a needle and thread to catch and pull away the entire film. Of all techniques used, this is probably the least harmful (and most delicate) procedure and no further treatment is required. Other cures include putting something into the eye, usually ground glass, household bleach, or acid. All animals are treated if an afflicted animal is found and the contagious nature of the disease is usually treated as its sole cause, though a few people speculate that wet weather will bring it on.

Footrot is a new disease, only recently introduced into the area — probably in association with overgrazing — and, of all diseases, it is the one on which my opinion was most frequently asked. Differences in medications are discussed at great length but cures, rather than prevention, are the major concern. The affected feet are treated with Bluestone, or copper sulphate, and although it is widespread, it seems not to be a very serious problem as yet. Five of my informants treated for it, and four others had occasionally seen an animal with it. In the Gaelic-speaking areas, the disease was unknown.

This concludes the data on animal health. My hypothesis to do with animal health states that if different types of animals are kept in a given environment, susceptibility to disease will be a factor in the decision to keep a specific type of animal and selective breeding will be largely determined by this consideration. This is more true for sheep than for cattle because cattle breeding is not directly controlled by the farmers, though they may choose the hardier breeds from the Artificial Insemination Service. Nor is disease susceptibility so much a consideration with them, since cattle are accorded better care and the morbidity rates are much lower. Informant testimony indicates that the thrust of the breeding programs is towards developing "hardier" sheep, i.e., those which can survive on very meager pasture and in difficult weather. Measures are taken against known scourges, such as braxy or fluke, but sheep are otherwise left to fend for themselves. Selection in breeding is determined primarily by hardiness and disease susceptibility is an important, but secondary, sorting mechanism, one which occurs both naturally and with the direct intervention of the farmers.

I have mentioned the curious distinctions between cattle and sheep; one of the most striking instances of this is in willingness to consult a veterinarian. My question was, "Under what circumstances would you call the vet?" When cattle were involved, the response was, under any and all circumstances that were the least bit doubtful, that is when the owner could not immediately identify the problem and solve it. Sheep farmers almost never called the vet and the reasons given for this were as numerous as my informants: they weren't sure what the animals might have died of, they tried treating them with home remedies, or, very commonly, they say that whatever the precipitating cause, the real cause was starvation and the vet wouldn't be any help for that. There is an underlying economic variable here, to do with the value of sheep vs. the value of cattle. One cow is worth ten sheep and a visit from the veterinarian would cost about one-fifth the value of one sheep or one-fiftieth the value of a full grown cow.

On this basis, a simple economic explanation for the distinction drawn between cattle and sheep seems reasonable. But during the Thirties, there was a government regulation in effect prohibiting the sale of livestock outside the country. Since the market for livestock is in Northern Ireland and that area is now defined as another country, cattle dropped in value until they were almost worthless. Calves were sold for 10/($1.50) and good cows went for a few pounds, maybe ten or fifteen dollars. Sheep did not lose their value to the same extent because there was a lively trade in smuggling wool across the Border. The veterinarians reported that their business in treating cattle was not affected: they were called just as frequently throughout this period as they are at present (although they did not get paid as often) and no one neglected a sick animal, even though animals had very little monetary value for almost a decade.

REFERENCES

Aalen, F.H.A. and Hugh Brody
  1969 *Gola:* The Life and Last Days of an Island Community.
  Cork: Mercier.

Agricultural Institute
  1967 *West Donegal Resource Survey,* 4 vols. Dublin: Agricultural
  Institute.

Alland, Alexander, Jr.
  1970 "That's the Way Our Grandfathers Did It." mimeo,
  presented to AAA Meetings, 1970.
  1972 C'est Ainsi que Faisaient Nos Grand-Peres. *L'Homme*
  XII:111 — 118.

An Roinn Talmhaiochta
  Agus Iascaigh
    1965 "Fence Off Liver Fluke," Leaflet No. 138. Dublin:
    Department of Agriculture and Fisheries.

Arensberg, Conrad M.
  1937 (1968) *The Irish Countryman:* An Anthropological Study.
  Garden City, N.Y.: Natural History Press.

Arensberg, Conrad M., and Solon T. Kimball
  1968 *Family and Community in Ireland.* 2d ed. (lst ed. 1940).
  Cambridge, Mass.: Harvard University Press.

Bacon, Francis
  Quoted in Loren Eiseley, *The Man Who Saw Through Time*, p.
  96. New York: Charles Scribner's Sons, 1973.

Barnes, J. A.
  1951 The Perception of History in a Plural Society. *Human
  Relations* IV:295-303.

Bax, M.
   1970 Patronage Irish Style: Politicians as Brokers. *Sociologisches Gids* 17:179-191.
   1973 *Harpstrings And Confessions:* An Anthropological Study of Politics in Rural Ireland. Mimeo. University of Amsterdam.

Bennett, John W.
   1969 *Northern Plainsmen:* Adaptive Strategy & Agrarian Life. Chicago: Aldine Publishing Company.

Bergson, Henri
   1914 *Dreams.* Translated by Edwin E. Slosson. New York: B. W. Huebsch.

Birmingham, George A.
   n.d. *The Lighter Side of Irish Life.* New York: Frederick A. Stokes Company.

Bohannan, Laura (Bowen, Elenore Smith)
   1964 *Return to Laughter.* Garden City, New York: Doubleday.

Bolger, P.
   n.d. Mimeo. Land Use & Agriculture. County Donegal.

Brody, Hugh
   1973/1974 *Inishkillane:* Change and Decline in the West of Ireland. Harmondsworth: Penguin.

Browner, Michael
   1970 *Irish Times,* 31 December.

Campbell, John R. and John F. Lasley 1969
   The Science of Animals That Serve Mankind New York: McGraw-Hill Book Company.

Chadwick, Nora
   1970 *The Celts.* Harmondsworth, Middlesex, England: Pelican Books.

Chance, Neville
    1971 Farmers Help Themselves. *Irish Farmer's Journal.* 27
    March 1971.

Cohn, Bernard S.
    1961 The Pasts of an Indian Village. *Comparative Studies in
    Society and History* 3:241-249.

Coimisiun Na Gaeltachta
    1925 Minutes taken in Dungloe, County Donegal, 17 August
    1925. Microfilm.

Collier, George A.
    1975 *Fields of the Tzotzil.* Austin: University of Texas Press.

Colson, Elizabeth
    1974 *Tradition and Contract*: The Problem of Order. Chicago:
    Aldine Publishing

Connell, K. H.
    1950 *The Population of Ireland, 1750-1845.* Oxford: Clarendon
    Press.

Cresswell, Robert
    1969 *Une Communaute Rurale de L'Irlande.* Paris: Institute de
    Ethnographie.

Cross, T. P. and C. H. Slover, eds.
    1969 *Ancient Irish Tales.* Dublin: Allen Figgis.

Daly, Patrick J.
    n.d. "Some Observations of Farming in Northwest Galway and
    West Mayo with Particular Emphasis on Sheep Production."
    Hill Sheep Production Seminar for Agricultural Instructors.
    Ballinrobe, County Mayo. mimeo.

Dillon, Myles, and Nora Chadwick
    1973 *The Celtic Realms.* LondonP Sphere Books Cardinal
    Edition.

Eiseley, Loren (see F. Bacon)
    1973 *The Man Who Saw Through Time.* New York: Charles
    Scribner's Sons, p. 96.

Ensminger, M. E.
1964 *Sheep and Wool Science*. Danville, Ill.: Interstate Printers and Publishers.

Evans, E. Estyn
1957 *Irish Folk Ways*. London: Routledge & Kegan Paul.
1967 (1942) *Irish Heritage*: The Landscape, The People and Their Work. 2d ed. Dundalk: W. Tempest, Dundalgan Press.
1976 Some Problems of Irish Ethnology: The example of ploughing by the tail. *In* Folk and Farm: Essays in honour of A. T. Lucas. C. 0. Danachair, ed. Dublin: Royal Society of Antiquities of Ireland. Pp. 30-39.

Fernandez , James W.
1972 Cited in Stevens (1975), p. 200 n.

Foster, George M.
1965 "Peasant Society and the Image of Limited Good," *American Anthropologist*, vol. 67 (2).

Fowler, H. W.
1965 *A Dictionary of Modern English Usage*. 2d ed. Oxford: Clarendon Press.

Fox, Robin (J.R.)
1962 The Vanishing Gael. *New Society,* October, pp. 17-19.
1963 The Structure of Personal Names on Tory Island. *Man* 192:153-156.
1966 "The Living Past in Donegal," *Clare Market Review*, Lent Term, 1966. Pp. 7-13.
1968 Tory Island. *In* Burton Benedict (ed.), Problem of Small Territories. London: Athlone.
1978 *The Tory Islanders*: A people of the Celtic fringe. Cambridge: University Press.

Freeman, T. W.
1957 *Pre-Famine Ireland*: A Study in Historical Geography. Manchester: University Press.
1969 *Ireland:* A General and Regional Geography. 4th edition. London: Methuen.

Friedl, Ernestine
1962 *Vasilika*: A Village in Modern Greece. New York: Holt, Rinehart and Winston.

Galt, Anthony
1974 "Rethinking patron-client relationships: The real system and the official system in Southern Italy." *Anthropological Quarterly* 47:182-202.

Gibbon, Peter, and M. D. Higgins
1974 The Case of the Irish "Gombeenman." *Economic and Social Review*, vol. 6:27-44.

Gilmore, David
1977 Patronage and Class Conflict in Southern Spain. *Man* (n.s.) 12:446-458.

Glassie, Henry H.
1982a *Passing the Time in Ballymenone*: culture and history of an Ulster community. Philadelphia: University of Pennsylvania Press.
1982b *Irish Folk History*. Philadelphia: University of Pennsylvania Press.

Goody, Jack
1977 *The Domestication of the Savage Mind*. Cambridge: Cambridge University Press.

Graham, Jean M.
1970 "South-West Donegal in the Seventeenth Century." *Irish Geography* VI(2):136-152.

Griffith, R.
1857 *General Valuation of Rateable Property in Ireland*. Dublin: H.M.S.0.

Hannan, Damian
1970 *Rural Exodus:* A Study of the Forces Influencing the Large-Scale Migration of Irish Rural Youth. London: Geoffrey Chapman.

Hawthorne, Nathaniel
n.d. *The House of the Seven Gables*. New York: Signet, New American Library.

Hobsbawm, Eric and Terence Ranger, eds.
   1983 *The Invention of Tradition.* Cambridge: University Press.

Honigmann, John T
   1976 The Personal Approach in Cultural Anthropological
   Research. *Current Anthropology* 17:243-261.

Hunter, David E., and Phillip Whitten, eds.
   1976 *Encyclopedia of Anthropology.* New York: Harper & Row.

Inglis, Brian
   1956 *The Story of Ireland.* London: Faber & Faber.

Joyce, P. W.
   1913 (1968) *A Social History of Ancient Ireland,* Vol. II. New
   York: Benjamin Blom.

Kane, Eileen
   1968 An Analysis of the Cultural Factors Inimical to the
   Development of the Nationalistic-Revivalistic Industrial
   Process of Rural Irish Gaeltachts. Ph.D. dissertation,
   University of Pittsburgh.
   1971 "Change in the Gaeltacht." *Irish Times,* 31 March-2 April
   1971.

Killanin, Lord, and Michael V. Duignan
   1967 *Shell Guide to Ireland.* London: Ebury Press.

Kinsella, Thomas (trans.)
   1969 *The Tain* (from the Irish epic *Tain Bo Chuailnge*) Oxford:
   Oxford University Press.

Leach, E.R.
   1954 *Political Systems of Highland Burma.* London: G. Bell
   and Sons Ltd.
   1972 Buddhism in the Post-Colonial Order in Burma and
   Ceylon. *In* Post-Traditional Societies. S. N. Eisenstadt, ed.
   Pp. 29-54. New York: W. W. Norton.
   1976 *Culture and Communication.* Cambridge: Cambridge
   University Press.

Lévi-Strauss, Claude
    1966 *The Savage Mind.* Chicago: University of Chicago Press.
    (Original: *La Pensee Sauvage*, Paris, 1962).
    1976 How Myths Die. *In* Structural Anthropology Vol.II. Pp.
    256-268. New York: Basic Books.

Leyton, Elliott
    1977 "Studies in Irish Social Organisation: The State of the
    Art." *Social Studies.*

Lucas, A. T.
    1957 "Cattle in Ancient and Medieval Irish Society." *O'Connell
    School Union Record*, 1937-58. Pp. 75-85

McGill, Patrick T.
    n.d. *History of the Parish of Ardara.* Donegal: Donegal
    Democrat.

MacManus, Seumas
    1969 *The Story of the Irish Race.* New York: The Devin-Adair
    Company.

Malinowski, Bronislaw
    1948 Myth in Primitive Psychology. *In* Magic, Science and
    Religion and Other Essays. Garden City, New York:
    Doubleday & Company. Pp. 93-148.

Maloney, Clarence (ed.)
    1976 *The Evil Eye.* New York: Columbia University Press.

Maybury-Lewis, David
    1970 Science by Association. *In* Claude Levi-Strauss: The
    Anthropologist as Hero, E. Nelson Hayes & Tanya Hayes,
    eds. Cambridge, Mass.: M.I.T. Press, pp.133-139.

Messenger, John C.
    1962 A Critical Reexamination of the Concept of Spirits: With

Special Reference to Traditional Irish Folklore and Contemporary Irish Folk Culture. *American Anthropologist* 64:367-373.

1968 Types and Causes of Disputes in an Irish Community. *Eire-Ireland* 3:27-37.

1969 *Inis Beag*: Isle of Ireland. New York: Holt, Rinehart & Winston.

Micks, William L.
1925 *An Account of the Constitution, Administration, and Dissolution of the Congested Districts Board for Ireland.* Dublin: Eason & Son.

Millman, Lawrence
1977 *Our Like Will Not Be There Again*: Notes from the West of Ireland. Boston: Little, Brown and Company.

Mitchell, G. F.
1971 "The Larnian Culture: A Minimal View." *The Prehistoric Society* XXXVII, Pt. 11:274-283.

Morton, H.V.
1931 *In Search of Ireland.* London: Methuen and Company.

O'Connor, Frank
1970 (1959) *Kings Lords & Commons.* London: Gill & Macmillan

O'Faolain, Sean
1970 (1942) *The Great O'Neill.* Cork: Mercier Press.
1972 (1947) *The Irish.* Harmondsworth, Middlesex: Penguin Books.
1977 "A World of Fitzies," *Times Literary Supplement*, April 29, 1977:502-503.

Orans, Martin
1965 *The Santal:* A Tribe in Search of a Great Tradition. Detroit: Wayne State University Press.

Orme, A. R.
1970 *Ireland.* Chicago: Aldine.

Paine, R.
  1971 "A Theory of Patronage and Brokerage," in R. Paine, ed.
  Patrons and Brokers in the East Arctic. St. John's,
  Newfoundland: Social and Economic Papers.

Parsons, Talcott and Edward A. Shils
  1962 [1951] *Toward a General Theory of Action*. New York:
  Harper & Row.

Pitt-Rivers, Julian
  1961 *The People of the Sierra*. 2d ed. 1972. Chicago: University
  of Chicago Press.

Redfield, Robert
  1968 The Folk Society (first published 1947), *In* Readings in
  Anthropology Vol. II, 2d ed. Edited by Morton H. Fried. Pp.
  497-517. New York: Thomas Y. Crowell

Rose, Richard
  1971 *Governing Without Consensus*. Boston: Beacon Press.

Sacks, Paul Martin
  1976 *The Donegal Mafia*: An Irish Political Machine. New
  Haven: Yale University Press.

Schapera, I. ed.
  1937 *The Bantu-Speaking Tribes of South Africa*. London:
  Routledge & Kegan Paul.

Scheper-Hughes, Nancy
  1982a *Saints, Scholars, and Schizophrenics:* Mental Illness in
  Rural Ireland. Berkeley: University of California Press.
  1982b 'Ballybran' Letters, *R.A.I.N.* August 82, No. 51, pp.12-
  13.

Schwartz, Norman B.
  1977 A Pragmatic Past: Folk History, Environmental Change,
  and Society in a Peten, Guatemala Town. *American
  Ethnologist* 4:339-358.

Shanklin, Eugenia [Cramer]
  1973 Sacred and Profane Livestock in Southwest Donegal. Ph.D.
    dissertation, Department of Anthropology, Columbia
    University.
  1974 Where There Are No Innocent Bystanders. *Group* (News
    Journal of the Eastern Group Psychotherapy Society, New
    York). July:1-16.
  1976 Donegal's Lowly Sheep and Exalted Cows. *Natural History*,
    Vol. 85, No.3 (March), pp. 26-33.
  1979 A Good Social Role is Worth a Thousand Pictures. *In*
    Images of Information: Still Photography in the Social
    Sciences. Ed., Jon Wagner. Beverly Hills: Sage Publications.
    pp. 139-145.
  1980 The Irish Go-Between. *Anthropological Quarterly* Vol.
    53:162-172.
  1981 Two Meanings and Uses of Tradition. *Journal of
    Anthropological Research*, Vol. 37, No.1:71-89.

(Killanin, Lord, and Michael V. Duignan)
  1967 *Shell Guide to Ireland.* London: Ebury press.

Silverman, S. F.
  1965 "Patronage and Community-Nation Relationships in
    Central Italy," *Ethnology* 4:172-189.

Snyder, Philip
  1975 The Milk of the Mountain: The Meaning of Place in the
    West Coast of Ireland. Ph.D. dissertation, Anthropology,
    Cornell University.

Stevens, P. Jr.
  1975 The Kisra Legend and the Distortion of Historical
    Tradition. *Journal of African History* XVI:185-200.

Swan, Harry Percival
  1969 *Highlights of the Donegal Highlands.* Letterkenny, Co.
    Donegal: W.J. Barr and Sons.

Tambiah, S. T.
  1972 The Persistence and Transformation of Tradition in
    Southeast Asia, with Special Reference to Thailand. *In* Post-

Traditional Societies. S. N. Eisenstadt, ed. pp. 55-84. New York: W. W. Norton

Tylor, Edward B.
1960 [1881] *Anthropology.* Abridged and with a foreword by Leslie A. White. Ann Arbor: Ann Arbor Paperbacks, University of Michigan Press.

Vansina, Jan
1973 *Oral Tradition.* Harmondsworth, England: Penguin Books.

Vengroff, Richard
1975 Traditional Political Structures in the Contemporary context: The Chieftaincy in the Kweneng. *African Studies* 34(1):39-56

Williams, Raymond
1976 *Keywords*: A Vocabulary of Culture and Society. New York: Oxford University Press.

Woodham-Smith, Cecil
1962 *The Great Hunger*: Ireland 1845-1849. London: New England Library.

Worden, A. N., et al, eds.
1963 *Animal Health, Production, and Pasture.* London: Longmans Green.

Zimmerman, Robert L.
1970 Lévi-strauss and the Primitive. *In* Claude Lévi-Strauss: The Anthropologist as hero, E. Nelson Hayes & Tanya Hayes, eds. Cambridge, Mass.: M.I.T. Press. Pp. 216-224.

INDEX

Active uses of tradition, 17-31
  comparing past "glories" with
    present realities, 28-30
  preserving components of
    behavioral or ecological
    systems, 19-24
  as sanction for innovation, 17-
    19
  sharing ethnic identity, 24-28
Africa, 1-2, 15-16
Aftergrass, 199
Agricultural agents, 47, 62-63
  as gombeenmen, 70
Agriculture, *see* Farming
All Hallows Day, 40
American school of cultural
    anthropology, 156-157
Ancestors, 50-51
Anglo-Normans, 39-40
Angus cattle, 150-151
Anthropological views of
    tradition, 8-17
  active vs. passive aspects, 14-15
  British view, 15-16
  functionalist view, 9-10
  myths and tradition, 13
  U.S. view, 15
Apprenticing, intermediaries and,
    55
Artificial fertilizers, 91, 112,
    205-206
Artificial Insemination Service,
    94-95, 138, 215
Asia, 1-2
Auctions, 116-117, 118

Bachelors, 104, 106
Bacon, 146
Bacterial diseases
  cattle and, 204, 206-207
  sheep and, 211-214

Behavioral system, tradition in
    preserving components of,
    19-24
Benign gossip, 182-183
Blackface sheep, 95, 126, 142,
    147, 148-150
Blackleg (bacterial disease), 206
Bluestone (copper sulfate), 215
Bogland, 7, 130, 132, 142, 143
Boycotting, 70
Braxy (bacterial disease), 211-212
Brigid, St., 41-42
Britain, 15, 19
  Battle of Kinsale and, 46
  COBO response and, 24-28, 53,
    153
  colonization by, 46-49
  Cromwell's War and, 48, 49
  religious division of Ireland by,
    53
  social anthropology and, 156
  tradition and anthropology and,
    15-16
Brokers, 60
Bronze Age people, 35
Buddhism, 15
Bureaucrats, intermediaries as,
    60-63,
Butter, 151
Buttermilk, 151

Catholicism
  Celtic calendar and, 40
  doctrine of holy intercession,
    58
  land ownership and, 53
  late marriage and, 85
  religious division of Ireland
    and, 48, 53

229

Dogs
  killer, 131, 134, 138
  sheep, 150
Dole, 60, 61, 151,152
Donegal tweed, 64
Dowry system, 147-148
Dysentery, 206, 212

Early marriage, 83-84, 104
Ecological system, tradition in
    preserving components of,
    19-24
Economic intermediaries, 63-73,
    74
Education, 106
  myths as, 32
Edward (case history), 129, 130,
    131, 140-141
Emigration, *see* Outmigration
Ethnic identity, 27, 153-154
  tradition as means of sharing,
    24
Evil eye, 58-59, 207-208
Ewe subsidies, 96, 97

Fair of Magheramore, 18-19, 23,
    25, 26-27, 40-41
Fairs, 2, 147, 152
  cattle sales and, 116, 117, 118
  sheep sales and, 117, 118-119
Farming, 6, 8, 46-47
  Charlie (case history) and, 129,
    130, 132-134
  Edward (case history) and, 129,
    130, 131, 140-141
  in "image of limited good,"
    143-144
  Francie (case history) and, 130,
    142-144, 145, 146
  innovative methods used in,
    145
  land tenure and, 46, 47
  late marriage and, 103-104
  males engaged in, 99-100
  Ned (case history) and, 131,
    134-136, 145
  Neolithic people and, 35
  physical resources available for,
    130-131

plantation system and, 46-47,
    48-49
potatoes and, 49-50
pre-Celtic period and, 35-36
production cycle for, 145
St. Brigid's Day and, 41,42
sample selection and
    characteristics of field site,
    77-83
Seamus (case history) and, 131,
    136-139, 145
Farm subsidies, 60, 95, 96
Fatalism, 143-144, 145
Females
  age-sex pyramid (1926 and
    1966), 100
  celibacy rate of, 85
  girl's chores in household, 110-
    111
  household stove and, 110
  leisure opportunities for, 111-
    112
  male-female division of labor,
    109-110
  marriage rate of, 100
  outmigration and, 154
Fertilizers, artificial, 91, 112, 205-
    206
Fieldwork (anthropological), 161-
    184
  asking directions, 169-170
  basic group formations, 174-
    178
  formal and informal
    identification systems, 170
  preconceptions and, 162-167
  ritualized activities, 178
  rules of gossip, 178-184
Fighting, intermediaries and, 55-
    56,57
Fine, the (joint family), 37
Finn Cycle (myths), 20-21
Flight of the Earls (1607), 46
Fluke (parasitic infestation), 131,
    204-205, 210-211
Footrot (bacterial disease), 215
Fortified settlements, 36-37
Francie (case history), 130, 142-
    144, 145, 146